Arches
& Light
the
fiction
of
John
Gardner

David Cowart

Southern Illinois
University Press

Carbondale and Edwardsville

Permission to quote from the following sources is gratefully acknowledged:

Alfred A. Knopf, Inc., for excerpts from "Song," *W. H. Auden: Collected Poems*, ed. Edward Mendelson, 1938. From works by John Gardner: *The King's Indian Stories and Tales*, 1974; *The Sunlight Dialogues*, 1972; *Grendel*, 1971; *Freddy's Book*, 1980; *The Art of Living and Other Stories*, 1981; *Mickelsson's Ghosts*, 1982. For the illustration of Gardner by Herbert L. Fink in *The King's Indian*, 1974.

Jacket photograph: By Joel Gardner, in *Mickelsson's Ghosts*, by John Gardner, copyright © 1982 by Alfred A. Knopf, Inc.

Andre Deutsch for excerpts from *Grendel*, by John Gardner.

Georges Borchardt, Inc., for excerpts from *Sunlight Dialogues* and *The King's Indian*, by John Gardner.

Lord John Press for excerpts from "Nicholas Vergette" from *Poems*, by John Gardner, 1978.

Martin Secker & Warburg, Ltd., for excerpts from *Freddy's Book*, *Michelsson's Ghosts*, and *The Art of Living and Other Stories*, by John Gardner.

Twentieth Century Literature for reprinting of chapter 6, "The Dying Fall," in a slightly altered version.

Library of Congress Cataloging in Publication Data

Cowart, David, 1947–
    Arches and light.

    Bibliography: p.
    Includes index.
    1. Gardner, John, 1933–   —Criticism and
interpretation. I. Title.
PS3557.A712Z62   1983   813'.54   83-335
ISBN 0-8093-1127-5

For Georgia, as always,
but also for our parents:
Margaret, Eugene, Jack, and Jewel

. . . *une technique romanesque renvoie toujours*
à la métaphysique du romancier.
La tâche du critique
est de dégager celle-ci
avant d'apprécier celle-là.

—Sartre

Contents

Acknowledgments

I would like to express my appreciation for the help of many good friends in the preparation of this book. I first read Gardner at the instigation of Raymond and Mary Carney; it was thanks to them and to Patricia Leighten, who lent me her copy of *Grendel*, that I had something to go on when Richard Layman called one day in 1978 and asked me to write an essay on Gardner for *American Novelists Since World War II*. His coeditor for that volume, Jeffrey Helterman, later took the trouble—when the present book was in the writing—to read *On Moral Fiction* so that I would have someone to discuss it with. I have also to thank Ellen Greiner, who shared her expertise on children's literature; Buford Norman and Barbara Postles, who sent periodicals I might otherwise have missed; and Ina Hark, who discussed *Grendel* with me.

I am indebted, too, to Robert A. Morace and Kathryn Van-Spanckeren, whose request for an essay to include in *John Gardner: Critical Perspectives* provided the stimulus for beginning something longer and more substantial on this author. I came to their attention through the good offices of my colleague and friend Donald J. Greiner, who subsequently read and annotated several chapters, providing much inspiration and good counsel. I hope he will not mind my adapting the title of my chapter 8 from the title of one of his essays. Another colleague, John Ower, supplied the epigraph for that chapter, and I borrowed the epigraph for chapter 7 from Thomas Pynchon.

John M. Howell's *John Gardner: A Bibliographical Profile* has saved me a great deal of time. A model of scholarly exhaustiveness, his book has been of tremendous value—more than can be acknowledged in the odd footnote. My thanks, too, to George Geckle, chairman of the University of South Carolina Department of English, and to Chester Bain, dean of the College of Arts and Humanities, for release time and for a research grant in the summer of 1982.

Thanks finally to my wife Georgia who has cheerfully read and critiqued every chapter as it was completed, despite a heavy schedule of teaching and research of her own.

1

"Flooring the Ancient Abyss"
John Gardner and Moral Fiction

Art derives a considerable part of its
beneficial exercise from flying in the
face of presumptions.

—Henry James

In 1974, on the death of a close friend, the sculptor Nicholas Vergette, John Gardner wrote an elegy in which he expressed a lifetime's reflection on morality in art, for Vergette and the writer
had shared certain convictions. In the poem, "Nicholas Vergette
1923–1974," Gardner observes that his friend, like all thoughtful
sons of the twentieth century, had faced a "world . . . meaningless
and scant."[1] But unlike his fellow artists, Vergette had declined
merely to hold a mirror up to such vacuity; preferring to make a
better world, Vergette had set about "flooring the ancient abyss
with art." He had planted flowers, built walls, and turned out
sculpture, paintings, ceramics, and collages. No believer in "the
old stiff-minded gods," he was nevertheless a man of faith. The
sculptor had "faith in his hands" and "in his friends," and he had
touched the writer, John Gardner, with his vision: "I saw what he
saw: the grass and ourselves and the stars one work." But though
that last word, "work," hints at a divine Laborer, a cosmic Artist,
the Whitmanesque affirmation is muted, for the poem focuses ultimately on the achievement of the human artist. Gardner knows,
as Vergette did, that the only sure thing is the "ancient abyss" and
the floor the best artists, themselves godlike, lay, reinforce, patch,
and extend. "The floor he built / and came to believe in so fully he
dared us to dance on its stones / we test with tentative steps. It
will hold." Vergette, in other words, was a moral artist. Gardner
praises his work and his spirit because they testify to a belief that

1

the poet himself shares, a belief in art's responsibility to the human community.

Gardner advocated a literary art as supportive as Vergette's solid floor, and he did so consistently throughout his extraordinary career. Born in 1933, Gardner grew up, one of four children, on a farm near Batavia, New York. His parents contributed to his literary and musical bent. Gardner's father, when not attending to his farm, gave public recitations of poetry; he was also lay reader at the local Presbyterian church. The author's mother was a high school English teacher. Née Priscilla Jones, she is of Welsh stock, and her son delighted in his Welsh heritage. The characters in *The Resurrection*, *Nickel Mountain*, *The Sunlight Dialogues*, and "Come on Back" owe much to Gardner's family and neighbors.

In childhood the author was called "Buddy" or "Bud." The nickname was appropriate since, as John Howell notes, *Budd* is Welsh for "poet."[2] From an early age Gardner wrote poems and made up stories. He recalled for an interviewer that his brothers, sister, and the other farm hands were a demanding audience. If they liked his work, they would do his chores for him; if they did not, they would pelt him with straw and, presumably, whatever else came to hand in the farmyard. "It teaches you to please the crowd."[3] The hands had Saturday afternoon off to listen to the Metropolitan Opera broadcast, and opera remained one of the passions of the adult Gardner. Among his many literary productions are libretti for the operas *Rumpelstiltskin* and *Frankenstein*, by Joe Baber. When, in 1977, an interviewer asked Gardner how he wanted to be remembered, the author replied, "As the greatest librettist of the twentieth century."[4]

That statement may not have been entirely serious, but music was always important to Gardner. It may have gotten him through the most terrible experience of his childhood. He was eleven when, pulling a cultipacker on which his little brother Gilbert was sitting, he heard his sister cry out, turned, and saw the immense implement crush the pelvis of the boy, who had fallen. Gilbert did not survive. Gardner describes a similar—perhaps identical—incident in "Redemption," published over thirty years later. The story hints that Gardner managed to sublimate his guilt through music, for it ends with its young protagonist studying French horn and gaining a sense of the power of art to absorb energies otherwise depleted by guilt. Gardner did in fact study French horn at a preparatory school operated by the Eastman School of Music in Rochester. His familiarity with the Rochester music scene would also contribute to his short story "The Music Lover."

On his graduation from Batavia High School in 1951 Gardner attended DePauw University in Indiana but transferred to Washington University in St. Louis after his marriage, a few weeks shy of his twentieth birthday, to Joan Louise Patterson, a second cousin. (Their courtship may have provided the model for "Joan Orrick's" recollections in the story "Stillness.") In college Gardner at first took an interest in chemistry but soon turned to literature, writing, and philosophy. He graduated from Washington University, having made Phi Beta Kappa, in 1955. A Woodrow Wilson Fellowship enabled him to study creative writing at the University of Iowa, where he took two advanced degrees. Parts of his Master's thesis, "Four Stories," would later be reworked for inclusion in *Nickel Mountain* (1973). By 1958 he had also completed two novels, "Sparrows" and "The Old Men." Neither has been published, but the outlines of "The Old Men," which was Gardner's Ph.D. thesis, appear in *Dissertation Abstracts*. The first sentence of the abstract provides evidence that the concerns seen in "Nicholas Vergette 1923–1974" do not represent a late development: "*The Old Men* is a novel which takes as its general theme the place of man in the universe and attempts to work out the nature and ramifications of man's two essential choices, affirmation and denial." [5] Though the young author describes his novel somewhat clumsily ("Through the juxtaposition of slightly or sharply distorted internal visions of reality, normative vision becomes dependent on character relationships and agreement of various distortions"), "The Old Men" would seem to be the product of an advanced artistic sensibility. Far from peopling his novel with simplistic characters standing for affirmation or denial, Gardner fills it with characters who represent a remarkable variety of intellectual, psychological, and emotional maturity. The development of two morally confused characters is central. One "seeks spiritual involvement with the universe"; the other "seeks not involvement but detachment." Both are mistaken, and the novel turns on their discovering and accepting the halfway point between the obligations and the limits of ethical accountability. Thus the character "who began as a life affirmer, totally irresponsible through cosmic inclusiveness of responsibility," and the one described as "a life denier, irresponsible through detachment," move towards a "morally responsible" middle ground, which the author endorses.

But Gardner would wait eight years to see a novel of his in print. Before the appearance of *The Resurrection* in 1966, he taught briefly at Oberlin, Chico State, and San Francisco State. During this period he and a colleague at Chico State, Lennis Dunlap, edited *The Forms of Fiction* (1962), a textbook. He also began writing scholarly articles and preparing translations of medieval literature, including *The Complete Works of the Gawain Poet* (1965) and *The Alliterative Morte Arthure* (published in 1971, but completed much earlier). Gardner began *The Sunlight Dialogues* late in 1964 and completed it early in 1968. He then turned to *The Wreckage of Agathon*, finishing it late in 1969, and before the year was out he had begun *Grendel*. He was, however, still the author of only one published novel, *The Resurrection*, which had generated little excitement among reviewers (Granville Hicks, in the *Saturday Review*, called the book "pretty muddled").[6] *The Resurrection* had been accepted by David Segal of New American Library; when he moved to Harper & Row he took his enthusiasm for Gardner with him, bringing out *The Wreckage of Agathon* in late 1970. Segal soon moved again, to Knopf, where, before his death, he set in motion the publication of *Grendel* (1971) and *The Sunlight Dialogues* (1972). *The Wreckage of Agathon*, with a first printing of 6500 copies, attracted more attention than Gardner's first novel, which had had a first printing of only 2500 copies. In addition to respectful reviews by

Robert Wernick in *Time* and Paul West in the *New York Times Book Review*, the novel received strong praise from *Newsweek's* Geoffrey Wolff, who described it as, in the main, "astonishingly good."[7] It suffered its share of carping, however, and one reviewer dismissed it as "a total bore."[8] But with *Grendel*, which appeared the next year, the tide of critical caution began to turn. Reviewers were charmed, and *Time* and *Newsweek* cited it among the year's best novels. After a first printing of 7500 copies, it went through nine hardback and thirteen paperback printings in this country and England by the end of 1977. It had also, by then, been translated into French, Spanish, and Swedish.

Any remaining doubts about Gardner's stature as an important new novelist were dispelled by the appearance of *The Sunlight Dialogues* in 1972. Surprisingly, in view of the charm, wit, and brevity of *Grendel*, its lengthy and demanding successor was the first Gardner novel to gain a wide readership. It quickly became a bestseller and was chosen by a major book club, the Literary Guild. Although the *New Yorker's* anonymous reviewer and Victor Howes in the *Christian Science Monitor* thought the novel flawed, Tony Tanner praised it in *Saturday Review of the Arts*, and R. S. Bravard declared in *Library Journal*: "With this large, complex, fascinating work, Gardner moves into the first rank of American novelists, more than living up to the promise of his two fine previous novels."[9]

If Gardner's next book, *Nickel Mountain* (1973), does not measure up to its predecessors (he first drafted it at the age of nineteen), it has had the greatest appeal of any of his novels. Encouraged, presumably, by the reception accorded *The Sunlight Dialogues*, which had had a first printing of only 8775 copies, Gardner's publisher brought out 27,500 copies in the first printing of *Nickel Mountain*, and had to go into a second printing within less than a month. The book was also chosen by the Book-of-the-Month Club, which required two printings to satisfy demand. It was pirated in Taiwan and soon translated into Danish, Finnish, French, Hungarian, Spanish, Swedish, and other languages.

The literary success did not lead Gardner to abandon his academic career. He had begun teaching at Southern Illinois University in 1965 and continued there, with odd semesters or years as a visiting professor elsewhere, for over a decade. He also received a number of important fellowships: in addition to the Woodrow Wilson that had enabled him to go to the Iowa Writer's Workshop in 1955, he received a Danforth in 1970, a Guggenheim in 1973, and, at Bennington College, a Hadley Fellowship in 1974. Gardner published several more books in these years. No Mauberley "lacking the skill / To forge Achaia," he even produced an epic poem, *Jason and Medeia* (1973). "Parts of this poem," he explains in the Acknowledgments, "freely translate sections of Apollonios Rhodios' *Argonautica* and Euripides' *Medeia*, among other things." The poem also contains adaptations or reworkings of material from William H. Gass and Gary Snyder. The following year saw the publication of another scholarly book, *The Construction of the Wakefield Cycle*, and of his first collection of short fiction, *The King's Indian Stories and Tales*. These stories, written in 1971, represent the attainment of Gardner's full powers. In them, and in their arrangement, one discovers a mastery beyond that attained even in *Grendel* and *The Sunlight Dialogues*. The collection was warmly received, with good reviews in *Library Journal*, the *New York Times Book Review*, and *Time*, but because the book contains many secrets inaccessible to reviewers and casual readers, it has tended to be somewhat undervalued. Indeed, by the late seventies it had had only two hardcover and two paperback printings. Teachers wanting to assign the paperback in recent years have been disappointed to learn that it is out of print.

In 1975 Gardner published *Dragon, Dragon and Other Tales*, a collection of the stories he had given his children each Christmas, and *The Construction of Christian Poetry in Old English*, which he had begun in 1973; he also began work on *October Light*, which appeared late in 1976 and won the National Book Critics Circle Award for fiction. The critical esteem complemented Gardner's growing popularity. After a first printing of 25,000 copies, *October*

Light went through seven more hardcover printings within twelve months, in addition to two Book-of-the-Month Club printings. It was eventually brought out in paperback by both the Quality Paperback Book Club and Ballantine. The same year—1976—also marked the publication of *Gudgekin the Thistle Girl and Other Tales*, another collection of children's stories, which was followed in 1977 by *A Child's Bestiary, In the Suicide Mountains*, and *The King of the Hummingbirds and Other Tales*. These books delight adults as well as children with their craftsmanship and humor; though the tales often have morals, they avoid the overt moralizing that spoils so many children's stories. Thus Gardner's stories for children are remarkably consistent with the adult fiction.

Nineteen seventy-seven was an extraordinary year for Gardner. In addition to receiving the National Book Critics Circle Award, he saw the first production of Joe Baber's opera *Rumpelstiltskin*, for which he had written the libretto, and the publication of both *The Poetry of Chaucer* and *The Life and Times of Chaucer*. The Chaucer books were the product of a 1973 revision of an immensely long manuscript dating back to 1963. Gardner also completed revisions on *On Moral Fiction* (1978), another manuscript with a long history. Concurrently with all of this literary activity he lectured in Salzburg and at Bread Loaf, and, in the first part of the year, taught simultaneously at two colleges, Skidmore and Williams. But this *annus mirabilis* came to a dark close, with Gardner's undergoing an operation for cancer and spending six weeks in hospital.

The author's career did not slow down following his illness. He remained creatively involved in opera, poetry, and drama—especially radio drama. Major fiction continued to appear, no less frequently, really, than before. Though his interest in genres other than fiction—not to mention his health and his teaching duties at SUNY Binghamton (where he remained from 1978 until his death in 1982)—ought to have reduced his output, he continued to publish important fiction every year: *Freddy's Book* in 1980, *The Art of Living and Other Stories* in 1981, and *Mickelsson's Ghosts* in 1982. None of these books elicited much more than politeness from critics, and the lengthy and demanding *Mickelsson's Ghosts* received fairly rough treatment, including negative or largely negative reviews in *New York*, *The New York Times Book Review*, and *The New York Review of Books*. Robert R. Harris's remarks in *Saturday Review* were especially nasty: "It is a good bet that John Gardner enjoys writing his novels far more than the public enjoys reading them. *Mickelsson's Ghosts* is dreadfully long and padded, and it often degenerates into drivel."[10] But Curt Suplee, in an appreciative article in *The Washington Post*, argued that "the new novel is one of his best, striving toward his vision of fiction as 'a vivid and continuous dream,' deeply serious yet surprisingly exciting."[11]

Gardner frequently mentioned a work in progress entitled "Shadows," which he began in 1974. According to his remarks in interviews, it concerns a hard-drinking detective, not unlike Ross MacDonald's Lew Archer, and in it the author attempts to handle a subject he has never been comfortable with before: "real sexual love." As he told Stephen Singular, "The only great artist who ever surmounted an inability to deal with this was Melville. Shakespeare mastered love. Mozart was great. He *knows* about men and women. Chaucer, terrific on it. Dante, fantastic. Homer, just unbelievable. It's one of the motivating forces—and I don't have it. It's partly puritanical shyness. 'Nickel Mountain' is a kind of love story, but it really shies away from it. I couldn't handle it. But maybe this is changing. 'Shadows' . . . is the first love story I've ever written flat out. A real love story requires a woman who is the equal of the man. And my women . . . this has been a weakness."[12]

But if sexual love presented difficulties for Gardner, he handled other modes of love—especially familial—with great mastery. Love, like art, can counter the terrible insecurities of human existence, and Gardner's whole career was dedicated to the advocacy of such balms as the human condition affords. Though he understood that life perches briefly over a great abyss, he persisted in describing himself as a man of faith. Thus he exemplifies the intellectual heroism recognized by F. Scott Fitzgerald: "the test of a first-rate intelligence is the ability to hold two opposed ideas in the mind at the same time and still retain the ability to function. One should, for example, be able to see that things are hopeless and yet be determined to make them otherwise."[13] Gardner believed, quite simply, that life is its own *telos*. He believed, moreover, in his own personal vision of what man—through the agency of enlightened artists, those unacknowledged legislators of mankind—can make of himself.

The world is "meaningless and scant" only as long as man fails to make it otherwise, and twentieth-century man has failed signally. Modern man, according to George Steiner, finds himself in Bluebeard's castle. In his quest for knowledge of the real he has pried into room after mysterious room and now, perhaps, stands before the last, fateful door. Behind this door lies knowledge that cannot be handled, knowledge that brings annihilation. Wondering "whether society and the human intellect at their present level of evolution can survive the next truths," Steiner suggests "that abstract truth, and the morally neutral truths of the sciences in particular, might come to paralyze or destroy Western man."[14] Steiner refers to advances that may show us the genetic, cortical programming of humanity for apocalypse. Will we discover that biologically we *must* make war, that our genetic proclivities, given the increasing deadliness of our arsenals, *guarantee* our self-destruction?

Gardner denied that such "abstract truths" constrain man absolutely. He explores the choices available to man in stories and novels that frequently concern artists who must deal with just the kind of terrible knowledge adumbrated by Steiner. John Napper, for example, pursues graceless reality to the pit only to "jump back" and realize that *his* is the task of creation. The artist must, in his work, make the world over from scratch. This creation is by no means irresponsible or escapist, because the world becomes what art says it is. To put it another way, the artist must shoulder moral responsibility for what he creates at first hand—his art—and for what he creates at second hand—the world shaped by that art.

Gardner thus modifies the traditional dictum that art uncovers changeless, preexistent truths; he makes of the proposition "life imitates art" something more than a parlor witticism. Behind the seemingly visionary affirmation lie certain commonplaces about the relativity of truth in different ages. Sir Francis Bacon reminds every age that will read him of the "idols of the theatre," the errors of perception and judgment that stem from the character of the age. Ours is an age of disillusionment and despair, and twentieth-century man makes the mistake of distrusting all suggestions that there might be grounds for faith impervious to the theory of evolution, the second law of thermodynamics, Heisenberg's uncertainty principle, and the death of God.

Gardner refused to despair. The more terrible the revelations of science, the greater the opportunity for art to effect a cultural restoration. Ours is not the first age to learn that "the new science calls all in doubt." Bacon's age saw its share of stunning scientific revelations (faith reeled before the fact of heliocentrism), but the response of Renaissance artists was to shape a splendid new secular image for society to emulate. Instead of a rudderless bark of anomie, society became what its artists hinted it could become: resurgent, purposive, expansive.

Gardner's conviction that an age is as healthy as its art underlies his major themes. The first of these, law-and-order versus wild, anarchic freedom, is probably most common in Gardner's work. In interviews the author frequently mentioned that order and anarchy vie within his own soul. "I am on the one hand a kind of New York State Republican, conservative. On the other hand, I am a kind of Bohemian type. I really don't obey the laws. I mean to, but if I am in a hurry and there is no parking here, I park."[15] Small wonder, then, that this dichotomy structures several Gardner novels. The central conflict in *The Wreckage of Agathon*, between the fascistic Lykourgos and the Bohemian free spirit Agathon, recurs in *The Sunlight Dialogues*, in which Chief Clumly represents the law and Taggert Hodge an impossible ideal of anarchic freedom. In *October Light* Gardner examines a whole spectrum of political and social choices facing America in its Bicentennial year, and in *Freddy's Book* he describes a state evolving towards totalitarianism despite the best intentions of its revolutionary founders. In *Mickelsson's Ghosts*, finally, the battle between order and anarchy takes place in the mind of a single character. Peter Mickelsson is a philosopher, a rationalist devoted to ordering the world through intellection, but he finds himself slipping into chaos.

Endemic to human society and civilization, the conflict that exercises Gardner is not exclusively political or social. It is also metaphysical, and Gardner's willingness to raise the question of whether the phenomenal world is fundamentally orderly or chaotic is evidence of his integrity, for the modern physicist's answer to the question makes credible affirmation difficult indeed. If modern science reveals uncertainty, randomness, at both the subatomic and cosmic levels, the fate of man, the *amphibium*, is to live in a state of contingency and to suffer the vagaries of chance. His plight, thus defined, is nothing new. "Man never is, but always to be blest," said Pope, but our knowledge of the real makes increasingly untenable the optimism about a future blessed state. Gardner's characters, then, must often come to terms with terrible sufferings visited on them by chance and with the fact that succor, in this life or hereafter, will not be forthcoming. Characters in *The Resurrection* and "Nimram" struggle with unjust, wasting diseases; the boy in "Redemption" becomes the accidental murderer of his brother; several of the characters in *Nickel Mountain* suffer accidental death or maiming, while the protagonist lives in daily dread of his second—and surely fatal—heart attack. Only in *Grendel* is what afflicts humanity actually reified: the monster that mocks and undermines human attempts at establishing and preserving a civilized order represents something anarchic at the very heart of things.

Gardner engaged in a career-long quest for fictive strategies to gainsay this horror. He did not claim to have discovered ultimately satisfying answers, but he always viewed the surrender to despair as unthinkable. What he offers in his fictions—besides optimism, which comforts only those temperamentally predisposed to it—is a kind of Lawrentian reverence for life, often projected, as in *The Resurrection*, *Grendel*, and *October Light*, in celebrations of nature and its cyclical renewal. He also affirms the power of art to redeem life, however embattled and beset. In nearly everything Gardner published, art figures as part of the program to defeat pain, depression, death, and entropy.

Though he never wrote a full-scale *Künstlerroman*, Gardner frequently examines the education of an artist: John Napper, Brother Ivo, Jonathan Upchurch, Benjamin Nimram, Vlemk the Box-Painter. Gardner's artists must choose between some narrowly defined existential truth and some finer, more complex, less accessible truth that is no less real for being created, at least in part, by the artist in the process of uncovering it. Those who realize their ability and responsibility to reshape the world are the moral artists, and often they must struggle directly or indirectly with immoral artists, those who have been miseducated; thus the Shaper competes with Grendel, Brother Ivo with Brother Nicholas, "Dr. Thorpe" with Dr. Hunter, and Jonathan Upchurch with Luther Flint.

In addition to these instructive juxtapositions of moral and immoral artists, Gardner argued his beliefs about moral art directly and polemically in the critical book *On Moral Fiction*. This declaration of literary values has been met with a certain amount of angry scorn, for many perceive it as the work of an aesthetic reactionary. But doubtless the iconoclastic child who insisted that the emperor's new clothes were nonexistent was also thought to be ridiculously simple-minded. Gardner, at least, is not alone in his iconoclasm. His book is bracketed by Tom Wolfe's attacks on contemporary painting (*The Painted Word*, 1975) and on modernist design and architecture (*From Bauhaus to Our House*, 1981). All three books are commonsense expressions of dismay at what has become of the arts in our time. Where Wolfe merely debunks, however, Gardner offers theoretical and practical alternatives, and like the epochal Preface to *Lyrical Ballads*, his manifesto could represent the beginning of something very important indeed, a fresh new direction for literature.

Some manifestos cause revolutions, some merely yawns. Although it has not yet filled the streets with sansculottes, *On Moral Fiction* has generated its share of controversy. It probably outrages more readers than it pleases, but it does not surprise those familiar with the career of its author, whose every public statement, every poem, and every work of fiction illustrate the book's argument. Gardner advocates a literature of affirmation in the face of widespread conviction that the ultimate meaninglessness of man's existence necessarily dooms all attempts at discovering or creating a morality more secure than that espoused by the middle class and despised by intellectuals. In the absence of absolute religious, philosophical, or scientific grounds for human values in the modern age, literary artists from Eliot to Barth and from O'Neill to Beckett have for some decades now documented a Waste Land of despair and creeping nihilism. Those who have not placed such matters in the foreground of their fiction have made them the premises of a literature that increasingly deals with nothing more substantial than its own artifice. Conceiving of the novel as essentially a form of play, writers like Vladimir Nabokov or Gardner's friend and rival William Gass devote themselves entirely to pattern, convolution, and verbal gamesmanship to the deliberate exclusion of real-world exigencies.

Not that Gardner despised fabulation. It should be clear by now that he found simple realism somewhat misguided. He did not eschew lexical play or technical experiments, nor did he ignore or underestimate the bleak facts of our existence, but he does see writing that concerns itself exclusively with these matters as literature of at best the second rank. Whatever our existentialist posturings, Gardner realized, we act as if we had values. If these values are provisional, we nevertheless allow them to shape our lives. Gardner believed that literature has a responsibility both to explore *ad hoc* values and to seek less provisional ones.

> Moral art in its highest form holds up models of virtue, whether they be heroic models like Homer's Achilles or models of quiet endurance, like the coal miners, the steelworkers, the Southern midwife, or the soldiers in the photographs of W. Eugene Smith. The artist so debilitated by guilt and self-doubt that he cannot be certain real values exist is an artist doomed to second-rate art, an artist of whom the best that can be said is that he's better, at least, than the consciously nihilistic artist or (worse, perhaps) the artist who believes in morality but has got it all wrong, so that he holds up for emulation what ought to be despised.[16]

Gardner claimed for literature enormous powers of moral suasion. "If we celebrate bad values in our arts," he remarked in an interview, "we're going to have a bad society; if we celebrate values which make you healthier, which make life better, we're going to have a better world."[17] Art, then, molds values and behavior. In saying as much, one does not go so far as to say that art ennobles everyone exposed to it. Too many great criminals—from Hitler and Goebbels to Jack Abbot—have been connoisseurs. But broadly speaking the art that flourishes within a society influences that society, teaching it how to perceive itself and the world in which it subsists. Gardner thus argued for an art to foster those positive actions and values that on the personal level minimize pain and enhance life and on the broader societal level contribute to vision and purpose, to great ideas and benevolent, lasting institutions. Art that meets these criteria—nearly all classical art does so—he saw as unquestionably the greatest and best. Contemporary art generally fails to make the grade.

In novel after novel, Gardner follows his own counsel. By way of an example one could again cite *Grendel*, in which he allows the *Beowulf* monster to give his own version of his storied encounter with the Geatish hero. As first-person narrator, Grendel is a perfect spokesman for the nihilist world view that, having displaced the more wholesome Christian and heroic world view of the original epic, breathes through so much of modern life and art. Grendel, in other words, is a parody of the modern artist. But while he is insisting on the dreary existential truth (nothing has meaning; life masks a void), another kind of artist, the Shaper, is teaching a rude culture to perceive itself as heroic and purposive, providing his people with the kind of vision that enables them to found a civilization whose exemplar, the heroic Beowulf, defeats Grendel and transcends the existential and supposedly ineluctable realities he represents.

In *Grendel* and in his other works, Gardner puts theory into practice. In *On Moral Fiction* he applies the theory to the literary competition, and like Sir Philip Sidney, who did the same thing in *The Defense of Poesie* and *An Apology for Poetry*, Gardner generally finds his contemporaries wanting. Most of the controversy over Gardner's book has been caused by this aspect of it, for the author treads on many a toe. Indeed, even those most sympathetic to the argument find the book alternately delightful and infuriating. The problem with judging contemporaries—aside from the possibility that the least charitable reviewers will call one self-serving—is that at every turn one will bump up against the prejudices of one's audiences, which happens for the most part to be the audience for contemporary fiction. Gardner runs the fewest risks when he criticizes minor figures like Vonnegut, Brautigan, Barthelme, and the like; he outrages more and more of his audience as he proceeds to point out what he finds lacking in Bellow, Barth, Updike, and Pynchon.

The results of his frankness were predictable; contumely from the parties judged, anger and near hysteria on the part of their apologists. One must keep in mind that the book's reviewers were often those responsible for the public taste in fiction over the last few years; even so, some reviews were positive. Edmund Fuller, the dean of humanists, gave Gardner a favorable review in the *Wall Street Journal*, and Henrietta Buckmaster, noting that Gardner's "morality is never moralistic," praised the book in the *Christian Science Monitor*.[18] But most reviewers were less kind. Roger Sale, in the *New York Times Book Review*, called the book "repetitive and predictable. . . . One finds oneself nodding in agreement at times, but much more often . . . one finds oneself just nodding off."[19] "When Gardner moves from the general to the specific," remarked Max Apple in the *Nation*, "it is sometimes as easy to say no to him as to the missionary on the corner."[20] Only Earl Rovit, in an otherwise largely negative review in *Library Journal*, makes a positive comment about Gardner's judgments on contemporary fiction. Conceding the author's sincerity but calling the argument "repetitive," "opinionated," "tautological, over-ambitious, and ultimately less than persuasive," Rovit finds the "offhand impressionistic comments on the fiction of his contemporaries . . . harsh but invariably shrewd and worthy of attention." But even this observation is soon qualified: "The larger attempt to embrace the artistic and intellectual tradition of the West in terms of reductive commonsense pieties is beguiling in its cranky egotism, but tainted by preachy pretension and self-righteousness."[21]

Perhaps looking to critics for an adequate response to the challenge of this book is a mistake. Reviewers are almost never given the space or the time necessary to counter an argument. They judge—often crabbily—and move on. But Gardner's fellow authors, as seen in the remarks of Max Apple above, are even less charitable. In an article on Gardner in the *New York Times Magazine*, "The Sound and Fury Over Fiction," Stephen Singular gives a sympathetic account of *On Moral Fiction* and provides a forum in which a number of prominent contemporary novelists can defend themselves.[22] John Updike, for example, has little patience with "whatever life-affirming thing" Gardner has in mind; fiction, in his view, chronicles truth, and the truth is bleak. John Barth describes *On Moral Fiction* as "a shrill pitch to the literary right wing that wants to repudiate all of modernism." Bernard Malamud finds its author "lacking in generosity and, sometimes, taste." Nobel laureate Saul Bellow merely sniffs, "If I'm not Gardner's ideal novelist . . . I'm full of regret. I can't suit every taste." Joseph Heller, finally, declares Gardner "a pretentious young man" who "talks a lot and has little of intelligence to say . . . . He writes dull novels and dull, carping criticism."

Journalists have a way of taking advantage of controversy and making honest differences of opinion sound like vendettas. As quoted by Singular, none of these contemporary masters makes an attempt to engage Gardner in any substantial way, and to a certain extent they are justified, inasmuch as Gardner's evaluations of them can frequently be faulted as hasty or, to borrow Rovit's carefully chosen word, impressionistic. It is odd, however, that none of Singular's respondents, with the slight exception of Barth, makes the argument that in fact their work *is* moral in the terms that Gardner proposes. The reason, perhaps, is to be found in the tone of the remarks: Gardner is a crackpot, to be dismissed, not argued with.

The chorus of denunciation—or, alternately, the studied indifference—argues a certain nervousness on the part of those Gardner criticizes. They and their supporters feel threatened, because his ideas give every promise of annunciating a new literary dispensation. In response to the question "How Is Fiction Doing?", posed by the editors of the *New York Times Book Review* late in 1980, John Barth conceded unhappily that the kind of fiction associated with his name was entering a recession, though he expressed the hope that the new trend would spend itself within a decade. Barth did not mention Gardner by name, but the choice of terms makes clear that the author of *On Moral Fiction* was on his mind: "A Proposition-13 mentality pervades the medium; our literary Howard Jarvises are in the ascendancy, preaching 'the family novel' and 'a return to traditional literary values.' And, in the Reagan country of at least the early 1980's, one may expect more of the same: The decade of the Moral Majority will doubtless be the decade of Moral Fiction." [23]

Barth suggests, erroneously, that moral fiction must be didactic
or moralistic. "I do not mean," Gardner observes in *On Moral Fiction*, "that what the world needs is didactic art. Didacticism and
true art are immiscible."[24] Elsewhere he compared didacticism to
the sermon one might hear in a cathedral; it contributes little or
nothing to the aesthetic impact of the "arches and the light."[25]
Barth's analogy between literary and political conservatism is also
mistaken. The political conservatism seen in the ascendancy of
Ronald Reagan and the Moral Majority is three parts blind, unreflective, pinch-mouthed prejudice to every one of tested, thoughtful commitment. But literary values, even at their shallowest, are
seldom divorced from reflection. Politics is an odd blend of chicanery and complacency; literature, among its practitioners and serious consumers, is all passion and principle. Gardner, the champion of this literary conservatism, described himself politically as a
mixture of conservative and liberal values. His novel *October Light*,
with its sympathetic treatment of liberal causes like civil rights and
the women's movement, is hardly the product of a sensibility congenial to the Moral Majority.

Barth's remarks in the *New York Times Book Review* jibe strangely
with the wistful article he had published in the *Atlantic* earlier the
same year. In this article he expresses regret at the misunder-
standing caused by the phrase "literature of exhaustion," which
he had coined in the same pages twelve years previously. Now he
calls for a "literature of replenishment"[26] but seems unwilling to
recognize that he and the author of *On Moral Fiction* might have a
common cause. Gardner, however, wanted not only literary replenishment but also cultural replenishment, and he saw the one
as fostering the other. For him, art of the highest moral order at
once shapes and expresses the finest aspirations of a culture. It
provides "models of virtue." Thus Gardner insisted on the long
view in evaluating contemporary art; he asked the big questions
and advocated a return to a judgmental as opposed to a purely or
largely exegetical criticism. Art, said Gardner, influences life, and

moral art is that which reduces the individual's existential insecurity at the same time that it contributes to the larger cause of civilization. If the most respected and influential art of an age is an endless rehearsal of futility and bleakness, then the age will be one like ours, one in which purpose, heroism, sacrifice, *pietas*, and a host of other indispensable values will be sadly lacking. But if art endorses ideals, if the artist comes up with ways of affirming man's worth and even man's greatness in the face of all that an indifferent, hostile, or capricious cosmos can visit on him, then the age will be one such as we associate with the names of such eminently moral artists as Homer, Sophocles, Dante, and Shakespeare.

These dwell in Gardner's literary pantheon. But to say as much is not to concede that their high priest is an aesthetic reactionary. If Gardner looked to the past, he did so only to shape a criticism that could with greater authority look to the future. Sir Philip Sidney, after all, finding little to praise in the work of his contemporaries, also looked to the past for standards of literary excellence. He wrote before Shakespeare or even Marlowe had made his mark, and his critical work, like Gardner's, had to wait more than a decade for publication (*On Moral Fiction*, according to Singular,[27] was first written in 1965, thirteen years before the literary environment would become receptive enough to its iconoclasm to allow publication). When Sidney's criticism appeared in 1595, the greatest literary efflorescence in history was under way, and it was, in retrospect, largely consistent with Sidney's taste and Sidney's judgments. One can only hope that another great literary and cultural renaissance will validate Gardner.

As artist and as critic, Gardner sought, like that little known but enlightened sculptor Nicholas Vergette, to build something over the "ancient abyss," the void into which most modern artists seem content merely to gaze. In Gardner's 1974 novella "The King's Indian," part of a collection dedicated to Vergette, the author mentions the dying sculptor at one point and contrasts him with the vicious Luther Flint, the artist who devotes himself exclusively to facile trickery. Flint, who leaves not a single floorboard over the abyss at the end, is the fictional counterpart of the numerous contemporary artists Gardner takes to task in *On Moral Fiction*. As for Gardner himself, he moved beyond the laying of floorboards to planning the arches and light.

2

Et in Arcadia Ego
Gardner's Early
Pastoral Novels

The woods of Arcady are dead
And over is their antique joy;
Of old the world on dreaming fed;
Gray Truth is now her painted toy.

—Yeats

Gardner produced novels, short stories, children's books, an epic poem, opera libretti, and, most recently, radio, film, and television scripts. As a scholar he produced books and articles on poetry, drama, and fiction, as well as translations from Middle English dialects, Old English, and Greek. His willingness to handle virtually any literary form complements an awareness of the possibilities of literary hybridization. In *Grendel* (1971), the best known manifestation of that awareness, Gardner converts an epic poem in Old English into a novel narrated by the original hero's monstrous antagonist and in doing so demonstrates—and comments on—the differences between the literature of the past and the literature of the present, the literature of heroic possibilities and the literature of anti-heroic futilities. But before combining novel and epic in *Grendel*, Gardner combined novel and pastoral in *The Resurrection* (1966), *The Wreckage of Agathon* (1970), and *Nickel Mountain* (1973).[1] In each of these, by availing himself of the conventions of pastoral and the novel's flexibility in the handling of point of view, he deals creatively with the artistic problem of treating in a positive manner the morbid subject of a protagonist's death.

One initially takes the subtitle of *Nickel Mountain*, "A Pastoral Novel," as a means of distinguishing it from the other early novels.

The one is pastoral because it concerns the country and rural folk, while the others, with their sophisticated and articulate protagonists and their overt concern with "ideas," are something else. But such a division is not particularly accurate. However one defines pastoral, it is more than a simple depiction of rustic virtues contrasted with urban vice, and in fact the pastoral setting need not necessarily be Arcadian. It is simplified, but it need not be idealized. Thus a pastoral can be set wholly or partly in a prison—particularly when, as in *The Beggar's Opera* ("a Newgate pastoral") or *The Wreckage of Agathon*, the author's intent is satiric. The shepherds become criminals, and they "complain" behind bars rather than on grassy swards. For that matter, a shepherd in a more conventional pastoral seldom bears any resemblance to his counterpart in real life. Writers of pastoral commonly take advantage of the simplicity of a carefully controlled setting to scrutinize the behavior of people who are often sophisticates translated into a world whose simple artifice contrasts with the complex artifice of the world they normally inhabit.[2] The setting may simply complement an elegant poetic dialogue, or it can function as a commentary on the sophistication and superficiality brought into it.

The pastoral setting can also provide perspective on the perennial human concerns of art, love, and death, and ultimately this perspective is its chief appeal for Gardner not only in *Nickel Mountain*, the ostensibly pastoral novel, but also in *The Resurrection*, in many ways the most pastoral novel of the three. Pastoral traditionally involves stripping away the distractions of urban civilization; thus there is a perfectly good literary reason for moving James Chandler out of San Francisco and his academic-urban milieu and back to the country. Once established in the rural setting, Chandler commences a treatise on aesthetics, just as certain shepherds in Spenser propound theories of poetry. But art is long, life is short, and death stalks swains like other men. Thus in *Arcadian Shepherds*, the famous painting by the seventeenth-century French artist Nicolas Poussin, shepherds in an idyllic landscape contemplate a tomb bearing the inscription *Et in Arcadia Ego*. The message is simple: "in Arcadia I, death, also hold sway." In pastoral poetry and in operas like Monteverdi's *Orfeo* the protagonists usually learn this grim fact through the sudden death of a comrade or a beloved. In *The Resurrection* the protagonist must face his own mortality. The point, however, is not to correct idealized notions of country life but to isolate the question of Chandler's death in a simplified setting where it may be recognized and accepted as part of a natural process.

The poignance of Chandler's death depends in large measure on the subtlety with which Gardner manipulates point of view in the novel. The book begins with the equivalent of Poussin's painting: a description, in a brief prologue narrated from a purely objective point of view, of Chandler's grave. The rest of the book is divided into three parts of twelve chapters each. With one or two minor deviations, each chapter is narrated from the point of view of a single character. As might be expected, most of the chapters are narrated from the point of view of the protagonist, James Chandler, but his chapters are not evenly distributed. While all twelve of the chapters in part one are narrated from his point of view, the number is halved in part two, and in part three only two chapters show the action as he sees it. The progression reflects Chandler's own fading from life; even his name, from the Latin *candela*, is a reminder that life is a wasting taper.

Point of view is a way of rendering consciousness. In life the world is marshalled around one's consciousness, and the self is the ultimate referent of external phenomena. Chandler had realized as a child that "beyond the farthest hill or cloud, beyond the farthest star he saw through his window at night, stretched the shell of his own mind." [3] But when consciousness departs, the "world" must be displaced into other consciousnesses—at least in fiction. Thus Gardner apportions the chapters not narrated from Chandler's point of view roughly in terms of age: the older the character, the fewer the chapters from his point of view. The secondary characters who are near death themselves, John Horne and Emma Staley, have only one chapter apiece. Chandler's aged mother has three, his middle-aged wife four, and nineteen-year-old Viola Staley six. But with Viola this declension stops, for none of the youngest characters, the children of the doomed man, is used as a center of consciousness in even a single chapter. A reason for the author's scrupulousness on this point is suggested by the main character of *Nickel Mountain*, who pauses over "what he'd never have doubted once, the idea that Henry Soames would live practically forever."[4] With an unconscious conviction of their own immortality, children have little understanding of death, even when it touches them. In *The Resurrection* the children's comprehension of the novel's central subject is inchoate; the author would have risked inappropriately ironic or sentimental effects if he had used one of them as a center of consciousness.

But Chandler himself repeatedly harks back to his childhood on his grandfather's farm, a truly pastoral landscape where he had had a child's intuitive knowledge of his place in the natural order. There, waking up mornings, "leaning out of the window smelling the air—flowers, apples, hay drying in windrows on the hill to the west," he had discovered "the interpenetration of the universe and himself. . . . It was himself . . . all the rich profusion of it" (p. 133). Sometimes, however, he had found nature more disquieting. Once, standing with his father on a roof, he had seen something terrible: "In the sky—it was this that they'd come up to see—there were birds, hundreds of thousands of them: hawks, starlings, sparrows" (p. 165). To his earnest query, "What does it *mean?*," his father had had no satisfactory answer. The wheeling birds become a motif in the book, and as death approaches, the image of vast multitudes of them careering in the sky repeatedly invades Chandler's mind. In one reverie he sees "a sky full of screaming blackbirds, hundreds of thousands of them, and he stood looking up at them, terrified. But even as he quaked, one part of his mind stepped back, calm, professorial, thinking, 'It means something perfectly obvious but what is it?'" (p. 135). The answer comes to him when he remembers an outing at the California coast one bleak day. Again he had seen birds by the "hundreds of thousands . . . caracoling over the water, below them, and screaming" (p. 153). In this landscape he had seen "miles of gray-green, dwarfish trees, the cliffs to the right, the ocean falling away to Japan, the wide storm of birds. What Chandler . . . had seen that instant was Death, wheeling and howling" (p. 155).

Chandler's birds are symbolically the vast hordes of the dead, which he will soon join. Like Yeats's mackerel-crowded seas, his bird-filled skies remind him of his place among dying generations. "Everything in this world," remarks a minor character in the book, "was made to go to waste" (p. 197). But what of the resurrection of the book's title? Resurrection is a word with religious and specifically Christian associations—and indeed James Chandler shares at least a pair of initials with Jesus Christ. Yet nothing in the book gainsays the finality of Chandler's death. An agnostic, he "couldn't turn on belief again now, merely because it would be comforting" (p. 41), and he explicitly repudiates the idea, hinted at by the grotesque John Horne, of being "born again." Although the problematic word in this book's title denotes a rising from the dead—as the word's etymology implies—it refers, as Gardner uses it, to the act of the living, who, letting the dead lie, rise and go on with the business of living. Chandler makes a mythic flight from west to east, from the region of the setting sun and death to the region of the rising sun and life, but to no avail. For him time's arrow points inexorably west. The hay he notices as a child has been harvested and laid out to dry on "a hill to the west," up on the roof with his father he sees "huge black clouds . . . sliding in from the west" (p. 165), the blighted landscape with caracoling seagulls is a westerly prospect, "the ocean falling away to Japan," and he even dies, bleeding, clutching Viola's foot, "an image out of some grim, high-class Western" (p. 232).

Gardner's scrupulously refuses his character and his reader any of the comforts that existential man views as false. Nevertheless, the tone of the book is positive, for Gardner insists that the spectacle of a man dying bravely, without recourse to superstition, is edifying. The point is made by Chandler himself in his aesthetic treatise: "All that belongs to Burke's realm of *the Sublime* (the large, the angular, the terrifying, etc.) we may identify with *moral affirmation*; that is to say, with human *defiance of chaos*, or the human assertion of *the godlike magnificence of human mind and heart*" (p. 201). Chandler's treatise is obviously an attempt to come to terms with his own death. That he never quite succeeds in doing so is a testimony to his honesty and to that of Gardner. But Chandler does convince himself that life is not futile as long as one can find grounds for "moral affirmation" in the face of yawning chaos. The terms in which he expresses his conviction are intended by Gardner to be applied to his book—a work of art that attempts to be both aesthetically and morally rewarding. As Chandler defies chaos by continuing to write, so Gardner means to defy the chaos he invokes in his awesome and terrible image of the birds. As thrilling as they are terrifying, the book's great images of mindless chaos are ultimately bracing—sublime in the Burkean sense.

Yet the bird-filled sky, Chandler's memento mori, need not be viewed exclusively as a sublimely terrifying image. The earliest appearance of this motif in the book is a casual allusion to "that last line of 'Sunday Morning'" (p. 129). The reference, of course, is to Wallace Stevens' famous meditation on the mystery and richness of the mortal state. Stevens fills his poem with descriptions of the natural world and the ephemerality of its beauties: fruit ripens, dew melts, April's green fades; the poem ends with several lines describing deer, and quail, and berries, and "casual flocks of pigeons" that "make / Ambiguous undulations as they sink, / Downward to darkness on extended wings." These are Chandler's serried birds in a more elegiac mode, and ultimately Gardner's book, like Stevens' poem, tempers the bleakness of its reflections on mortality by affirming not only the beauties of the natural world but also its generative vitality. The woodsman who makes the remark about all things being "made to go to waste" is obviously less impressed by the waste than by the sheer quantity, diversity, and tenaciousness of the teeming life around his woodland pond. The teeming pond and the bird-filled sky are finally part of Gardner's strategy in *The Resurrection*. To encounter the pastoral world, James Chandler must travel to the east, to the country, to his childhood, and back in time. That the trees are "just beginning to bud" (p. 18) when he returns to Batavia to die is a bitter irony yet also a comforting renewal: death and resurrection.

Though bucolic, Chandler's natal region cannot compare as a pastoral landscape with the Laconia of 800 B.C.E., the idyllic setting of *The Wreckage of Agathon*. Like Sidney's *Arcadia*—in which a helots' revolt also figures—this book addresses itself to the question of what constitutes just government. Sparta was the least urban of all the Greek city states; its ancient rival Athens was always vastly more sophisticated. Consequently, just as James Chandler is translated from San Francisco to Batavia, Agathon must be translated from Athens to Sparta. Yet Sparta mixed great natural beauty with political rigidity, and Gardner does more than move Agathon to the country: he moves him to a prison in the country. He thus qualifies the temperate nature common to pastoral. If pastoral conventionally places its characters in a simplified natural setting, then the concrete circumstances of the setting will vary from age to age, as "nature" is redefined. Agathon's prison merely updates the glossy natural world of older pastoral. As Solon's maxim has it, *"Imprisonment and execution are not great evils, merely mirrors, too clear for cowardly eyes, of reality as it is."* [5] Formerly the pastoralist could assume an orderly and beneficent natural world; though pastoral began in ancient times, pastoral stereotypes derive largely from the eighteenth century, when a serene optimism about the natural order made for particularly wholesome and salubrious pastoral landscapes. But if men define nature differently, as they do in every age, if they begin to view it as something brutal, random, and uncaring, then an entirely different literature will come out of placing characters in simplified natural settings. The same disinclination to idealize that results in such uniquely contemporary forms as *film noir* and black comedy also results in what might be called black pastoral, typical settings for which include the Mexican jail of *The Power and the Glory*, the claustrophobic hell of *No Exit*, and the bleak wasteland of *Waiting for Godot*.

Gardner's novel is in a sense a corrective to common stereotypes of ancient Greece and the pastoral mode; armed with a modern sensibility, he invades and reshapes a landscape in which the pastures, sheep, and shepherds ought still to be spotless. Of course such iconoclasm is not without precedent. Already Swift, with his acute sense of the world's fallen state, was capable of debunking Augustan celebrations of nature with his scatological pastorals—and it was Swift, reputedly, who suggested the idea of "a Newgate pastoral" to John Gay. Gardner's book, like Gay's opera, reveals that the difference between criminals and politicians is that the criminals happen to be in jail, the politicians in office; indeed, the criminals and politicians even have sporadic contact with each other. Each of these works, too, has a protagonist who is a lovable rogue. Like Gay's Macheath, Agathon has a weakness for women, and as Macheath has a long-standing relationship with Peachum and Lockit, who burlesque prominent politicians of eighteenth-century London, so Agathon has a relationship of long standing with Solon and Lykourgos. Both *The Wreckage of Agathon* and *The Beggar's Opera* posit some degree of identity between the man in office and the man in jail, and while Agathon's name means "the good," he and his antagonist are not melodramatic illustrations of the Lowellian formula: "Truth forever on the scaffold, Wrong forever on the throne." Agathon represents something potentially as destructive as that which Lykourgos represents. Both, significantly, are crippled: Lykourgos is one-eyed, Agathon is lame. The physical impairment is symbolic of flaws in both their world views —Lykourgos' adherence to the ideal of law and order and Agathon's personal creed of freedom and goodwill.

The journal entries written by Agathon and his reluctant disciple Demodokos are the equivalent of shepherds' plaints. They even come close to being the kind of dialogue between the spokesmen for two sides of an artistic or amatory question that often figures in more conventional pastoral. The journal entries also make for an interesting treatment of point of view, for the novel's action and the title character are presented exclusively through two first-person narratives. Agathon the seer and Demodokos the apprentice-seer or "peeker" are not exactly master and disciple, since Peeker is for the most part contemptuous and disloyal, though towards the end both he and the reader come to see the roguish Agathon as someone essentially noble, a Quixote undaunted by the world's demands that he behave responsibly. The novel's two voices generate ambiguity, especially regarding Agathon's character and the real significance of his imprisonment and resistance to authority. Peeker speaks for practical considerations. He is a street-wise apple vendor who recognizes with perfect clarity that Agathon is a filthy, lecherous, half-cracked old reprobate. His account at once serves as a corrective to the subjectivity of Agathon's narration and helps to keep his master from becoming in the reader's eyes a gentle, martyred soul like Socrates or Dietrich Bonhoeffer. Peeker also takes their imprisonment seriously. Agathon, on the other hand, understands it much better than his fellow prisoner, for he has a much better grasp of the political realities that have led them to prison. If Peeker's is the voice of practicality, Agathon's is the voice of philosophy and intuition. The irony of the situation—as in life generally—is that practicality tends to be blind to the long-term truth that makes it useless or stupid (Peeker's pathetic faith in and cooperation with the seemingly decent ephor does him no good whatsoever), while philosophy is ultimately more practical in that it recognizes the things on which day-to-day practicality is contingent.

One may ask why Gardner chooses these two for his first-person narrators. Why, in particular, Peeker, who has no part in the novel's political and amorous action? Why not Dorkis and Iona, leaders of the revolution, or Lykourgos, spokesman for the political order Agathon seems to be fronting? The reason is that with Agathon and Peeker Gardner secures the advantages of the two basic types of first-person narration and simultaneously avoids their pitfalls. A nonparticipant or innocent narrator like Peeker allows for gradual revelation of character and action, especially when he describes his experiences immediately, in his journal, rather than in retrospect. The ambiguities and uncertainties of real life are preserved and pierced only by degrees: like Nick Carraway in *The Great Gatsby*, Peeker comes to know the truth about events and the main character at the same rate the reader does. But with such a narrator one sacrifices some of the information and immediacy that a protagonist telling his own story can provide. Gardner therefore allows Agathon's narrative to complement Peeker's—though with questionable reliability, since a narrator's account of events in which he figured prominently will tend to be colored by his own interest or prejudice. The American husband in Ford's *The Good Soldier* or the title character in Gardner's *Grendel* demonstrates the unreliability of the narrator who is also a major character. Even more striking examples of the untrustworthiness of first-person accounts are to be found in recent history—in the various books written by participants in the Watergate scandal. John Dean, Richard Nixon, John Ehrlichman, and Leon Jaworski all purvey different versions of the truth.

The reference to Watergate is more relevant than it may seem, for to a certain extent Agathon's Sparta coincides with America in the Nixon years. The reader begins to realize as much when he notices the anachronisms and historical inaccuracies with which Gardner—a writer with credentials in classics—deliberately peppers the novel. His characters, for example, quote or allude to pre-Socratic philosophers such as Anaxagoras and Heraclitus, both of whom lived at least a hundred years later than the period described in the story. Similarly Hoplites go mounted, and women participate freely in political and social life. By means of such calculated "carelessness" Gardner prevents his readers from mistaking *The Wreckage of Agathon* for an historical novel, a scrupulously accurate account of ancient Greece in the Mary Renault mode. The novel is an allegory, and the author means for the contrasts between law-and-order despotism, revolutionary resistance, and private conscience to point up similar contrasts in the United States of the late 1960s. In those days, with Lykourgian pronouncements issuing from the White House, American Spartans crushed helots in Vietnam and on the campus while Agathons named Berrigan, Hayden, and Hoffman played the gadfly.

But Gardner avoids the trap that makes works like *MacBird!* and *Our Gang* ephemeral. As the 1960s fade into the past, his novel seems richer, like *The Beggar's Opera*, for outlasting its original topicality. Nixon and Agnew are gone, but Lykourgos we have always with us—as Castro if not Batista, as the Ayatollah if not the Shah. The helots recur as Tupamaros and Sandinistas, and Agathon is legion in the gulags. In other words, *The Wreckage of Agathon* is ultimately about political antinomies that are universal. These antinomies are also universally destructive, at least in the extreme forms in which they figure in the book, and Gardner presents them in terms of what they do to the pastoral countryside. Laconia quickly becomes a black-pastoral landscape dotted with burning grain stores and swarms of displaced persons.

The snowballing disorder in the country is an image of the condition towards which all things tend, from political systems to whole galaxies. Lykourgos has a certain narrow understanding of this entropic drift, for when Agathon tells him quite sensibly that "that which is unnatural, Nature destroys," the lawgiver replies: "All life is doomed, *finally*" (p. 52). But a wiser man, the tutor Klinias—a name, incidentally, out of Sidney's *Arcadia*—has instilled in Agathon a simple precept: "Never judge particular cases by general laws" (p. 68). Life, Gardner says, is a particular case, entropy a general law. With this point in mind, one can make certain choices among the ethical positions represented by Lykourgos the tyrant, Iona the revolutionary, and Agathon the putative bum. Agathon seems to sense that what is so destructive is the mutual extremism of the tyrant and the revolutionary; he recognizes that a paradoxical kinship exists between Lykourgos and Iona. "Her eyes," he remarks at one point, "were as cold, as aleatory, as the Kyklops eye of Lykourgos" (p. 57). Thus it is that only twice in the book does the protagonist act decisively: both times he attempts to forestall murder, even though he must betray friends to do so. Agathon is committed to life, and Gardner insists that the business of life is to defy entropy, not to endorse it.

Characters in Gardner's fiction have much to answer for if they have "aleatory" eyes, if they ally themselves to chance rather than choice, to the randomness that is entropy's end product. Chance is the nemesis of Henry Soames, the protagonist of *Nickel Mountain*. By becoming a husband and father he has, to paraphrase Sir Francis Bacon, given hostages to chance, and because his wife and child look to him as their protector, or "pastor," *Nickel Mountain* is "A Pastoral Novel," as its subtitle indicates, in more senses than one. Of the three books under consideration here, it comes closest to the definition of pastoral in Dr. Johnson's dictionary—even though the great lexicographer speaks not of the novel but of "a poem in which any action or passion is represented by its effects on a country life." The novel is set in rural upstate New York, and its characters, farmers and dairymen, are real agricultural people. Without turning the book into a neo-Arcadian tract, the author also observes the conventional distinctions between country and city. The reader learns at the outset that Callie Wells would like to go to New York and that she would be in danger there, since an acquaintance has gotten into trouble: "I'd hate to tell you what happened to *her* in New York City" (p. 8). Later Henry Soames reminisces on what he has seen in the city: impersonal multitudes, concrete, despair. The novel makes no overt claims for the rural life, but as the reader comes to know Henry Soames and his community he cannot fail to recognize that these people have a sense of shared values and of community that is of inestimable value in surviving the manifold shocks of modern life. The characters are not, however, idealized or sentimentalized like the shepherds of the classic pastoral. These are real people in a real setting, their lives hard but solid. If from time to time the author reminds the reader that his characters spend a good deal of their time clomping around in "good honest shit" (p. 216), the effect is not shocking, as it is in Swift's "Strephon and Chloe" or "Cassinus and Peter."

Although the protagonist, Henry Soames, keeps no farm, agriculture runs in his blood, for his grandparents farmed, and his father worked for a time as a dairyman. Henry also marries into a farming family, and he shares his neighbors' anxieties about weather and crops. Moreover, caring for a "flock" that is highly vulnerable to various dark forces, Henry takes his stewardship far more seriously than any ordinary shepherd. He is a "pastor" in a quasi-religious sense, and Gardner drives home the point by repeatedly comparing him to the archetypal Good Shepherd. Driving up Nickel Mountain makes Henry "feel like Jesus H. Christ charioting to heaven" (p. 31). At his wedding "George Loomis would be there beside him, looking him over, telling him to look like Good King Jesus" (p. 81). Later George probes for a sanctimonious motive in Henry's taking Simon Bale in: "I guess that makes you Jesus, don't it" (p. 194). George also sketches in an imaginary exchange between himself and Henry: "I'd say: 'You think you're God!' And you'd say, 'Yes.' I'd be stopped. Cold. What can you say to a man that's decided to be God?" (p. 225). All the allusions to Henry's Christlike role are rooted in the remarks of his friend Kuzitski: "A man wants something to die for" (p. 11). Henry quotes Kuzitski to Callie Wells and Willard Freund: "it's what poor old Kuzitski used to say: It's finding something to be crucified for. That's what a man has to have. . . . Crucifixion" (p. 42). (The point is made in a more narrowly evangelical sense by John Horne in *The Resurrection*.) But Henry's own pastoral pretensions are at this point qualified, made ridiculous, for "He was," the author says, "a fat, blubbering Holy Jesus, or anyway one half of him was, loving hell out of truckers and drunks and Willards and Callies—ready to be nailed for them" (p. 42).

As Henry progresses from a picture of modern alienation (physically and spiritually sick, isolated, despised) to an unwitting hero who chooses, as George Loomis asseverates, to take on the responsibilities of an absentee God, he makes a transition from the fat blubbering Holy Jesus of the novel's opening pages to something closer to the original. The reader participates in Henry's transition from pariah to pastor through Gardner's handling of point of view. The book comprises fifty-one chapters in eight titled sections. In the first four and the last two of the titled sections the narrator limits himself to the perceptions of a single character. But in the other two—sections five and six, over a third of the book—point of view shifts continually, not merely from one of the eighteen chapters to the next, but from page to page and paragraph to paragraph. The change in narrative technique does not, however, constitute an abandonment of the discipline manifested elsewhere, for the alternations in narrative strategy allow the reader to move with Henry Soames and his neighbors from isolation to community. Thus the book opens with a fourteen-chapter section narrated scrupulously from Henry's point of view. Confined to the protagonist's world, the reader experiences Henry's alienation and misery at first hand. The transition from isolation to community begins in section two, "The Wedding," but the reader knows only that poor pregnant Callie Wells must, to save appearances, take her monstrously fat employer as a husband. Narrated from Callie's point of view, this section avoids the tone of desperate misery one might expect because the narrator's obvious fondness for the Wells, Jones, Thomas, and Griffith clans, and for the whole celebration, shifts the reader towards a greater sense of well-being. Section three remains ominous. Troubled by the possibility of Callie's death or Willard's return and still horribly isolated, Henry waits through his wife's long and painful delivery. Again, the reader shares his isolation through carefully controlled point of view. But with the birth of the child the last chapter in this section begins: "And so, it seemed to Henry, it was different now" (p. 121).

After a long section narrated from the point of view of George Loomis, another isolate (he has no family, only "things"), the novel shifts gears. Gardner abandons the restricted point of view of the first four sections and devotes the middle third of the book to a depiction of family and community life. The characters do not overcome isolation entirely (the reader gets glimpses of George Loomis's solitary life, and after Simon Bale's death Henry slips into anomie), but in his attention to the customers at the diner, to unfortunate neighbors like Simon Bale, and to the community-wide anxiety about the continuing drought, the author turns away from individual alienation to celebrate the healing influence of the communal whole. In these chapters the point of view is either omniscient or continually shifting from character to character. The narration immerses the reader in these different lives: Henry, Callie, Simon Bale, George Loomis, Doc Cathey, Nick Blue, Old Man Judkins, the Goat Lady. Life flourishes, and it manages to carry Henry along through his dark night of the soul after the death of Simon Bale.

The novel concludes with two balanced sections—each four chapters long—that return to narration from a single character's point of view. Section seven, devoted to the return from college of Willard Freund, presents a rather unattractive picture. Willard is having an affair with a psychoanalyst's neurotic daughter, and he has lost his ingenuous enthusiasm about race cars to become cynical and superior in his attitude towards the community that produced him. Deracinated, he has moved spiritually from the country to the city, and the narration from his point of view emphasizes his isolation. Willard's old friend Henry, meanwhile, has moved from alienation and despair to quiet confidence in his home, his family, and his place in the community. Henry is the rich man suggested by his name, which derives from Germanic roots meaning *home* and *kingdom*. If at the end Henry is again alone—for the book's last section, like its first, is narrated strictly from Henry's point of view—his solitariness is qualified by all that he has learned and experienced. This last section's title, "The Grave," brings us full circle to the opening of *The Resurrection*, and the message once again is that no Arcadia can exclude death. Henry's solitude at the end reflects the nearness of his own death, which he must face alone. But he need not face it in loneliness, for now he has lived, now he understands the natural order, now he belongs to a community in which life and death are accepted as part of the same process that brings seasons and crops. Henry is alone, as the limited point of view emphasizes, but he is not alienated. With his son beside him, curious about dead rabbits and opened graves, Henry sees that "life goes on." He accepts, he affirms.

Henry may not be particularly intelligent, but he is infinitely wise. Like James Chandler at his moment of epiphany, Henry affirms not the beauty of the world but the world itself. "The world had changed for Henry Soames because little by little he had come to see it less as a yarn told after dinner, with all the relatives sitting around, and more as a kind of church service—communion, say, or a wedding" (pp. 299–300). The world has become sacramental. These words come from the book's penultimate chapter, which contains a good deal of sacramental language. Feeling "like a man who'd been born again," a man with a "new life," Henry perceives "the holiness of things" (p. 301). A secular savior, he saves not only Callie and Jimmy but also himself. He tries to save Simon Bale, a man obsessed with the idea of a Christian salvation. Ironically, though he could never realize it, Simon is privileged, like his namesake Simeon in the New Testament, to see the "savior" before his death. But the appropriation of religious language and symbols must not mislead the reader, for Henry is strictly a temporal savior. His serenity at the end is merely the believable reward for the "pastoral" life in all senses of that word.

In these early pastoral novels—prolegomena to his greatest pastoral, *October Light* (1976)—Gardner sets himself the task of making positive stories out of the grimmest possible material: a man struck down in his prime by a terrible disease, a derelict rotting to death in a filthy prison cell, and a shabby isolate wrestling obesity. Gardner realized that his creed as a novelist—affirmation—was nugatory unless it could be practiced in the face of the ugliest truths about the human condition: the death, disease, cruelty, selfishness, and hardship that flesh inherits. His adaptation of pastoral conventions allows him, with the weight of a venerable literary tradition at his back, to focus more clearly on the questions, moral and mortal, that he addresses in these novels. He also, in at least two of the books, enlists nature in her more temperate aspects as a source of comfort and reassurance. Doggedly positive in novel after novel, Gardner struck many of his contemporaries as ridiculously quixotic, but in time they may find him, like Don Quixote himself, more admirable than absurd.

3

Artists Divine and Otherwise
Grendel

Schopenhauer has analysed the pessi-
mism that characterises modern
thought, but Hamlet invented it. The
world has become sad because a puppet was once melancholy.

—Wilde

According to John Gardner, the credit for Grendel's defeat ought properly to go to the Shaper, not to the beefy and humorless Beowulf. Proof against the small-scale heroics of the territorial imperative, Grendel might have continued to harass the Scyldings indefinitely had art not shaped a more substantial heroic ideal to nurture a deliverer. But Gardner goes beyond making the Shaper his hero. He makes Grendel the narrator of his novel, and in that role the monster becomes in effect the Shaper's rival artist. Thus the battle between Grendel and Beowulf, a contest of strength, takes second place in importance to the indirect competition between Grendel and the Shaper—a contest of art. The story ultimately concerns the triumph of good art over bad, for in it Grendel manages only self-indictment. He unwittingly produces a case history of the bad artist, as John Gardner would define such a monster.

Gardner inadvertently misled a few critics with his remark, in an interview, about Grendel's becoming an artist when Beowulf twists his arm and makes him sing: "At the end of the novel Grendel himself becomes the Shaper. Beowulf bangs his head against the wall and says, *feel*. Grendel feels—his head hurts—so Beowulf makes him sing about walls. When the Shaper dies a kid is chosen to succeed him, but the real successor is Grendel."[1] But

Grendel is in fact an artist throughout the book, as one can see by a kind of argument-from-design: only an artist could have produced such an artful narrative. Susan Strehle, who sees that "the novel traces the development of Grendel's artistry," points out how the later chapters "include long sections of poetry in a variety of literary forms."[2] Yet in singling out those later, "lyrical" chapters to illustrate her point, Strehle seems to imply that the early chapters are less artistic and that Grendel emerges as an artist only in the latter part of the novel. One must realize, however, that the book's incrementally poetic structure is the calculated effect of an artist whose control manifests itself equally in every part of the narrative. Grendel introduces and often refers to himself as one perennially engaged—like any poet or novelist—in "spinning a web of words."[3] Even at the beginning, he embellishes his tale with poetic devices, especially alliteration: "These brainless budding trees, these brattling birds" (p. 6), "stirrings of springtime" (p. 8), "life-bloated, baffled, long-suffering hag" (p. 11). From the first line's "old ram" that "cocks his head like an elderly, slow-witted king," simile and metaphor also figure prominently in his artistic repertoire.

   Though Grendel is an artist throughout his narrative, he has not been an artist all his life. His artistic vocation dates from his first encounter with the Shaper; consequently he describes his career before the coming of the bard—in chapter 2 and most of chapter 3—in language more prosaic than that obtaining in the rest of the narrative. On that first appearance at Heorot, the Shaper sings of great Scyld and the line he founded, and Grendel, confused and troubled, cannot get the poetry out of his head as he makes his way home. "At the top of the cliffwall I turned and looked down, and I saw all the lights of Hrothgar's realm and the realms beyond that, that would soon be his, and to clear my mind, I sucked in wind and screamed. The sound went out, violent, to the rims of the world, and after a moment it bounced back up at me—harsh and ungodly against the sigh of the remembered harp—like a thousand tortured rat-squeals crying: *Lost!*" (p. 45).

This scream is, I think, Grendel's earliest attempt at an artistic response to experience. It is the uncouth utterance, the "barbaric yawp," of a fledgling poet. But at the same time that he reports on his nascent artistry, Grendel works in figures of speech that quietly discover a later mastery. Indeed, the barbaric yawp is preceded by a simile that reveals the presence of the mature artist behind the description of the immature one: "The yellow lights of peasant huts were like scattered jewels on the ravendark cloak of a king" (p. 44). It is a rather sophisticated simile at that, since it hosts a secondary comparison—the metaphoric "ravendark"—and expresses admirably the future status of far-flung peasant villages.

Grendel, then, is the Shaper's epigone. But where the Shaper changes men, and for the better, Grendel does not. However verbally gifted, he lacks the power of a transforming imagination, as he himself dimly realizes when he slyly comments on his early imitation of the Shaper:

> 'Well then he's changed them,' I said. . . .
> 'He reshapes the world . . . . So his name implies. He stares strange-eyed at the mindless world and turns dry sticks to gold.'
> A little poetic, I would readily admit. His manner of speaking was infecting me, making me pompous. 'Nevertheless,' I whispered crossly—but I couldn't go on, too conscious all at once of my whispering, my eternal posturing, always transforming the world with words—changing nothing. (pp. 48–49)

What kind of artist, having such knowledge and such power, declines to "shape" a wholesome world in which men strive to be loyal, heroic, far-seeing, and decent? According to Gardner, only a woefully benighted or downright vicious artist could fail so signally in his responsibility to the community. Too many modern writers, Gardner implies, seem to have shrugged, like the poet of an earlier generation, and said: "Play no tricks upon thy soul, O man; / Let fact be fact, and life the thing it can." The bad artist, like Grendel, lets "fact be fact" and changes nothing; the good artist, like the Shaper, insists that life is what we make it and changes everything. He is our true deliverer.

The bad artist, in Gardner's view, is not merely careless, conceited, or immoral. He is *monstrous*. The author could have made his rival shaper an ordinary mortal, but he pointedly makes him the supreme antagonist, the monster that by definition embodies nature gone malign and riotous. But Grendel plays a variety of symbolic roles—including some that might appear mutually exclusive. He is, for example, a distillation or projection of humanity's least appealing appetites at the same time that he is an embodiment of the entire nonhuman universe, conceived as sentient and single-mindedly malevolent. If the malignity of the universe is something conferred on it by the human imagination, man nevertheless advances the cause and the conception of his own humanity by such projections. The dragon delivers a cynical lecture on humanity's curious debt to Grendel: "You improve them, my boy! . . . You stimulate them! You make them think and scheme. You drive them to poetry, science, religion, all that makes them what they are for as long as they last. You are, so to speak, the brute existent by which they learn to define themselves. The exile, captivity, death they shrink from—the blunt facts of their mortality, their abandonment—that's what you make them recognize, embrace! You *are* mankind, or man's condition: inseparable as the mountain-climber and the mountain" (pp. 72–73).

The ironies of "you *are* mankind" are profound. Grendel dwells inside man as much as outside, and the monster's exclusion from the meadhall and the human community it represents is recognizably man's attempt to banish, through the instrumentality of civilization itself, his own baser instincts. Grendel reifies those parts of man's inner being that he trusts least or fears most, those passions or appetites driven deep into the unconscious, from whence they manifest themselves without harm only in dreams or works of the imagination. This monster, after all, is the creation of art, or rather of the artist who dreams public dreams for us, making us shiver at the ghastly things he calls up, with such insouciance and sangfroid, from the depths of the unconscious. Contemplation of monsters in works of the imagination is thus indirectly instructive and chastening; to the extent that some kind of vicarious release figures, it is even cathartic. But along with common repressions, works of art also reflect private concerns that are not necessarily unconscious or pathological. John Gardner, for example, is surely drawn to this avatar of Cain—and moved to tell his story in the first person—by the complex of emotions deriving from the fact that years ago he accidentally killed *his* brother.[4] "It hath the primal eldest curse upon't, / A brother's murder," says Claudius in *Hamlet*, and one need not have committed murder in the first degree to suffer the guilt—as the misery of the brother-killer and flawed hero Unferth reveals.

But one finds such superficial psychologizing less interesting and important than the perfectly conscious symbolism whereby Gardner projects himself into the novel as two kinds of artist, both quite appealing in different ways. Why does Gardner make his villain so winsome and droll? The answer lies partly in the author's willingness to do justice to the kind of artist Grendel represents. Behind Grendel are a host of witty and appealing modern writers—among them such "black-humorists" as Nathanael West, John Barth, Kurt Vonnegut, and Joseph Heller—who sugarcoat their bleak themes with amusing patter. But more specifically, Grendel is allowed to be charming and frequently cogent because he is modeled on a writer for whom Gardner felt a reluctant admiration: Jean-Paul Sartre. Gardner considered the French philosopher a mistaken thinker with the ability to

> write like an angel. That's the thing that fascinates me. Sartre is my great love-hate, kind of because he's a horror intellectually, figuratively, and morally, but he's a wonderful writer and anything he says you believe, at least for the moment, because of the way he says it. . . . What happened in *Grendel* was that I got the idea of presenting the Beowulf monster as Jean-Paul Sartre, and everything Grendel says Sartre in one mood or another has said, so that my love of Sartre kind of comes through

as my love of the monster, though monsters are still monsters—I hope.[5]

One notes here a tremendous ambivalence towards the thing decried; monster or *philosophe*, Grendel is an intimate part of John Gardner—whether as intellectual freight for the conscious mind or as mythic projection of the unconscious. (Given the French pedigree for Grendel, incidentally, one begins to recognize in the creature rendered by Gardner's illustrator, Emil Antonucci, the lineaments of the splendid monster in Cocteau's *Beauty and the Beast*.)

The existentialism of Sartre provides a point of reference for Gardner's plan, in *Grendel*, "to go through the main ideas of Western civilization."[6] Craig J. Stromme, taking Gardner's hint that these great ideas number roughly twelve, has argued that they are taken up seriatim in the novel's twelve chapters,[7] but one suspects that the author of *Grendel* has not conceived its philosophical content so schematically. After all, the important ideas explored in the book number rather more than twelve: Gardner manages to scan major social and economic ideas like chivalry, feudalism, and mercantilism; theology from primitive animism to Kierkegaard, with side glances at oriental religions; metaphysics from Hume to Sartre and from Heidegger to Whitehead; and political philosophy—the origins, legitimacy, and accountability of the state—from Plato to Locke and Hobbes, and from Machiavelli to Marx and Georges Sorel. Surprisingly, this ranging of the ideational vast neither confuses nor distracts, for the ideas examined are dramatically integrated and subordinated to the aesthetic question—how to construe the moral responsibility of the artist—that for Gardner subsumes all others.

Like Samuel Johnson in *Rasselas*, the author of *Grendel* surveys, in the various ideas taken up, the possibilities for optimism about the human condition, and in this respect the novel does not differ radically from the Ur-story, *Beowulf*. Projecting a fatalistic awareness of man's mortality and the mutability of all his glories, the *Beowulf*-poet also "surveys" the claims of statecraft, familial love, heroism, and loyalty to gainsay the passing of all things: great men, great beauty, great nations. *Beowulf* at once endorses and questions the values of the society it describes; it glorifies the ancient, heroic ideals espoused by the pagan ancestors of its Christian audience at the same time that it reveals how little those ideals mean without the rationale provided by Christian faith. With *Grendel* the situation is exactly reversed. Where the earlier audience could look back on the pagan past and congratulate itself on its spiritual enlightenment, the modern audience looks back on a Christian past and laments its disillusionment. The desperate spiritual situation of the Scyldings mirrors our own.

In *Beowulf* the spiritual critique of the poem's action emerges through a strategy of Biblical allusion. For example, the poet draws a direct parallel between Hrothgar's splendid meadhall, Heorot, and God's creation as described in Genesis. When he subsequently hints that Heorot will one day perish in a terrible conflagration, the reader may recall that Christian prophecy describes a similar fate for the world. The poet, however, makes no direct reference to Revelation, because—though he frequently alludes to the Old Testament—he consistently refuses to mention the New Testament and its message of redemption for a fallen world. Thus he pretends, as it were, to be an artist with only half of a Judaeo-Christian heritage at his disposal. From this odd vantage he imagines pagans capable at best of a fitful monotheism, for the Scyldings stood in desperate need of the Christian message that had recently—perhaps within living memory—come to *Beowulf*'s audience. Critics have argued that the *Beowulf*-poet suppressed New Testament references so that the audience, wondering at his reticence, would the more readily see the heroic deliverer, Beowulf, as an allegorical Christ. Gardner himself, in *The Construction of Christian Poetry in Old English*, cites the many details that justify an allegorical reading of the poem:

> The hero is unquestionably 'Christlike': as Beowulf alone overcame the demonic enemy of all (699), Christ overcame the

devil; as Beowulf's mother might well say that 'the God of Old was kind to her in her childbearing' (942b sq.), so the Virgin might say; as Beowulf's men give up all hope in the ninth hour (1600a), so did the disciples at the crucifixion; and as Beowulf was survived by twelve, so was Christ. . . . In his first great battle, Beowulf killed nine sea monsters; Christ in his first great battle expelled defectors from nine angelic legions. . . . The Grendel's Mere episode is parallel to Christ's crucifixion and harrowing of hell . . . . And the dragon episode may have to do, on its deepest level, with Armageddon and Last Judgment.[8]

In the ultimate victory the deliverer triumphs over "the dragon, that old serpent, which is the Devil" (Rev. 20:2). Indeed, Beowulf's three monstrous antagonists remind one of Milton's chthonic trinity: Satan, his self-begotten paramour Sin, and their incestuous issue Death. (Though probably inapplicable to *Beowulf* directly, the Miltonic paradigm provides an intriguing clue to the identity of Grendel's absentee father.) Like Christ, the hero must lay down his life to defeat the satanic dragon, but as the poet ends his story, the allegory, which Gardner suggests may be "ironic," is allowed to disperse. When Beowulf prepares for his burial as a mortal and a pagan, and when his people learn of their bleak future, the poet provides a final reminder of the emptiness of heroism and glory unvalidated by the Christian dispensation.

Gardner scrupulously follows the action, details, and symbolism of the original poem. In *Beowulf*, for example, the number twelve figures importantly: Grendel's ravages last "twelve winters"; Hrothgar's gifts to the successful hero include a helmet, sword, mailshirt, battle-banner, and eight horses; and eleven companions and a traitor appear in the dragon sequence. Numerologically significant, the recurring number is the product of four and three, numbers symbolic of the four earthly elements and of triune godhead. These numbers represent the material and the spiritual; multiplied together, according to the medieval numerologist Hugh of St. Victor, they produce a number symbolic of the universe.[9] Thus Gardner, in his novel, recounts the twelve months of the twelfth year of the monster's war on Hrothgar and the Scyldings, and the squaring of the symbolic number underscores its cosmic significance. "Twelve is, I hope, a holy number" (p. 92), says Grendel with unconscious irony.

The twelve chapters of *Grendel* are each narrated under a different astrological sign, from the sign of the ram to the sign of the fish. The account of a year's cycle, it takes advantage of the profoundly mythic rhythms of the annual revolution of the seasons. The beginning in Aries has its precedent, of course, in *The Canterbury Tales* and in *The Waste Land*, and indeed Gardner is mediating between Chaucer's world view and Eliot's. If the novel's trajectory towards that ancient life-symbol, the fish, seems to rehearse Eliot's own spiritual journey, both the narrator and the author stop short of embracing, as Eliot did, the Christian faith. The journey thus chronicled—the mental traveling, so to speak—complements the progression or passing-in-review of those "main ideas" that culminate in a modern world view that is, broadly speaking, "existentialist," for the narrator, as we have seen, is an arch-existentialist who witnesses and shakes his head, sadly or contemptuously, over the unfolding of those ideas. But Grendel's philosophical perspective, so enormously influential in shaping the dominant outlook of our time, is itself subtly undercut—like the heroic pretensions of *Beowulf*'s ancient Danes—by an artist sensitive to the tragic implications of a flawed world picture. Like his spiritual ancestor, the creator of *Beowulf*, Gardner embraces an art undergirded by a philosophy rather more sanguine than the one he is constrained, by historical and literary circumstance, to deal with.

The novel's epigraph, from William Blake's "The Mental Traveller," also hints that Grendel's view will not prevail. Blake's poem concerns a miraculous "Babe" whose growth and decline, according to W. M. Rossetti, represent the career of any public idea—first attacked, then deferred to, and at last supplanted by a newer idea.[10] Like Grendel, Blake's Babe inspires fear and revulsion in certain phases of his life cycle; the ghastly "Woman Old" who attends him even reminds one of Grendel's mother. In fact, the poem can be made to annotate the novel at several points. For example, one of the great public ideas the Babe represents is Christianity, and Blake adumbrates, especially in the stanzas following the one Gardner cites in his epigraph, features of Christ's passion in the Babe's career: "She binds iron thorns around his head, / She pierces both his hands and feet, / She cuts his heart out at his side." Eventually the Babe becomes a "bleeding youth" and the formerly anile companion a "Virgin Bright." In linking his ideational Babe to Christ, Blake asserts that the world will always martyr the bringer of a new dispensation. Hardly orthodox in his religion, he also hints that Christianity itself will eventually give way to something new; beneath the trappings of this or that religion, however, lies a truth that will not change, for the Babe remains the same from cycle to cycle. Gardner follows the poem in providing the otherwise demonic Grendel with certain Christlike attributes. After all, he is arguably the product of a virgin birth, and, as will be seen in more detail presently, he undergoes a kind of crucifixion.

Lines toward the end of the poem also sound relevant to Grendel, for the Babe, poised between the end of one cycle and the beginning of another, seems particularly fearsome:

> But when they find the frowning Babe,
> Terror strikes thro' the region wide,
> They cry 'The Babe! the Babe is born!'
> And flee away on Every side.
> But who dare touch the frowning form,
> His arm is wither'd at its root.

In this passage one sees not only Grendel, but also—especially in the last two lines—Grendel's victor, for at the tearing off of an arm, Grendel's day passes, and Beowulf's day begins. Thus the epigraph allows Gardner to remind his reader that however persuasive and final the prevailing world view seems, it is still destined, like all the world-swaying ideas before it, for the scrap heap or the museum—just as the comfortless and fatalistic ethos of the heathen Scyldings eventually gave way, in the time of the *Beowulf-poet*, to the sunnier idea of Christian humanism. The something immutable that Blake intuited beneath the surface of perishable Christianity is still valid, Gardner would insist, even though there is as yet no new formulation of it consistent with the modern temper.

Like Blake's poem, Gardner's novel is circular in form. Certain chapters begin and end with the same words and phrases, and the novel as a whole, having rehearsed one full cycle, Aries to Pisces, ends where it began. The message as well as the medium, the circle is an ancient symbol of eternity, perfection, and faith—and not least because it is the emblem of the annual round, the yearly progression of the seasons. This cycle, culminating in spring's yearly triumph over wintry death, provides Gardner with the substructure of his novel and the great counter to Grendel's dreary metaphysics. Beowulf, brutal pedagogue, inculcates the lesson of the natural cycle and its message of hope: "*Where the water was rigid there will be fish, and men will survive on their flesh till spring. It's coming, my brother. Believe it or not. Though you murder the world, turn plains to stone, transmogrify life into I and it, strong searching roots will crack your cave and rain will cleanse it: The world will burn green, sperm build again*" (p. 170).

Yet Gardner has at no point suggested that anything about the natural cycle cancels the absoluteness of death for the individual. The stirring arrival of spring, with its resurgence of life, does not prevent the passing of the Shaper (who dies like Leonardo, with a sovereign in attendance) or the decline into the feebleness before death of Hrothgar and his mighty kingdom. In the emphasis placed on the discontent of Hrothgar's nephew Hrothulf Gardner foreshadows the destruction of Heorot and all it represents. A more subtle augury of the same event appears in a portentous description of a hunt. In the chapter narrated under the sign of Sagittarius, one of Hrothgar's bowmen slays a hart, the majestic creature from which the king's great hall takes it name. The hart "lies as still as the snow hurtling outward around him to the hushed world's rim," and even Grendel worries over its death. "The image clings to my mind like a growth. I sense some riddle in it" (p. 127). But the inevitable destruction of Heorot and the world it symbolizes does not invalidate the affirmation Gardner puts into the mouth of Beowulf. Life's return, spring after spring, provides no inconsiderable counterbalance to the horrors of personal and, in time, cosmic oblivion. Only Death himself, only an entity excluded absolutely and by its very nature from the communion of all living things, could loathe the season of renewal as Grendel does.

Nature's rhythms are stable and comforting, even though they include death along with life. From the vantage of its conclusion, the novel's opening scene reveals itself as a distillation of the entire story, for Grendel here protests too much his hatred of the spring. The "old ram" of the first line stands his ground in the face of Grendel's threats because of something bigger and vastly more powerful than either: "The season is upon us" (p. 5). But to a being like Grendel, blind to or contemptuous of nature's contradiction of himself, the vernal season can only bring pain and frustration. The ram's stubbornness anticipates that of the goat in Chapter 10, which refuses to be intimidated as it climbs towards a height occupied by Grendel. With frightful bloodshed the monster systematically destroys the goat, but the creature keeps coming, even after it is technically "dead," and thus becomes an emblem of life's blind, undeniable tenacity—life, under the wintry sign of Capricorn, fighting its way upward, towards the vernal efflorescence.

"It is the business of rams to be rams and of goats to be goats" (p. 165), Grendel reflects cryptically before he meets Beowulf for their fated struggle, the mythic agon of winter and spring. But to identify the monster as an incarnation of winter, or death, scarcely does justice to the extraordinary complexity of Gardner's mythmaking. In Grendel's history the author has gone beyond eclectic demonology to anatomize the development of religion itself, from primitive, animistic belief to sophisticated theology. Intimately bound up with the origins of religion, the seasonal progression that structures the novel provides an ideal backdrop for Gardner's treatment of the religious impulse in its various cultural phases.

One sees the breadth and subtlety of this author's handling of primitive religion in the way he associates Grendel, or at least Grendel's arm, with the theories of Sir James George Frazer concerning the legendary Golden Bough, the talisman required by Aeneas to visit—and return from—the underworld. Frazer theorized that the Golden Bough was really the mistletoe that grows parasitically on various trees, especially the oak that figures in the Virgilian account.[11] Frazer's parasite reminds one of Grendel when first encountered by man. Trapped in an oak tree, he is taken at first for a "growth" or "fungus" (p. 24), then as an "oaktree spirit" (p. 25). Grendel shares with the Golden Bough an invulnerability to weapons. As the Cumaean Sibyl tells Aeneas, no blade can hew the Golden Bough; it must be plucked, and only by one smiled on by fate. Thus the blades of the Scyldings are ineffective against Grendel, and only the heroic Beowulf, a Nordic Aeneas favored by fate, is able to strip off a "branch." As Aeneas hangs up the Golden Bough at the gates of Elysium, so the Scyldings hang up Grendel's arm at Heorot. When Grendel's mother bears it off, necessitating the desperate pursuit to her subterranean cave, it even becomes, in a sense, Beowulf's ticket to the underworld.

The world of *Grendel*, however plausibly that of ancient Scandinavia, is also purely archetypal. Thus Grendel's discoverers, the youthful Hrothgar and his companions, enact, as it were, a tableau: primitive man encountering a supernatural world that requires propitiation. "Go get the thing some pigs" (p. 26), Hrothgar orders. Quickly promoted from oaktree spirit to hellish inventor of fratricide, Grendel becomes part of a more elaborate theology and its complementary demonology, as we see when the Shaper relates the Cain story and when the priests pray to the "ghostly Destroyer" (p. 127) to deliver them from the world-rim-walker. As the increasing sophistication of the characters telescopes man's entire social evolution, the rise of Grendel and Grendel-propitiation condenses the development of all religion. "He's in a period of transition" (p. 26), observes one of Grendel's discoverers. The joke behind this amusingly anachronistic remark is that the men, too, are in a period of transition.

If to the Scyldings Grendel remains always the arch-enemy, to the reader he seems at times more divine than demonic, for he undergoes a crucifixion that would seem to link him to myths of the divine scapegoat. When he hangs by one foot from his cross of living wood, the double oak tree, he is the living representation of that traditional emblem of divine sacrifice, the "hanged man" of the Tarot. Though Grendel's suffering here invites comparison to that of the crucified Christ, his passion seems closest to that of the Norse god Odin, who obtained power and knowledge—notably of poetry—through his self-crucifixion on Yggdrasil, the world tree or *axis mundi*. The roots of the world tree descend into the void, and visions of gnarled roots and the abyss into which they disappear recur to Grendel at various times in the years after his escape from the tree. "I recall something," he remarks at the end of chapter 9: "A void boundless as a nether sky. I hang by the twisted roots of an oak, looking down into immensity" (p. 137). The vision returns when the Geatish hero bests him. "I am . . . falling through bottomless space—*Wa!*—snatching at the huge twisted roots of an oak . . . a blinding flash of fire . . . no, darkness" (p. 169). At the end, breathing his last, he looks into the void that will presently swallow him: "With my one weak arm I cling to the huge twisted roots of an oak. I look down past stars to a terrifying darkness" (p. 173).[12]

Odin's passion was the price of his knowledge of certain esoterica, and Grendel, too, learns from his painful experience. Indeed, the suffering of gods is frequently associated with the acquisition of knowledge. Prometheus suffers for bringing knowledge to man, and Christ suffers—on a cross symbolically identified with the Tree of Knowledge—for man's impious seizing of an apple from that tree. Thus Grendel's existential knowledge of the universe dates from his passion in a tree. "I understood that the world was nothing: a mechanical chaos of casual, brute enmity on which we stupidly impose our hopes and fears. I understood that, finally and absolutely, I alone exist. All the rest, I saw, is merely what pushes me, or what I push against, blindly—as blindly as all that is not myself pushes back. I create the whole universe, blink by blink.—An ugly god pitifully dying in a tree!" (pp. 21–22).

But Grendel's passion is unredemptive, and the knowledge he gains amounts to little more than a projection of his own self-absorption. A parody-scapegoat, he merely impersonates a savior. Such an inchoate messiah—generically called the "trickster" because his suffering is usually occasioned by his cruelty, pranks, and general destructiveness—is not uncommon among primitive peoples. In his essay "On the Psychology of the Trickster-Figure," Carl Gustav Jung notes "his fondness for sly jokes and malicious pranks, his powers as a shape-shifter, his dual nature, half animal, half divine, his exposure to all kinds of tortures, and—last but not least—his approximation to the figure of a saviour."[13] Jung believed that the trickster modulates, in the mythology of more advanced societies, into more benign gods, including authentic scapegoat-figures who sacrifice themselves for the good of man. He saw the trickster as a "'forerunner' of the saviour, and, like him, God, man, and animal at once. He is both subhuman and superhuman, a bestial and divine being."[14] Few tricksters fit the model as perfectly as Grendel. But though he suffers like the divine scapegoat, Grendel never rises to savior-status. The redemptive function is displaced, partly onto the Shaper and partly onto Beowulf. One can even think of these two as God-the-Father, creator of the heroic ideal that will save the people, and God-the-Son, agent of the deliverance.

One can complete the trinity by including the shaping spirit that broods over experiential chaos to bring fictive order: John Gardner. The implied affinity between artistic and divine creation is of course a commonplace; Gardner himself once remarked that "the true story teller . . . is a model for all artists—intuition in the service of King Reason—therefore the eternal artist, God on earth."[15] But the divine artist must vie with the demonic competition. Viewing Grendel as a trickster-god who does not evolve into something more benign is essentially the same as viewing him as an artist, the Shaper's unwitting apprentice, whose talent is perverted. Without ever really understanding why, Grendel "cannot help but admire" (p. 12) the Shaper. Refuting the things affirmed by the Shaper proves difficult for the monster, however well he knows that the empirical facts of existence run counter to the way the bard represents them. Angry to see how "lies" allow man to flourish, Grendel assumes the task of reminding humanity— through his art as well as his predations—of the elemental and brutal reality of which he is himself the chief symbol.

In doing so he resembles certain no-nonsense modern artists. Gardner frequently denounced the modern artist's complacent and Grendel-like asseveration of the grimness of things. "Surely," opines John Updike, "morality in fiction is accuracy and truth. The world has changed, and in a sense we are all heirs to despair. Better to face this and tell the truth, however dismal."[16] But when artists devote themselves, like Grendel, to reminding us of the ultimate meaninglessness of existence, they undermine values that, however provisional, alone make civilization possible. Art is often described as subversive, but the subversiveness is properly aimed at narrow-minded pieties and smugness. If art poses a threat to something vastly more substantial than the values of the middle class, and if, moreover, it does so out of a smug complacency about the sacredness of its mission ("truth"), then according to Gardner it has lost touch with its real mission—the enhancement of life.

The message of the modern artist who recognizes only the responsibility to tell the dismal truth resembles—superficially—that of the artist in the Middle Ages or Renaissance who frequently re-

minded his audience of life's impermanence and the world's transitoriness. Shakespeare's Cardinal Wolsey, moralizing on his own
rise and fall, expresses conventional sentiments:

> This is the state of man: to-day he puts forth
> The tender leaves of hopes, to-morrow blossoms,
> And bears his blushing honors thick upon him;
> The third day comes a frost, a killing frost,
> And, when he thinks, good easy man, full surely
> His greatness is a-ripening, nips his root,
> And then he falls, as I do.[17]

The killing frost would seem to be, like Grendel, an emblem of the
impersonal and arbitrary hostility of the cosmos, for a recognition
of the role of accident in the affairs of men links the art of the past
with that of the present. But a Shakespeare or a Chaucer saw the
mischance that stalks the brightest of human hopes as merely the
work of Fortuna, goddess of vicissitude, and they could take comfort in the knowledge that her power extended only to the sublunary sphere. In the literature of their day, man was counseled directly or indirectly to remember the world beyond, where Fortuna
held no sway: "Lay not up for yourselves treasures upon earth."
Now, however, the artist reminds man of mutability and tran-
sience without the qualifying message of religion, and the result is
a literature of despair and the cultural vitiation it fosters.

Gardner, of course, cannot offer religion as an antidote to the
aesthetic and moral paralysis of the modern age. Indeed, his
novel contains, in the dragon, a highly dyslogistic parody of the
Judaeo-Christian god. "Dragons don't mess with your piddling
free will" (p. 63), declares this cynical deity. "BE STILL" (pp. 61,
62), he screams, echoing the Psalmist's "be still and know that I
am God" (Ps. 46:10). Gardner would seem to have little patience
with conventional religion—though he is not above invoking the
fish symbol in connection with the heroic Beowulf. Yet Beowulf,
the ostensible savior, will hardly satisfy a twentieth-century audi-

ence predisposed to dubiety regarding the prospects for "affirmation." For all his magnificence, he is merely a cardboard cutout.
Gardner expects his readers to see that the real savior of his people and confounder of their nemesis is the artist, or collective artist, who shapes the heroic ideal that produces a Beowulf. Admit-
tedly the Shaper, somewhat eclipsed by Grendel's depredations,
cannot sing this plague away; in fact the monster demonstrates repeatedly the mendacity and weakness of the bard. But Grendel
himself can never shake off the poet's magic, and one does well to
remember, with Pound's Sextus Propertius, that much of history
survives only because poets thought it worth celebrating. A real
Beowulf may once have lived, but men would long have forgotten
him had he not found his memorial in art—art like that which
doubtless shaped *his* heroism, provided *him* with values and ideals.

Gardner need not remind his reader of Beowulf's debt to art explicitly. For one thing, to do so would violate a fundamental canon
of art: indirection. Beowulf strides into the story undiminished because that stalking horse, Unferth, has already served as illustration of the hero's debt to the art that first conceived his heroism as
something beyond the territorial imperative.[18] Though Unferth
lacks the wit to realize his own origins, one is not fooled by his
disclaimer: "Poetry's trash, mere clouds of words, comfort to the
hopeless" (p. 88). These words, ironically, are perfectly true, yet
Unferth—not to mention Beowulf—is nonetheless a "creation," in
every sense of the word, of poetry. After all, Unferth is "a new
kind of Scylding" (p. 86)—the kind that will pursue the monster
to its den, whatever the odds. The appearance of this new kind of
Scylding follows that of the Shaper, for heroes are made, not born.

Gardner, then, advocates an art like the Shaper's, an art that improves as it delights, making its audience less crippled by the
Angst, insecurity, cruelty, and disorder that diminish our humanity. Dramatizing the argument, Grendel and the Shaper engage in
what the Germans call a *Sängerkrieg*, a battle of song. Their competition, like that of the vicious Beckmesser and the noble Walther

von der Vogelweide in Wagner's *Die Meistersinger*, involves not only skill and invention but also aesthetic principles. The attentive reader, alert to the novel's contest of art, will see how much the world stands to gain from the victory of the moral artist.

4

Paradise Lost
The Sunlight Dialogues

We live, but a world has passed away
With the years that perished to make us men.

—Howells

In the prologue to Gardner's fourth novel "the oldest Judge in the world"[1] receives a visit from the aged and broken Fred Clumly, the former police chief whose ruin—and salvation—the body of the novel will recount. The Judge, his title always capitalized, his identity left obscure for hundreds of pages, believes that "the world is a vast array of emblems . . . as the old hermetic philosophers maintained" (p. 4). He himself invites anagogic interpretation as a kind of degenerate deity, a once-powerful god reduced to making feeble boasts to the indifferent "son" he sees in his sinister male nurse: "I made that man. I created him, you might say. I created them all. The Mayor, the Fire Chief, all of them. I ran this town. I made them, and then when the time came I dropped a word in the right place and I broke them" (p. 5). In his conversation with Clumly the Judge dwells on entropy, described later in the novel as "the secret process of ruin that whispered in every leaf, that gnawed inside walls or boldly howled in the woods at night—the process of death, to name its name" (p. 451). Himself the victim of irreversible decline, the Judge believes that "nothing in the world is universal any more; there is neither wisdom nor stability, and faithfulness is dead" (p. 5). The old man with him has many reasons to believe this gloomy assessment, yet one doubts that he does. Though he does not attempt to contradict the Judge, he has discovered—as will the reader in the seven-hundred-odd pages to come—that the universal sway of entropy need not preclude wisdom, stability, and faithfulness. Clumly has learned wisdom from the Sunlight Man, faithfulness from his dead wife Esther, and stability of character from his long career as a police officer and the ordeal that capped it.

That ordeal, as it takes shape in the body of the novel, is a great contest with entropy in all its forms. As police chief of Batavia, New York, Clumly must attempt to preserve order in the face of a gathering and portentous lawlessness. In addition to his exhausting duel of wits and will with the Sunlight Man, he must cope with a crime rate that seems to grow exponentially. From tire-slashing and dog-poisoning to prostitution, burglary, arson, manslaughter, and outright murder, crime is a continual presence, increasingly alarming, increasingly out of control. Periodically, too, characters mention marching neo-Nazis, the Watts riots, the Texas Tower murders, and Richard Speck, killer of eight nurses—for the year is 1966, and the disorder of Batavia, New York, enacts in miniature the burgeoning chaos of the country as a whole.

In depicting the entropic drift as an inexorable march of crime, confusion, death, and decay, Gardner anticipates the technique of *Mickelsson's Ghosts*, his only other novel on the scale of *The Sunlight Dialogues*. Published a decade later, *Mickelsson's Ghosts* also focuses on a decayed town that becomes the symbol of a larger deterioration. The books differ, however, in narrative technique. Gardner narrates *Mickelsson's Ghosts* entirely from the point of view of his protagonist, so that the novel seems (no doubt intentionally) airless and claustrophobic. *The Sunlight Dialogues*, narrated from multiple points of view, is less taxing to read, though it remains Gardner's longest and most intricate fiction. Both books feature a brilliant but troubled title character who strives to discover in life something more than the dreary mortal round: "The beginning of things in the blood-washed breaking of membranes, the precarious middle span with its tortuous, ultimately futile imposition of order, the protracted close of life—entropy, chaos, the final loosening of the sphincter."[2] Both Peter Mickelsson and Taggert Hodge, the Sunlight Man, teeter on the brink of insanity.

Mickelsson, who has survived a bout with real psychosis, in the end embraces the kind of madness necessary to continued existence in a world given over to entropy. Gardner affectionately calls him a "lunatic"—the word he favors to describe one healthily determined not to be content with certain of the more deleterious aspects of reality. But madness in *The Sunlight Dialogues* is not in any way appealing, either in Hodge, who is mentally borderline, or in his wife Kathleen, who is completely and irretrievably insane.

In the later novel Gardner focuses on the deterioration of a single character, Peter Mickelsson, but in *The Sunlight Dialogues* he provides a Faulknerian overview of a whole family's decline. Indeed, the influence of Faulkner is fairly extensive. Will Hodge Jr.'s pursuit of R. V. Kleppmann, for example, recalls Ike McCaslin's stalking of Old Ben in "The Bear." The chase culminates, in a chapter entitled "Wilderness," in an encounter with the quarry after ritual relinquishment. "It was as if he had thrown away his compass, in the classical way, and had ventured into the thickness of the woods prepared for whatever he was destined to meet" (p. 568). Faulkner is most tangibly present, however, in the novel's strongly regional character and in the portrait of a once-powerful and gifted family, the Hodges, whose aristocratic pretensions become less and less tenable over three generations. Gardner hints, even, at a Snopes-like infiltration in the tough, amoral social climber, Millie Jewel, who marries into and helps to humble this proud family.

With the admixture of a number of violent deaths, the Faulknerian atmosphere of decadent gentility modulates into something like the creeping doom of Jacobean tragedy. Taggert Hodge's revenge on Clive Paxton, revealed late in the narrative, seems in retrospect to have set wheels in motion, causing violent death—in the guise of the inscrutable Nick Slater—to follow the Sunlight Man wherever he goes. Chief Clumly grimly pursues the Sunlight Man and his henchman over a growing pile of bodies: Mickey Salvador, Mrs. Palazzo, Mr. Hardesty. The number of violent deaths in the story—eight, not counting the Runian sisters, whose ghosts figure tangentially—is itself an index of the entropic loss of control in the representative human enclave of Batavia. In addition to the murders and fatal accidents one notes the earlier or later or off-stage deaths—violent or natural—of Gil Jewel (Millie Hodge's favorite brother, a suicide at eighteen), Albert Hubbard, Ben Hodge Jr., Chief Sun-on-the-Water, Esther Clumly, and a missing state trooper. Except for an unnamed illegitimate baby, buried in secret on the bank of the Tonawanda, the narrator mentions no births. The freight of corpses and the general air of fatality evoke the plays of Kyd, Tourneur, and Ford, and this atmosphere reflects Gardner's perception of his age:

> Maybe it's just my imagination, but it seems to me we are a play out of the seventeenth century. Seventeenth-century civilization is us. The Middle Ages was the end of a different civilization. Someplace in the sixteenth century the Middle Ages stopped. In the fifteenth and sixteenth centuries all the genres break down. It becomes impossible to write a straight romance or a straight anything. And everybody who is anybody starts form-jumping. Chaucer, for instance, starts putting together the epic poem. That's *Troilus and Criseyde*—it's a whole crazy different kind of thing. Well, and Malory comes out with *Morte d'Arthur*, which is a freaky new kind of form, a breakdown of all kinds of other forms. The mystery play arises. The literary genres of the Middle Ages didn't work anymore because the metaphysics and social ethic that supported them was no longer believed.[3]

Like the authors he cites who responded to the breakdown of belief systems by experimentation with old genres, Gardner engages in "form-jumping" of his own. *The Sunlight Dialogues*, by his own testimony, combines epic, novel, and Disney cartoon. He conceives Clumly and his wife, for example, as Disney grotesques: occasionally frightening or sad but for the most part purely droll. The policeman, in particular, is at once pathetic and ridiculous as the real and fancied depradations of the Sunlight

Man take their toll. Clumly seems at times hopelessly inept, an Elmer Fudd taking pratfalls while the clever Sunlight Man tricks and humiliates him time and again. These comedic details become unsettling, however, when juxtaposed with touches borrowed from Dante, Malory, and Homer. "Though I don't mention it in the novel," Gardner remarked, "Chief Fred Clumly . . . once read Dante on a ship, though he no longer remembers it. It sank deep down into the swamp of his mind and now throws strange light on his modern-seeming problems. The narrator of the novel has obviously read and pondered hard on Malory's *Morte D'Arthur*, which presents a medieval world view totally opposed to Dante's." [4]

Malory tends to emphasize the tragic turns of Fortune's wheel and the passing of ancient virtue; Dante focuses on the cosmic order that makes creation ultimately comedic. The Malory influence—one should remember that Gardner authored the *Cliff's Notes* on *Morte D'Arthur*—moves the narrator to give his story something of the air of medieval romance, with the police as knights errant, Chief Clumly as their beleaguered king, and the Sunlight Man as the magician or enchanter they must do battle with. Malory is also behind the pervasive sense of loss and decline in the novel—the infinite sadness attending the order that has passed (the one associated, as will be seen presently, with the Old Congressman and his Edenic estate). Dante, on the other hand, is present in Clumly's conviction that the ideal of order has some absolute validity and perhaps in his unconscious tendency to classify men as lost, redeemable, or saved according to their ability and willingness to abide by the law. He comes closest to remembering his Dante when he dreams of pursuing the Sunlight Man into the Sea of Metaphysics with a crew of "unbelievers, heretics, usurers, perverts, suicides" (p. 93). Awake, Clumly has noticed that his wife, like Penelope with her weaving, stitches and unstitches her sewing every day; asleep, he becomes Dante's Ulysses, who abandons his wife to sail into the unknown, "to follow knowledge," in the familiar Tennysonian phrase, "like a sinking star." Eventually, like Dante, Clumly accepts the chastisement and instruction of a moral guide—the Sunlight Man—and rises to a higher understanding of his world. But the Florentine poet depicts himself learning the most important spiritual lessons from a woman; thus Clumly's wife, however neglected, remains his bulwark of love and fidelity. "Mrs. Clumly," explained Gardner, "is the Beatrice of *The Sunlight Dialogues*. She guides everybody because she loves."[5]

Even more recognizably than it echoes Malory and Dante, the novel parodies the epic as practiced by Homer. Its epic features include the great canvas, the many characters, and the breaks in the action for lengthy recitations (the "dialogues" are largely monologues). Like *The Iliad* and *The Odyssey*, or for that matter Gardner's own *Jason and Medeia*, *The Sunlight Dialogues* begins *in medias res* and runs to twenty-four books. Like all great epics, it is an expression of national character and national experience, anticipating Gardner's Bicentennial novel, *October Light*. Though it has no central parallel to the Homeric poems, it contains numerous analogues that range from Joycean parody to tragic echo of the originals. Several Homeric Odysseuses complement the Dantesque Ulysses of Chief Clumly. Will Hodge Jr., for example, falls prey to a Circe at the bachelor pad of his friend Buz Marchant; his encounter with R. V. Kleppmann in St. Louis echoes that of Odysseus with Tiresias in the underworld. Walter Benson reaches home and wife after long travail and must immediately take measures to rid his house of that more successful latter-day Antinous, Oliver Nuper. Taggert Hodge, too, toils home- and wifeward, though his odyssey ends tragically. But Hodge, whose wife has been effectively taken from him by her father, is less an Odysseus than an Achilles, outraged at the appropriation, by a high-handed, powerful man, of a woman rightfully his.

"Most of fiction's great heroes are at least slightly crazy, from Achilles to Captain Ahab . . . . Achilles, in his nobler, saner moments, lays down the whole moral code of *The Iliad*. But . . . violence and anger triggered by war, the human passions . . . overwhelm Achilles' reason and make him the greatest criminal in all fiction."⁶ Like Achilles, Taggert Hodge lapses into criminal anger and violence, and in the dialogues that give the novel its title he, too, lays down a sophisticated moral code. Since the dialogues are widely spaced and the book long, a brief descriptive analysis will be helpful, if only to dispel the impression that their matter is unusually complex or abstruse.⁷ Though distributed over the four strange meetings of Clumly and the Sunlight Man, the dialogues actually constitute a single extended discourse, the themes of which, broadly speaking, are reality and freedom. Explored in terms of two sharply contrasting cultures, Hebrew and Babylonian, with side glances at political, social, and cultural assumptions in contemporary America, these themes bear directly on the conflict, central to the novel, of order and entropy. In the dialogues the Sunlight Man expounds a philosophy that seems little more than a mistaken attempt to convince himself that the patterns of cultural decay he has studied do not augur cosmic dissolution as well. If the ultimate reality, prefigured in the fate of civilizations, is a kind of cosmic cachexia, then the absolute freedom espoused by the Sunlight Man proves meaningless.

This spokesman for the ideal of absolute, anarchistic freedom first confronts Fred Clumly and the values of Main Street in a Presbyterian church at "the corner of Liberty and Main" (p. 312). The Sunlight Man lectures Clumly on the differences between ancient Hebrew and Babylonian culture. They differed in their conception of man's relations with the unseen, and this difference resulted in radically opposed sexual mores, marital customs, laws regarding property, and political life. The Babylonians believed that "there was the world of matter and the world of spirit, and the connection between the two was totally mysterious, which is to say, holy" (p. 320). Babylonian deference to the unknowable reality subsumed by that "world of spirit" resulted in the high development of intuition, astrology, divination, and other modes of living harmoniously in a numinous but enigmatic universe. Thus the Babylonian ideal was to maintain a kind of spiritual freedom, so that one stood ready to act with the gods whenever the divine will manifested itself. The Hebrews, by contrast, attempted to codify man's relations with the spirit world. The Hebrew ideal was to obey the religious and civil law, to comply with the divine will through voluntary surrender of freedom. But the Hebrews erred, according to the Sunlight Man, in assuming that the divine will is so easily known and codified. The very attempt at such codification amounts to a distortion of the way things are, a failure to recognize the gulf between the material and spiritual planes. The Sunlight Man illustrates the error of the Jews—and, by extension, all who have inherited their political, religious, and metaphysical assumptions—with a parable based on Plato's Simile of the Cave. He tells of a thief, long imprisoned in a cellar, who gains his freedom but finds the aboveground, sunlit world insupportable; he retreats to the cellar again, a broken man. "He'd misunderstood reality," explains the Sunlight Man, "and so he died." The moral of the story, as applicable to the modern world as to the ancient, confronts Clumly and all who dote on the Hebraic ideal of law and order in Main Street America with their fundamental error: "I doubt that anything in all our system is in tune with, keyed to, reality" (p. 327). The lecturer concludes with the assertion that his view, with its repudiation of all constraints on freedom, will prevail in the long run, however Clumly and the minions of narrow-minded, law-and-order bigotry prevail in the short run. "I love justice. You love law. I'm Babylonian, and you, you're one of the Jews" (p. 328).

The other dialogues expand on points made in this one. In his second meeting with the police chief, the Sunlight Man picks up where he left off, explaining Babylonian divination: "After divination one acts *with* the gods. You discover which way things are flowing, and you swim in the same direction" (p. 419). He comments further on the relation between the Babylonian virtue of maintaining one's freedom and the Jewish virtue of obeying the law, and again he notes the sexual, social, and political ramifications of the two philosophies. The modern age, he argues, errs in elevating the rational and despising the intuitive. The scientific bias and the distrust of intuition undermine attempts at reestablishing a Babylonian valuation of freedom.

The third dialogue—the Dialogue of the Dead—takes place appropriately enough in a cemetery crypt, where the Sunlight Man tells Clumly about *Gilgamesh*, the Babylonian epic whose description sounds like that of *The Sunlight Dialogues*: "A technique made up of careful segmentation, with elaborate echoing, repeating and counterpointing, with texture enriched still more by rare and artificial words" (p. 531). *Gilgamesh* demonstrates, among other things, the impossibility of escaping death and the futility of action that goes contrary to the will of the gods. But the Sunlight Man now begins to move beyond his Babylonian obsession, to speak more directly to the immediate conflict between himself and Clumly. He concludes another bizarre parable by foreshadowing the climactic moment of the fourth dialogue, when Clumly, getting the Sunlight Man's gun away from him, will have his enemy in custody again for the first time since the escape. This penultimate dialogue ends with the question of what Clumly will do in that situation. Will he "act on the side of the universe" and release this enlightened child of the cosmos, or will he "act for humanity" (p. 536) and do his legal duty? The Sunlight Man faces the same choice—to kill Clumly (an act for the universe, since Clumly serves a system at odds with cosmic reality) or to kill Clumly and himself (an act for humanity, since the one is an inept policeman, the other a criminal). The Sunlight Man leaves the question hanging, heightening the suspense for Clumly, for the reader, and not least, one suspects, for himself.

The fourth dialogue is quite brief; indeed, the dialogues become progressively shorter, for time is running out, and Clumly, though one may not notice at first, has become a better pupil. The encounter takes place at Stony Hill, a place walled like Gilgamesh's city of Uruk, and in the silo that Taggert Hodge and his wife had climbed on in the days when life smiled on them. The Sunlight Man discourses briefly on the towers of Babylon and their symbolic meaning, then proceeds to his conclusion: ultimately the towers fell, and in their fall they augur the fate of all civilizations. The towers of America will fall too, perhaps the last towers of Western civilization. The dialogues culminate, then, in a bleak vision of cultural entropy, and the force of that vision undercuts the Sunlight Man's claims for a cosmic order immune to the same dissolution, the same meaningless apocalypse. His last, vague reference to "the secret powers of the universe" (p. 697) seems halfhearted, and the Sunlight Man, despondent, leaves unresolved the question of his anarchist ethic's relevance or value in a universe without order.

At this point, as foretold, Clumly possesses himself of the gun, only to pass up the chance to reclaim his position as chief of police by bringing the Sunlight Man in. "You're free" (p. 634), he says, but the simple statement echoes ironically. The Sunlight Man is in fact anything but free, for he has squandered his freedom with every attempt to demonstrate it. Early in the novel he describes himself as "capable of gratuity" (p. 111), but the capability is evidently self-canceling. Later, he baits his former sister-in-law, Millie, with the idea of perfect freedom of action, the idea of the gratuitous or motiveless act. Millie, who does not believe in it, observes in sardonic French that the mind, source of conceits like gratuity, remains "*toujours croché à l'animal*" (p. 520)—always attached to the flesh, which it cannot escape. However liberated the soul (or for that matter however alienated), the body claims its own, demanding to eat, to make love, to shed blood. A better French scholar than Hodge, Millie probably knows what happens to Gide's Lafcadio (in *Les Cuves du Vatican*), who commits a gratuitous crime to prove that he is perfectly free—then finds himself imprisoned not for but *by* his crime. Taggert Hodge, who muses to himself in the Batavia jail that "there are still vast areas of freedom" (p. 99), attempts to be Gide's immoralist, only to find himself increasingly hemmed in by the choices he has made, the acts he has performed. Thus the irony of Hodge's end is that after he has forced Clumly to empathize with him, the events that Hodge himself has set in motion—the escapes, the deaths, the bizarre tricks—create the atmosphere of terror that causes him to be gunned down by a nervous policeman just at the moment he decides to turn himself in.

In letting his quarry go, Clumly does not act, as the Sunlight Man had suggested in the third dialogue, "on the side of the universe." Rather he acts on the side of a less grandiose ethic of personal compassion. Perhaps, too, he recognizes the flaw in the Sunlight Man's advocacy of a cosmic criterion for enlightened action. For all his earnest talk about the necessary readiness to swim with the cosmic flow, to stay in tune with the gods, Hodge never quite manages to convince himself that "the secret powers of the universe" exist. In fact he senses all along the meaninglessness and absurdity of the universe. His Babylonian creed proves a prescription for existential despair, for being in tune with reality means not compliance with the gods but compliance with entropy and the abyss. The universe refuses to live up to Hodge's expectations. As Gardner explained in an interview, "he finds no order, no coherence in it. He's a wild, romantic poet with no hope of God."[8] He experiences the absolute freedom of existentialist philosophy, and it destroys him.

A deformed and enraged monster raiding the fringes of society, Taggert Hodge resembles that other existentialist, Grendel. Like Grendel, too, he has a mythic dimension. "Stiff as the fire-blasted face was, he could wrench it into an infinite number of shapes." With this shape-shifting and his "elfish, impenetrable grin" (p. 59), the Sunlight Man is another avatar of the trickster, that archetypal figure of folk-tale, legend, and primitive religion. As noted in the discussion of *Grendel*, the trickster develops along with human cultures, eventually evolving from a creature of pure malice and impishness into—in Jung's words—the "approximation . . . of a saviour." Grendel remains the trickster (Gardner displaces the salvational development to Beowulf and the Shaper), but the reader and the town of Batavia encounter the Sunlight Man just at the moment that he begins the transition from trickster to savior. Thus, along with his tricksterish jokes at the expense of the police—

stealing their guns and bullets, making fools of them—he has begun to affect the rhetoric of a Christ: "I am the Rock" (p. 60), "I am
the Truth" (p. 105), "Behold, I am the Door!" (p. 122). His antics in
the Batavia jail move one of the Indians imprisoned with him to
exclaim, "Jesus God" (p. 63), and when the same prisoner adds,
"Jesus Christ" (p. 65) a couple of pages later, one suspects Gardner of trying out the technique of telegraphing allegory through
the profane exclamations of secondary characaters—the technique that would reappear parodically in *The Smugglers of Lost
Souls' Rock*, the novel-within-the-novel in *October Light*. The fact
that only one of the Indians "believes" in the Sunlight Man suggests a parallel with the good and bad thieves with whom Christ
was crucified; Walter Boyle, the fourth prisoner, is the Barabbas
who goes free. When the police take the Sunlight Man away for
questioning, he goes off "between two of them, quietly, as if full of
remorse for the sins of all mankind" (p. 65). Soon he declaims: "O
Father, forgive them! They know not whom they screw" (p. 109).
When he cuts or gouges himself, drawing blood, he says, "Go
ahead . . . . Taste it. In remembrance of Me" (p. 110).

These allusions might appear purely ironic, part of Taggert
Hodge's program of mystification and calculated blasphemy while
imprisoned, but his identification with Christ continues, abetted
by the narrator, through the rest of the novel. One of his brothers,
for example, remembers Tag's childhood penchant for carpentry
(p. 136), and his nephew Luke, decrying the release of Nick Slater,
says: "You set him 'free,' you say, like some new Jesus" (p. 408).
Hodge's Christ complex reaches new heights in the scenes at Luke's
house. He washes Nick's feet, stages a grotesque Last Supper, and
performs magic tricks with Biblical quotations and liturgical patter.
As the Sunlight Man he speaks, especially in the four dialogues,
in obscure parables, and when Clumly refuses to arrest him after
the fourth dialogue, one hears an echo of Pilate: "I'm outside my
jurisdiction" (p. 634).

But what kind of deliverer is the Sunlight Man, and whom does
he save? To answer these questions, the reader should recall that

one of the things preying on Taggert Hodge's mind, and on the minds of his brothers, is the sad decline of Stony Hill, their ancestral home. The once-noble estate corresponds symbolically to the once-glorious habitation of Adam and Eve. "Stony Hill Farm, inside its stone walls, was as self-contained and self-perpetuating, even as serene . . . as Heaven itself. It was a garden for idealism" (p. 338). Paradise, etymologically, means a walled garden, and Stony Hill becomes the book's major symbol of that mythic state in which entropy does not exist. It had been Eden, "a world now utterly vanished—expanses where trees grew taller than any trees grow now, where fences stood out in precise detail and flowers were sharp particulars—a world where . . . there was Space stretching out endlessly . . . but no hint yet of the antique serpent, the old destroyer, Time" (p. 346). The last dialogue takes place here amid reminders of postlapsarian decay: it is "late afternoon," the grounds are "now a place of high weeds," and "the September air . . . smelled of apples" (p. 627).

The first inhabitant of this garden for idealism, the prelapsarian Adam who believes in and exercises free will, is the Honorable Arthur Hodge Sr., known as the Old Congressman. He had lived in a world that afforded a solid base for his accomplishments, a world brimming with potentiality; his sons inherit that world in a fallen state, a prison rather than an Eden. No longer capable of the multifarious faith that sustained earlier generations, the children of the twentieth century view free will as the quaint conceit of a more naive age, or the reinterpret it radically as the existential freedom that coexists with pure accident in the cosmos. Taggert Hodge, a would-be New Adam, cannot reestablish Eden because he can come no closer to his father's belief in free will than a cracked, "Babylonian" anarchism, which is only existential freedom in fancy dress. Embracing this spiritually dangerous doctrine, he soon finds himself less Christ than Antichrist, visiting apocalyptic fire—the climax to the fourth dialogue—on the world he has failed to redeem.

The political character of Taggert Hodge's anarchism reveals another dimension to the allegory, for Stony Hill is specifically the American Eden, its patriarch the American Adam. The Old Congressman had "embodied all that was good" (p. 461), as his son Will tells a hitchhiker named Freeman (another emblematic presence in the American landscape). He had embodied, in fact, an eighteenth-century Jeffersonian ideal of faith in man and in the universal order, an ideal that vanished with the coming of the modern age. Like *October Light, The Sunlight Dialogues* anatomizes the historical and contemporary American experience, especially as that experience reflects the fate of Western culture:

> If you're going to talk about the decline of Western civilization or at least the possibility of that decline, you take an odd place that's sort of worn out and run-down. For instance, Batavia, New York, where the Holland Land Office was . . . the beginning of a civilization . . . selling the land in this country. It was, in the beginning, a wonderful, beautiful place with the smartest indians in America around. Now it's this old, run-down town which has been urban-renewalized just about out of existence. The factories have stopped and the people are poor and sometimes crabby; the elm trees are all dead, and so are the oaks and maples. So it's a good symbol.[9]

Like the early promise of the Hodge family, with its gifted statesman and his Edenic realm, the American Dream has gradually become compromised. Of all the Old Congressman's children, Taggert Hodge feels most powerfully the loss of the golden promise, but in embracing an extreme version of freedom, the quintessential American ideal, he threatens merely to accelerate the decay.

In the entropic decline of Stony Hill and all that it stands for, one perceives the breakdown of a primal unity—a breakdown reflected in the pervasive division of character in the novel. The integrated man exists only in the mythic past; half-men abound in the present. To illustrate the general failure of integration, Gardner doubles several of his characters: Walter Boyle and Walter Benson, Will Hodge Jr. and R. V. Kleppmann, Clumly and the Sunlight

Man. Walter Boyle/Benson has compartmentalized the larcenous and law-abiding sides of his personality, so that he functions with little strain as a thief under one identity, a perfectly respectable bourgeois under the other. Will Hodge Jr. pursues R. V. Kleppmann until he begins to identify with his quarry, and Kleppmann remarks, "We're somewhat alike, you and I" (p. 574). Their little drama of pursuit, flight, and gradual coalescence mirrors that of Clumly and the Sunlight Man. One of the Sunlight Man's themes, in his dialogues with Clumly, is their essential identity, but the police chief is the one who first asserts: "We're closer than you think!" (p. 328). As Judy Smith Murr points out, "their confrontation . . . is more than a simple one between order and disorder— it is between an order that longs for disorder and a disorder in pursuit of order. Like Grendel and man, the Sunlight Man and Clumly need each other for definition." [10] Thus by degrees they merge. In the second dialogue, the Sunlight Man wears one of Clumly's shirts and a turban with a badge in its center. In their third meeting, the Sunlight Man introduces a parable, saying, "I was once a policeman" (p. 534); he goes on to describe himself as if he were Clumly—superannuated, going to pieces under pressure. The reader may note other similarities as well. Both are or were professionally involved with the law (Hodge was originally a lawyer). Both are afflicted with an unpleasant personal odor. Both marry cripples: Clumly's wife is blind, Hodge's insane. After the Sunlight Man springs Nick Slater, Clumly strikes Verne, Nick's brother, on the cheek with his pistol; late in the novel the Sunlight Man strikes Nick the same way.

The pervasive fragmentation of character suggests the rarity, perhaps even the impossibility, of wholeness. It also reveals a Jungian influence. Clumly discovers in his antagonist something that frightens or disgusts him in a particularly intimate way, for the Sunlight Man reifies that projection of the submerged half of the personality Jung calls the Shadow, repository of traits abhorred or feared by the conscious mind. Walter Benson and Will Hodge Jr. also act or encounter their own secret selves. One recognizes more

Jungian psychology in the Old Congressman and his four un-happy sons. Jung describes one mode of psychological wholeness as the integration of four "functions of consciousness": thinking, feeling, sensing, and intuiting.[11] That the Old Congressman's serenity becomes, in the second generation, four kinds of unhappi-ness provides disturbing evidence of entropic tendencies in con-sciousness itself.

Certain of the features that invite Jungian interpretation dis-cover a Blakean vision as well, for the stages in the decay of Stony Hill and its environs recall the stages in Blake's myth of the Fall, and the disunity of the four sons evokes the breaking up of Al-bion, Blake's universal man, into the four Zoas.[12] If the Old Con-gressman lived in Eden, then the first-generation fallen world in which his sons grew up corresponds with Blake's Beulah, the still splendid but no longer unitary environment of the *disjecta mem-bra* of Albion. The Old Man's grandchildren exist in what Blake calls Generation, the condition and locus of ordinary human life. Blake's final stage, the hellish Ulro, does not seem far when one considers the suffering of Generation-bound man: Luke's paralyz-ing illness, Ben Jr.'s death in the Korean War, Will Jr.'s lockstep towards thrombosis, and the incineration of Tag's children. To Blake, the stages of the Fall were accompanied by a painful transi-tion from visionary perception to ordinary physical vision, and this idea is behind Will Jr.'s recognition of his family's fate: "He understood, suddenly, what had gone wrong between him and Louise, and between him and his children, between his own mother and father, between, even, the Congressman and his sons. A kind of power failure, a sickly decline into vision" (p. 576).

Blake envisions the apocalyptic restoration of the universal man as the task of the imaginative, visionary artist, guided by and blending with Los, the most gifted and sensitive of Albion's off-spring. Gardner's Los is the Sunlight Man, one of his most com-plex artist heroes. If his pyrotechnics anticipate those of the vil-lainous Luther Flint in "The King's Indian," one must remember that all artists deal in illusion and trickery—Flint no more, really, that Jonathan Upchurch. Each of the Sunlight Man's performances is a work of art involving stagecraft, magic, scripting, lighting, and acting. These specimens of guerrilla theatre have an intended audience of one—Chief Clumly, the perfect representative of that bourgeois complacency traditionally targeted by art. The bourgeois of every age, guilty of gross oversimplification of moral and ethical matters, attempt to reduce complex questions to shallow formulae. Many artists, however, merely insult or bait bourgeois morality, then retreat into a superior smugness that is only more reprehensible. The best artists, by contrast, simultaneously challenge moral complacency and affirm some higher, more comprehensive morality.

Is the art of Taggert Hodge, the Sunlight Man, moral or immoral? Without doubt, it is deeply flawed. To the extent that he tries, even unconsciously, to inculcate fatalism before cosmic processes that prove mindless and entropic, the Sunlight Man deserves reproach as a bad artist, a Grendel, and like Grendel, as Pat Ensworth points out, he is eventually outclassed by a man with less imagination.[13] But Clumly's moral development derives at least partly from the positive aspects of the Sunlight Man's art. Thus in addition to the psychological pairing with Clumly, not to mention the double identity as quondam lawyer and criminal magus, Taggert Hodge has two selves as an artist as well. Unlike John Napper or Vlemk the Box-Painter, who grow from one kind of artist into another, Hodge combines the attributes of Grendel and the Shaper. Unique among the artist figures in Gardner's fiction, he is at once the bad artist and the good.

Though a law-breaker, "professional disturber of the peace," madman, murderer of Clive Paxton, and accessory to the murders of Mickey Salvador, Mrs. Palazzo, and Mr. Hardesty, he remains in part a moral artist, for personal morality has relatively little to do with the morality of one's art. Moral artists in Gardner's fiction, even the Shaper, do not lack warts, and one recalls that the Pardoner, greatest sinner among the Canterbury pilgrims, tells a fine moral tale. The art of the Sunlight Man qualifies as moral to the extent that it leads Clumly to greater compassion and greater humanity. The police chief enters the Sunlight Man's world of illusion—just as the reader enters Gardner's—and comes away emotionally thawed, a witness to the truth of Kafka's dictum that a work of art should be an axe to the frozen sea within us.

Unlike the thief in the parable who could not endure sunlit reality, Clumly faces it and survives. At the end, as Daniel Laskin explains, the unprepossessing policeman triumphs:

> For the experience has changed Clumly, has forced him to abandon his once easily held conception of law and order; the Sunlight Man has taken him on a spiritual journey. For Gardner, a man like Clumly is the most admirable kind of hero. He is an undistinguished man, a flawed person with long regrets and an uneasy feeling that his life has been wasted, his marriage a failure, his career insignificant. But in his pedestrian way—clumsy, glum, humble—he has been brave enough to submit his values to a test, honest enough to recognize their shortcomings, and strong enough to resist despair, and to embrace instead an amended view of life.[14]

Thus, though the Sunlight Man forces the police chief to recognize the larger context of the law and order he so prizes, Clumly deserves part of the credit for his own moral development, for he is not without intelligence and imagination. From the first time he hears the word "metaphysics" from the Sunlight Man, Clumly seizes on it, coming back to it repeatedly in his mind. He eventually becomes comfortable enough with the term to say of his drunkard father, "his problem was metaphysical" (p. 152), and he even recites a definition: "Of the nature of being or essential reality. Very abstract, abstruse, or subtle: often used derogatorily of reasoning" (p. 153). If he can understand his father's bibulous response to "essential reality," Chief Clumly is well on his way to sympathizing with the Sunlight Man.

In pursuing the Sunlight Man, Clumly himself grapples with essential reality—maddeningly elusive (and illusive) yet also, when finally confronted, blindingly solar in intensity. Clumly comes to understand what made his father a drunkard, for reality can be terrible indeed, but he also learns the complex reality of a fellow human being. Sitting in the police car before his speech to the Dairyman's League, he looks into the Grange and sees fire. The delusion of flames is one of the Sunlight Man's afflictions, and at this moment Clumly has achieved an extraordinary form of empathy with the man he has stalked as a criminal. Having become one with the Sunlight Man mentally and emotionally, he has done what T. S. Eliot, in *The Waste Land*, says one cannot do:

> I have heard the key
> Turn in the door once and turn once only
> We think of the key, each in his prison
> Thinking of the key, each confirms a prison

The lines echo Ugolino, in Dante's *Inferno*, who was imprisoned and starved in a tower that for Eliot symbolizes the self. In his note to these lines Eliot cites F. H. Bradley's *Appearance and Reality*: "My external sensations are no less private to my self than are my thoughts or my feelings. In either case my experience falls within my own circle, a circle closed on the outside; and, with all its elements alike, every sphere is opaque to the others which surround it. . . . In brief, regarded as an existence which appears in a soul, the whole world for each is peculiar and private to that soul."[15] Clumly's empathy with the Sunlight Man is no small achievement, then. It is also emotionally shattering, so that Clumly virtually goes to pieces during his speech to the Dairyman's League. Yet however broken emotionally and professionally, he emerges the hero, the character who makes the greatest moral advance in the novel. He learns about essential reality but refuses to surrender to it morally; doomed in the undertow of entropy, he loses the world but saves his soul.

5

From Angst to Affirmation
The King's Indian

Life shrinks or expands in proportion
to one's courage.

—Anaïs Nin

Among collections of short fiction, only Joyce's *Dubliners* surpasses *The King's Indian* in the subtle interrelation of story with story. Gardner has arranged these "stories and tales" with the kind of care and attention to cumulative effect one would expect in a volume of poetry. The book unfolds in three parts: "The Midnight Reader," containing five stories; "Tales of Queen Louisa," containing three; and "The King's Indian," a short novel (here cited in quotation marks to distinguish it from the collection as a whole). Few authors would bury a novel in a collection if they could publish it separately—especially a novel as good as this one. "The King's Indian," after all, exceeds *Grendel* in length and equals it in invention and wit. But Gardner wanted the novel to function as a culmination, the final articulation of a thesis developed throughout the collection. The artist, Gardner argues, must create new and exhilarating possibilities out of the unpromising stuff of reality. His is thus a double responsibility: the real world must receive its due, yet the artist must continually—like the hero of old—challenge its darkness, its refractory horrors. The artist who refuses to engage that darkness, however quixotic such a gesture may seem, is ultimately guilty of confusing a species of complacency with a rigorous adherence to truth. The life-enhancing art that Gardner advocates should not be dismissed as a compromise with the truth—even though, on the face of it, it would seem to be at best benign illusion. The Gardnerian artist is a figure of the

76

hero, the slayer of dragons. The hero has no chance of defeating the dragon, yet he does. The grim reality that most modern fiction merely documents—death, entropy, and other such nihilism-fostering facts of existence—is the dragon that can, Gardner insists, be slain by a sufficiently resolute, resourceful, and inventive artist-hero.

Dark Night of the Soul

In all of the *King's Indian* stories Gardner describes victories—very small at first but finally substantial—over the darkness that forever threatens to swallow man's precarious enclaves of love, security, and order. He concedes the most to this darkness in the stories of "The Midnight Reader." The title of this section hints at the subject of each of the stories in it: someone's dark night of the soul. Yet each ends with some glimmer of light, manifested most commonly in a moment of renewal—of "resurrection," in Gardnerian parlance—for the main character. "Pastoral Care," perhaps the most cheerless story, explores a depressing number of spiritual dead ends, and the renewal of its protagonist, a priggish minister, comes at a terribly high cost. "The Ravages of Spring," on the other hand, offers literal resurrection through cloning. This story's darkness lies chiefly in its gothicism; though most of the tale takes place in the daytime, the reader experiences it as nocturnal, partly because of the greenish light of the ghastly weather in which the action transpires and partly because of the horrors revealed. The resurrection in "The Temptation of St. Ivo" is so understated as to pass easily unnoticed; it comes after the hero bravely hazards the spiritual credit of a lifetime of discipline. In "The Warden," set in dungeons and amid nocturnal burial parties, renewal merely flickers, a chimera or mockery. As one of the characters in a later story reflects, "It's always darkest before the dawn,"[1] and indeed the darkest of the stories in "The Midnight Reader" is this, the penultimate one. The last of this group, "John Napper Sailing

Through the Universe," concerns a real-life painter, a friend of Gardner's, who wins an exemplary victory over despair. He wins it in his art, and this story heralds a spiritual and aesthetic dawn after the long night chronicled in "The Midnight Reader."

Anyone can suffer a dark night of the soul, but the phrase specifically refers to the spiritual travail of the religious man afflicted with doubts. Thus Gardner begins this section with a troubled minister who seems to exemplify Kierkegaard's dictum: "The specific character of despair is precisely this: that it is unaware of being despair." A nicely realized character, Eugene Pick is a mixture of vanity, arrogance, compassion, and ultimately humility. In the first part of the story several members of his congregation reveal to him their various degrees of spiritual desperation. He comforts each, but his grasp of their pietistic errors is somehow too comprehensive. The reader becomes increasingly uncomfortable with Pick's intellectual and spiritual superiority—and, to do him justice, so does he. That superiority falters, however, when Pick's liberalism prevents his avoiding complicity with a radical who plants bombs around the community.

The author sketches in the late-sixties background of the story with great economy: hippies, communes, Weatherman-style radicalism. "Reverend Pick," like many liberal ministers of that era, likes to challenge the conservative complacency of his congregation from the pulpit. But one Sunday the radical who has recently bombed a campus building comes to church—and likes what he hears. He visits the minister, quietly mentions his violent work, and leaves him with a vague allusion to the biblical story of the fig tree, cursed to perpetual barrenness by Christ. After pondering this mystifying story (why should the tree have figs out of season?), the minister preaches on it the following Sunday, interpreting the figless tree as moribund religion that cannot respond to the new dispensation when it arrives. As the religious establishment of Christ's time rejected His message, the religious establishment represented by Pick's congregation fails to devote its energies to challenging the status quo in the name of Christian justice.

Its members have devoted themselves to supporting missions that merely "soften up ancient cultures for colonialism and capitalistic exploitation" (p. 8) or to building programs that prove stupid and wasteful when the congregation shrinks rather than grows. The minister does not see the radical during the service, and perhaps he would have toned down his exhortations in the presence of someone really willing to act on them. But the radical, lurking in the entry vestibule, hears the sermon and its incitement to action. When the police station is bombed soon thereafter, the minister, appalled at having contributed to the crime, flees the town—only to learn that a church, perhaps his own, has subsequently been bombed. Even now, in complete disarray, he understands the theological implications. He had conned himself into thinking that he understood things well enough to remain exempt from the errors of his miserable parishioners. But in his smug superiority he, too, is a child of Adam. "The fall is endless. All systems fail" (p. 34). He realizes his own fallibility: *he* is the barren fig tree, his the "dead, sham religion" (p. 27) fruitless at the crucial moment. At the end of the story, stripped of his illusions of superiority, he must comfort a crazed hippie whose wife has been killed. For the first time, chastened by all that has transpired, he offers the comfort of his office—"pastoral care"—with genuine humility.

What impresses one in reading this story is the way it avoids simplistic contrasts between conservatism and radicalism, or rather the way it prevents the contrasts between the two from deflecting the story in directions not intended. It examines without making central the question that troubles the minister and his congregation: what is the church's mission when a society's institutions are challenged in the name of justice? It concentrates, however, on the main character's personal drama. Gardner himself probably did not agree with Pick's conviction that in a fallen world "all systems fail," for he viewed "neo-orthodoxy"—the attempt to get back to strict notions about Original Sin and the fallen state of man—as yet another surrender to the dark circumstances of our existence.

Hence the irony of Pick's situation: despite his enlightenment, the minister's perceptions are flawed according to the very doctrine he embraces. Still, the author values his own convictions less than the responsibility to remain true to the character and the fictional situation he has created. Thus the reader need only accept the truth about Pick, not the absolute validity of Pick's epiphany. On the other hand, no irony undercuts Pick's other lesson. Whatever the cogency of arguments that "the fall is endless" and that "all systems fail," one must act with love and humility towards one's fellow men, recognize and rise above one's own shortcomings, and proffer—if one is a minister—real and substantial "pastoral care."

From the all-too-real revolutionary sixties of "Pastoral Care" Gardner shifts, in "The Ravages of Spring," to an earlier era, when country doctors made their rounds with horse and buggy. Where Eugene Pick comes to his dubious conclusions about the universality of Original Sin in the fall of the year, the narrator-protagonist of the second story witnesses monstrous rebirth in the spring. A physician with a healthy, commonsense view of things, the narrator introduces himself as a "plain . . . man," a "country doctor," and an "unpoetic soul" (p. 35). He rejects the label of "Platonist" and, like Dr. Johnson, refutes Bishop Berkeley's subjective idealism by thumping a solid object. He frequently reminds the reader of his credentials as a sensible man, "not . . . given to foolish superstitions" (p. 45). He offers the testimony, as he twice remarks, of "a medical man and veterinarian" (pp. 47, 56), and he favors qualifications like "though I cannot assert as a medical man that . . ." (p. 58). Gardner's strategy, a classic one, is to establish the narrator's sanity and credibility; he thus disposes the reader to accept the tale, however fantastic. At the same time, as the story draws one in and uncovers its horrors, the first-person narration becomes increasingly claustrophobic. The effects achieved recall those invented or refined by the author invoked in the opening paragraphs, Edgar Allen Poe.

Like certain characters in Poe, Gardner's narrator declines to supply his real name, and one must refer to him as "Dr. William Thorpe," the false name he gives when he takes shelter from multiple tornadoes in a house full of the "klones" of a mad scientist, Professor John Hunter. If cloning has since the story's publication (which, incidentally, antedates such popular treatments of the subject as Ira Levin's *The Boys from Brazil* and David M. Rorvik's *In His Image: The Cloning of a Man*) become increasingly plausible biology, a commonplace subject of scientific theorizing and experimentation, the fact does not spoil the gothic effect. The glimpse Gardner provides of the villain's scientific paraphernalia, reminiscent of the hokey laboratory equipment seen in Frankenstein movies, convinces one that Hunter's work bears little resemblance to science in the real world. The story does not, in other words, depend very heavily on scientific trappings for its chills or for realization of its theme: the enormity of tinkering with nature. I suspect that Gardner understood that the rapid outstripping of his story's science-fiction premises would merely accelerate its placement among those works, by Mary Shelley, Jules Verne, H. G. Wells, and Poe, in which a dated or bogus science plays no small part in the overall effect on modern readers.

The story invites reflection on legitimate uses of the human imagination. Hunter and the narrator, as the madman himself points out, follow the same calling, and the story examines the contrast between two modes of scientific vocation: that of the decent, humanitarian doctor and that of the vicious, unhinged scientist. The one celebrates nature, the other violates it. The narrator refers early on to the story of Sir Humphrey Davy, the English chemist who, disgusted at the atheistic theorizing of the dissecting rooms, would stroll out to commune with nature and so bring his mind back to God. Like Gardner, the narrator hedges about God but not about the restorative powers of nature: "The walk was a piece of pure sanity. The mulch of the flowering spirit is under thy feet, neighbor!" (p. 36). Hunter, on the other hand, sides with the impious dissectors: "What is the intellect for if not to penetrate, dissect? There's your God, Dr. Thorpe! The human

intellect!" (p. 53). But Thorpe's enlightened humanity is the outlook that Gardner always endorses, and significantly this character
draws an analogy between his calling and that of the artist. "We
physicians," remarks Thorpe, "are all too often maligned by those
who confuse objectivity with callousness. We're as much like artists, it seems to me, as like scientists" (p. 59). Art, after all, calls
for the same detached observation, the same "objectivity," that science does, and insanity such as Hunter's involves by definition a
loss of this prized objectivity. In this story the mad scientist, like
the bad artist, is a maker of copies, an epigone. Dr. Thorpe, by
contrast, demonstrates his status as good scientist and good artist
by his humane outlook and by his gifts as a storyteller. His tale,
moreover, reminds its audience of the sanctity of nature and life—
even the lives of the horrible little clones he twice rescues.

Thorpe witnesses the rebirth of John Hunter in the three clones;
he subsequently witnesses a kind of resurrection when he draws
them out of the well into which a superstitious old woman has
lowered them as a cure for insanity. But the story ends ambigu-
ously, with the two surviving children clinging to his face in a
frightening manner, like giant leeches. The ending suggests that
they will be with him permanently hereafter. They represent the
tangible, disquieting proof that, whatever his decent instincts and
natural piety, things exist that cannot be accounted for by the so-
ber empiricism he announces at the beginning, reasserts periodically, and finally sees exploded in the course of his experiences.
Gardner distances himself from his character, I think, by hinting
that such empiricism, such objectivity, is only partially efficacious
in dealing with the mysteries of existence—at least for anyone
with artistic pretensions. A dash of subjectivity, of imagination,
is also indispensable, but this prerequisite is, alas, the point at
which physicians and artists part company.

Gardner edges closer to his protagonist in the next story, "The
Temptation of St. Ivo," whose title character may owe something
to the historical St. Ivo of Chartres, who died in 1116. Gardner
apparently intends no direct correlation, however, for the real St.

Ivo was scarcely out of his twenties when he became bishop of Chartres, whereas the fictional Ivo remains in his monastery at the age of fifty. The intricate patterning of this collection—the inter-relationships among stories—continues to manifest itself here: the protagonist again narrates his own story; the seasonal setting ro-tates to summer; two artists (real ones this time) face each other in the central conflict; and the climactic rebirth, though more under-stated than those of preceding stories, seems also more positive—if only because it comes to a saint-in-the-making, Brother Ivo.

The classic temptations of the saintly—of Christ, for example, or St. Anthony—do not eventuate in a fall, but Gardner's story concerns the difficult decision of a saintly monk to give in to temp-tation in the name of a higher good. Such a decision wrenches the soul, because the temptation to let the end justify the means may be merely the most insidious device of Old Nick to undermine a monk's disciplined adherence to the rules of his order. Ivo's fellow monk, ominously named Brother Nicholas, has lost faith in God, in an orderly universe, and in the virtues of disciplined mona-chism. He begins to whisper his growing nihilism to Brother Ivo, baiting him, even feigning homosexual passes to force the vir-tuous monk to break the vow of silence or at least to give in to wrath. Eventually he comes up with a strange threat: "*Brother Ivo, I've decided to murder the Phoenix. I've discovered where it lives. . . . you're the only man who can save the beast*" (p. 75). To save the Phoenix—or whatever Brother Nicholas means by the Phoenix—Brother Ivo would have to break the rule against leaving the mon-astery at night. "If he makes me break one rule," he explains to his confessor, "he'll make me break another. Rules are my only hope against his nihilism" (p. 82). The confessor complicates Brother Ivo's moral dilemma by suggesting that the errant monk's bizarre behavior represents some kind of plea for help. When the confessor turns out to be Brother Nicholas himself (a touch that recalls Death's invasion of the confessional in Bergman's *The Seventh Seal*), Brother Ivo must wrestle with yet more confusion and indecision.

Though he does not believe in the literal reality of the Phoenix, the gifted Brother Ivo has recently painted a very fine one as a symbol of the Resurrection. But Brother Nicholas, not nearly so accomplished as a manuscript illuminator, affects indifference. The conflict between these two reenacts once again that of the bad and good artist: Grendel and the Shaper, Dr. Hunter and Dr. Thorpe. More broadly, it is the unending contest between anarchism and the dream of order: Agathon and Lykourgos, the Sunlight Man and Chief Clumly. These have always been, for Gardner, the conflict between nihilism and despair, on the one side, and faith and hope on the other. But through Brother Ivo Gardner illustrates the necessity of the good artist's facing up to the darkness, of not hedging himself round with "rules," habits of mind that make his art easy—and false. Thus Ivo's boast, early in the story, "I've been painting the shadows the truth casts all my life!" (p. 75), modulates to a searing epiphany at a critical moment of confrontation with dark reality: "I am maddened by art . . . . The rules, techniques of a lifetime devoted to allegory have ruined me" (p. 88). Brother Ivo learns that one must not let rules—artistic or monastic—come between oneself and life; he who does so lives in a land of shadows, a fool's paradise.

As the six-fingered man tells Prince Christopher in *In the Suicide Mountains*, sometimes one must be willing to throw away one's life in order to gain it. Ivo accepts the challenge of Brother Nicholas and breaks the rule against leaving the monastery after dark. In the forest and in the night—both ancient symbols of error—he finds himself utterly adrift, unable even to locate Brother Nicholas. In leaving the monastery Brother Ivo has, like the Phoenix, immolated himself—or rather the lifetime of self-discipline and adherence to the rules by which he has lived. But in venturing forth against the darkness that Brother Nicholas claims is final truth, Brother Ivo has become a figure of the hero, the savior who risks all in confrontation with that darkness. He returns, therefore, like the Phoenix, reborn from his own ashes, riding (for he has met a knight) behind the secular representative of the principle he has discovered. A pale memory to the reborn man, the fires of immolation glimmer in the story's concluding sentence: "We're a strange image, it crosses my mind, floating through moonlit mist down the silent, grassy lane, plumes bobbing, steel armor on the knight and horse like the pale recollection of unreal fire" (p. 89).

The institution founded on strict adherence to rules, a monastery in "The Temptation of St. Ivo," becomes a prison in the next story. In "The Warden" Gardner shifts stylistically towards Kafka, creating a nightmare world of bureaucracy, massive impersonal institutions, and vague, unaccountable authority. As in Kafka, neither time nor place nor season is clearly specified. The country is vaguely east-European, the time pre-twentieth century, the atmosphere chill. The narrator, a mean-spirited bureaucrat named Vortrab, runs a dank, filthy prison manned by fractious guards and filled with prisoners who waste away, chained in dungeons, ignorant of the crimes with which the authorities have charged them. Vortrab's superior, the Warden of the title, refuses to have anything to do with the day-to-day operation of the prison; ignoring all knocks at his door, he leaves his increasingly desperate assistant to run the place with whatever authority he can muster.

Gardner's prison, like Camus' Oran, is the world itself. The Warden is its absentee god. When at the end his spectre appears, the forehead blasted away, the reader understands that the Warden has long since died, probably by his own hand. All of the inhabitants of this world share in the condition of imprisonment. "Doesn't it strike you that we—we, too, are prisoners?" (p. 93), asks Heller, the sympathetic guard. Vortrab pretends to disagree but silently assents. Later he thinks miserably: "I could not help but wonder, that instant, who was more lonely, more desperately helpless—the prisoner whispering in his pitchdark dungeon, or myself" (p. 104). Vortrab's spiritual imprisonment eventually finds expression in a bodily immurement indistinguishable from that of the other prisoners. By the end of the story Vortrab, like the Warden before him, can "no longer go home nights" (p. 119).

The inhabitants of this miserable world make choices with ethical ramifications: to alleviate suffering, to redress injustice, to "follow orders," to end it all. Though Vortrab lacks the initiative to make some kind of intellectual break with his situation, he comes into contact with several people who grope toward—or intuit the possibility of—such freedom. Each of these characters has found a mental or emotional escape route from the existential prison. Even the Warden, according to Vortrab's old father, had yearned for a mystical experience by which to escape. Only Vortrab proves incapable of a system of freedom. He dismisses as senile his artist-father's optimistic faith, as he does Heller's Jewish hope. Heller introduces him to an ancient, saintly prisoner known only as "the Professor," who has worked out an elaborate doctrine by which to rise above his present miserable circumstances. The Professor's transcendentalism contrasts with the abhorrence of illusion imputed, by those who remember him, to the brutally executed archcriminal and anarchist Josef Mallin, whose memory Vortrab finds especially troubling. Vortrab's father, who seems to think that Mallin still lives, remarks: "It will be a great blow to the Warden, no doubt. The minute the axe comes down on Joe Mallin, the Warden's life will go *fssst!*" (p. 102). The Warden's self-immurement dates, as it happens, from the obliteration of this representative of pure freedom by the oppressive system and its mindless, unreflective servants.

But Mallin, like Brother Nicholas before him, had grounded his ideal of absolute freedom in a repudiation of all illusion, including that of order. Like other anarchists in Gardner, he effectively destroys himself. Vortrab, so remote from Mallin ideologically, fails to make a crucial connection between himself and the dead man. Blindly following his "ancient regulations" (pp. 90, 112), Vortrab clings to his narrow idea of order—it is Chief Clumly's "rusty chickenwire" once again—and remains in the condition of exitlessness that Brother Ivo has the courage to break out of. In Vortrab's fear of destructive intellectual freedom and in his single-minded adherence to orderly rule-following, one recognizes an extremism differing little from that of Mallin, even though the two occupy positions across the political and temperamental spectrum from each other.

The dialectic between these representatives of order and anarchy is, as we have seen, a favorite Gardner theme, one the author explained in interviews as a projection of personal traits:

Characteristically there's a battle in my fiction between the hunger for roots, stability, law, and another element in my character which is anarchic. I hate to obey speed laws. I hate to park where it says you have to park. I hate to have to be someplace on time. And in fact I often don't do those things I know I should do, which of course fills me with uneasiness and guilt. Every time you break the law you pay. That compulsion not to do what people tell me, to avoid tic repetitions, makes me constantly keep pushing the edges. It makes me change places of living, or change my life in one way or another, which often makes me very unhappy.[2]

Although change often brings pain, Gardner avoided "tic repetitions" because they turn a spontaneous human being into a mechanical one, as incapable of creative response to emotional pressure or mental challenge as Vortrab, who suffers from a facial tic that acts up whenever the strain of inflexibility, the strain between the official Vortrab and the frightened man inside, becomes too great.

The story's final irony comes when Vortrab drives away the seller of a book that begins: "*Modern thought has made considerable progress by reducing the existent to the series of appearances which manifest it. Its aim was to overcome certain dualisms which have embarrassed philosophy, and to replace them by the singleness of the phenomenon*" (p. 119). These are the opening lines of *Being and Nothingness*, the major philosophical work of Gardner's *bête noire*, Jean-Paul Sartre. The benighted prison administrator might have attained a species of enlightenment from this book, for Sartre reasons from "*Cogito, ergo sum*," the most famous statement in the treatise by Descartes that Vortrab spends his evenings reading. One tormented by the antithesis of freedom and order might have learned something from a discussion of "certain dualisms which have embarrassed philosophy," and one troubled by the silence and indifference of a traditional source of authority might have begun to see into the real meaning of his isolation. But Gardner never invoked existentialism uncritically. He thought of it as the philosophy of despair and viewed Sartre with the kind of genial hostility that Nabokov reserved for Freud. How, then, should the reader construe the allusion to *Being and Nothingness*? It hints, I think, at the real depths of Vortrab's moral paralysis. The kind of enlightenment, of faith, that Gardner advocates in story after story and in book after book is one that registers the argument of existentialism yet opts still for optimism. Gardner concedes, in other words, that one must grasp the existentialist position before one can strive for a meaningful faith, and he invites the reader to gauge the extent of Vortrab's nescience by the fact that he has yet to arrive at even the first, existentialist rung of the ladder of enlightenment. Few in this story—perhaps only Vortrab senior and the Professor—get very far up the ladder. Heller at the end has sunk into an ambiguous despair. Last seen "pacing, occasionally pausing, deep in thought" (p. 119), he seems at the point of a momentous decision. His pacing may end in suicide, as the Warden's did, or it could eventuate in repudiation of the system that fosters such despair. "The Warden," then, is the bleakest story in the book (unlike every other story, it even lacks an illustration). Where other stories in this section feature some hopeful renewal, this one offers only a travesty of resurrection: the appearance of the Warden's mutilated shade. The Warden is resurrected even less hopefully in Vortrab, who in effect assumes the Warden's mantle when he says to Heller what the Warden once said to him: "If Order has value, you and I are the only hope!" (p. 119; cf. p. 90).

However dark "The Warden," the "midnight reader" reaches dawn in the elegiac "John Napper Sailing Through the Universe." This sketch features Gardner's own family and friends, with Gardner himself narrating. The reader encounters the artist John Napper (he did the illustrations for *The Sunlight Dialogues*) only in flashback, for in the story's wintry present he is no longer living. The story has little plot, but it does have a central event: Napper paints a portrait of Lucy Gardner, the author's daughter. At the beginning of the story, in present time, the author contemplates the portrait of Lucy and reflects that though his daughter will grow up to be a beautiful woman, "time will blast her, her flesh will sag like an elderly dog's" (p. 121). But however evanescent the real Lucy's "hour as art," the Lucy on canvas will remain unchanged: "a kind of snag in time" (p. 121), "a kind of gasp in space" (p. 130). Though the flowers that surround her painted likeness symbolize the transitoriness of mortal beauty, they too will remain forever fresh, made immortal by art.

Gardner's story doubles the *ars longa, vita brevis* conceit—the contrasting of life's ephemeral beauty with the lasting beauty of art—by doing for John Napper what John Napper did for Lucy Gardner. As Napper has immortalized Lucy in a work of art, so Gardner will immortalize Napper. At the same time Gardner redresses the literary injustice implied in Napper's anecdote about J. M. W. Turner, who, though a "secret philanthropist" (p. 130), served Dickens as a model for Scrooge. The author of "John Napper Sailing Through the Universe" makes up for Dickens' dyslogistic portrayal of Turner by turning another gifted painter into a literary character memorable, unlike Scrooge, for a host of positive and endearing traits.

Napper's philosophy of art, chief among these positive traits, complements Gardner's own. " 'John Napper Sailing Through the Universe' is my fundamental theory of art," Gardner observed. "What Napper says is at the heart of it: an artist can't just describe the world, 'bitter reality'; the artist has to create new and wonderful possibilities." [3] Gardner describes Napper's struggle with that reality by reporting on paintings—or rather the handling of light and dark in them—from different moments in the artist's career. In the earlier paintings the light seems to be in a losing battle with the dark. Described as "mostly black, with struggles of light, losing," this early work reveals "something suicidal," and Gardner wonders "why he kept fighting, instead of slitting his wrists" (p. 124). An impromptu "Napper retrospective" reveals "ghoulish faces, fuliginous lump-people, terrible previews of Hiroshima, mournful cityscapes the texture of, roughly, dried blood. Here and there, there was a scraggly flower, a crushed bit of light" (p. 125). A Turneresque "transitional work" depicts "a ship, small in an enormous sea and sky. The ship was in trouble. The universe was churning" (p. 130). The ship, of course, is John Napper, "sailing through the universe." He eventually breaks through to calmer seas and paints "big bright" pictures that represent his personal triumph over the darkness. His experience recapitulates the aesthetic development of "The Midnight Reader." Like Brother Ivo, he has faced the darkness and come back with a new strength:

> He'd gone to the pit, in those Paris paintings, fighting for his life, squeezing the blood from this turnip of a world to hunt out the secret life in it, and there was none there. He'd hounded light—not just visual light—straining every muscle of body and mind to get down to what was real, what was absolute; beauty not someone else had seen it but beauty he could honestly find himself, and what he'd gotten was a picture of the coal pocket. . . . And then, at the edge of self-destruction, John Napper had, I saw, jumped back. He would make up the world from scratch: Let their be light, a splendid garden. He would fabricate treasure maps. And he'd come to believe it. How could he not, seeing how it lighted his sad wife's eyes? It was majestic! Also nonsense. (p. 133)

Napper's resurrection inspires Gardner in his own struggle with the world's "bitter reality." With the same godlike *fiat lux!* Gardner too creates a "splendid garden" of art. Both Napper and Gardner recognize the craziness of such an enterprise, but determination such as theirs ultimately makes art heroic. Like the hero, Gardner's artist defies darkness and affirms light, and thus like the knight who flings his dagger into the dark in "The Temptation of St. Ivo," Napper makes his last appearance here in a kind of freeze-frame, "his smile thrown forward in the darkness like a spear" (p. 134).

Their desire to "make up the world from scratch" notwithstanding, neither Gardner nor Napper would advocate retreat from or obliviousness to the reality they find wanting. Both do it justice before moving on to "new and wonderful possibilities." In the stories of "The Midnight Reader," then, Gardner not only presents his own progression from darkness to light but also concludes the exercise in the real world—which he has found capable, in the nonfictional example of John Napper, of stirring enlightenment. In this metaphoric progression from midnight to dawn, the light that gradually gathers is nothing less than art itself.

A Kingdom Ruled by Art

If art is light in "The Midnight Reader," it is benign madness in the "Tales of Queen Louisa." Gardner always admitted that successful defiance of the world's darkness requires inspired madness on the part of the artist. He characterizes John Napper's triumphant vision as "nonsense" and twice describes him, to his face, as "crazy." Napper agrees. The collection's consummate artist, Jonathan Upchurch in "The King's Indian," closes his tale with the Holy Ghost's benediction on himself: "thou fucking lunatic" (p. 323). By the same token, the colloquial vocabulary of lunacy turns up in Gardner's interviews whenever he described his own commitment to affirmation.

Though he properly does not abandon the real world altogether, the moral artist must perforce make it over; he tends, therefore, towards romance or fantasy of the type seen in the last two-thirds of *The King's Indian*. Gardner makes careful distinctions among the forms of short fiction, and one finds that anything labeled "tale" in this collection complies in all particulars with the description of that genre in *The Forms of Fiction*, a textbook that Gardner co-edited with Lennis Dunlap in 1962. Gardner and Dunlap define the tale as a story—not necessarily "short"—that commonly departs from reality in some way, yet without generating resistance on the part of the reader. They cite fairy tales, romances, and Chaucer's *Canterbury Tales* by way of examples, and they quote Coleridge on the "willing suspension of disbelief." But however much the tale makes free with real-world plausibility, it must enlist the reader's credence in the moral and psychological validity of extraordinary and frequently supernatural character and action. The author accomplishes this end by "a curious mixture of vagueness and generality, on the one hand, and meticulously exact detail on the other. The author's scrupulousness in supplying concrete detail inspires credence, and the remoteness, together with the vagueness and generality, tends to prevent the reader from considering the reality or unreality of the setting."[4] Thus in the "Tales of Queen Louisa" the reader has little idea just where or when King Gregor and Queen Louisa reigned, yet at the same time he knows with some intimacy their physical surroundings and their daily concerns with war, peace, love, sanity, and family.

Gardner's attention to form has its complement in a conscientious attitude towards narrative technique. Like Henry James, he devoted much of his career to greater and greater mastery of this aspect of his craft. As early as *The Resurrection* Gardner demonstrates the subtle effects available to the writer who makes conscious decisions about point of view; and whatever the failings of *The Wreckage of Agathon*, its author solves narrative problems with admirable resourcefulness. In the "Tales of Queen Louisa," the only narratives in the *King's Indian* collection not told in the first person, Gardner explores the implications of rotating the center of consciousness among the principle characters in a set of related stories. He complicates matters by also making his central character, center of consciousness in the first tale, a lunatic. Because of Queen Louisa's rank and sensitivity the other characters, however sane, defer to her and thus compromise their own reliability when in subsequent tales they become the centers of consciousness. Only in the last of the Queen Louisa stories, not included in *The King's Indian*, does the author introduce a truly objective center of consciousness. In "Trumpeter," first published in *Esquire* in 1976 and collected in *The Art of Living* in 1981, the action flows through the consciousness of the palace dog, but because he understands neither the death that drives Queen Louisa mad nor the madness itself, he too fails to deliver anything definitive about the strange situation in her realm.

The perceptual shortcomings of the centers of consciousness in these stories do not preclude the reader's seeing the larger picture, since fictional characters can convey information they themselves do not grasp. Still, the proposition that truth varies according to the authority consulted becomes an epistemological scalpel of great keenness in the hands of an artist capable of exploiting the possibilities inherent in the manipulation of point of view. In *The Turn of the Screw*, for example, a lonely governess's fantastic tale is made plausible by means of carefully framed first-person narration. As a result the story can be read as an exciting ghost tale or as a case history in hysteria. Another example, Akira Kurosawa's *Rashomon*, is the perfect analogue to Gardner's "Tales of Queen Louisa." In Kurosawa's film the truth behind a violent crime becomes increasingly puzzling as one witness after another colors it with his own self-interest. Gardner too concerns himself with the elusiveness of pure objectivity: "*Who can swear / that his own apprehension of reality is valid?*" (p. 144).

In the first of these stories, "Queen Louisa," Gardner modifies the popular fairy-tale motif of the frog prince, for Queen Louisa perceives herself most of the time as a giant, ugly frog. She is at other times—when it suits her—a great beauty with red hair and freckles. That other, supposedly sane characters also see her as a giant frog complicates the fantasy in a delightful way, especially when some of these same characters start shape-shifting themselves. The three justices—at first merely described as sheeplike but subsequently perceived as sheep by characters and narrator indifferently—are pure Lewis Carroll. The queen's husband and lady-in-waiting also undergo metamorphoses. The story's narration, however, does not quite allow the reader to dismiss these illusions as projections of the madness of Queen Louisa, the center of consciousness. One might with greater accuracy say that the queen's madness rubs off on others (including the narrator and the reader), who begin to participate in it, seeing justices as sheep and His Royal Highness as a "red hound." Not only is this kind of lunacy fun, it also proves beneficial in dealing with certain kinds of unpleasantness.

Queen Louisa operates instinctively to protect and preserve her family, her little enclave of order, against a variety of anarchic threats. In this first story she suspects that her husband, transformed into a beast by lust, has become enamored of the lady-in-waiting. From the queen's point of view the lady-in-waiting is a witch, a Circe, and she confronts her rival at the enchanted monastery where presumably the adulterous trysts have taken place. The threat posed by the witch takes on a philosophical dimension when she begins mouthing existential jargon: "We're cosmic accidents! . . . Life is gratuitous, it has no meaning till we make one up by our intensity." The witch's depredations, as she explains with Grendel-like cynicism, are "to end the boredom! To end all those mornings of waking up vaguely irritable!" (p. 151). The last observation may hurt the most, for the story began with the queen's waking up "worried and irritable" (p. 137). Burdened with some "deeply buried secret of her soul's unrest" (p. 137), Queen Louisa suffers from the basic human complaint, the feeling of general disquiet and meaninglessness in what is called, in the third story, "a senseless and lawless universe" (p. 183).

But Queen Louisa, refusing to surrender to Angst, repudiates the witch's philosophy. The queen has earlier described herself as the daughter of a dragon and a Catholic, and this daft pedigree accounts for both her vulnerability and her spunk. In Gardner dragons are pure negation, the kind of nihilism that defeats all aspirations to morality and meaning, to finding life worth living. Catholics, by contrast, are archetypal theists, believers in the orderliness of the universe. The queen, like Gardner himself, is the living reconciliation of these two supposedly contradictory world pictures. Her madness, then, is the benign craziness of a John Napper. A positive thing, enabling her to triumph over the evil witch, it is analogous to the art that refuses to content itself with mirroring the world's "bitter reality," and indeed the queen reshapes the bitter reality of her marital situation (not to mention the still more bitter realities canvassed in subsequent stories) to create new possibilities for familial wholeness, harmony, and love.

Beginning in fragmentation and isolation and ending in wholeness and harmony, the story ultimately pits two kinds of absurdity against each other. That described by the witch is cosmic and existential—absurdity divorced from all questions of value and elevated to the level of cosmic principle. But the queen's madness differs radically from that of the universe. It is dominated by—is in some ways the expression of—the love imaged in the rose bush that flourishes in the dead of winter and grows stronger the more it is assaulted. That love resumes its normal, quiescent state after the defeat of the witch, and the rose becomes "an ice-clad stick" (p. 152)—a condition natural for roses in the dead of winter.

Lunatics (especially the artistic variety) may have a clearer view of things than the putatively sane, who tolerate all manner of folly and vice because it has somehow become the norm. Hamlet's madness, feigned or real, reflects this paradox, and there is method in the madness of Yeats's Crazy Jane, too. In Philippe de Broca's popular film *King of Hearts* a soldier elects to join the inmates of an insane asylum rather than continue to participate in the sane world's prosecution of the Great War. These examples tell one how to read the second of the Queen Louisa stories, "King Gregor and the Fool," in which Gardner examines commonly held notions of madness and sanity.

Nearly every page of this story teems with words denoting mental aberration: "foolish," "lunatic," "insane," "crazy," "idiotic," "mad," etc. Comments on sanity, accusations of insanity, and self-congratulation on mental stability—all in the ironic mode—vie for the reader's attention and acceptance. "It wasn't easy to be sane when the whole wide world around him was crazy" (p. 155), thinks King Gregor, lamenting the insanity of his wife and waxing furious at the liberties taken by his Fool, who trades on the polite falsehood of being "supposedly mad, and therefore not responsible" (p. 154). But these "lunatics," the queen and the Fool, effectively challenge the sanity of the king and his chief pastime, waging war.

Queen Louisa and her entourage come out to view the proceedings between King Gregor and his neighborly enemy, seen "jumping up and down like an idiot" (p. 164) at the prospect of a nice, bloody battle. Appalled, the queen stops the battle before it can get underway and remarks succinctly: "You people are all crazy" (p. 165). The Fool echoes her sentiments in a bit of nonsense verse:

> You think I'm small because I'm lazy;
> But big brave knights get killed. That's crazy!? (p. 167)

Faced with execution for his effrontery, the Fool claims the lines come from the Bible, and the subterfuge works. Ironically, this king who loves to make war has a great, if fatuous, respect for the Bible. Thus the royal household plays two jokes on him. The first is that only the pacifism of lunatics like the queen and the Fool—they are both, of course, "holy fools"—is in any sense biblical; the second is that they are saner than he about the things that matter. The story ends, therefore, with another moment of harmony, with the king in full possession of his dignity, the Fool off the hook, the royal husband and wife once again reconciled, and the war forgotten.

Queen Louisa continues her good offices in "Muriel." This time she succeeds in imposing her kind of harmony on political disorder. A group of discontented peasants, former friends of the queen's adopted daughter Muriel, wants to erase ideas of station out of a simple-minded notion that through their revolutionary activities they, too, can become privileged and live like nobility. The revolt of the peasants is decidedly unsophisticated and childish, and indeed the whole story can be read as an allegory of rebellion in the nursery quelled by the administration of corporal punishment by the paternal King Gregor with his knights and the maternal Queen Louisa with her switch. The punishment completed, Queen Louisa solves the political and social problems by absorbing the refractory peasants into the ranks of her "long-lost" children. Only the romantic outlaw-princeling Vrokror remains unredeemed, as if to hint at disruptive principles, existential realities, that no madness and no art can ever tame or integrate. But Vrokror's recalcitrance, as will be seen, qualifies only temporarily the general comedic harmony of the story's conclusion.

One must read these first three stories very closely to see the circumstance that, in driving the queen mad, sets all of the stories in motion. That circumstance, repeatedly hinted at but never made clear, even when the center of consciousness is sane, is the death of the original Princess Muriel. This fact comes out unambiguously only in "Trumpeter," which resembles Virginia Woolf's *Flush* in that it is a dog's-eye view of domestic arrangements in a remarkable household. As part of the inhuman world Trumpeter can register certain things—death for example—that he does not understand. His confusion over one of these provides this story and the others with an essential thematic focus. Gardner introduces the phenomenon that so puzzles Trumpeter with a canine view of the operatic and dramatic stage:

> He had seen the whole court sit erect for hours, dead silent except for an occasional whisper, an occasional cough, listening to people on a bright raised platform howl. He, when he tentatively joined them, had been kicked and sent outside. On that same raised platform he'd seen a man in black creep up cunningly on another, a dagger in his hand, and when he, Trumpeter, had hurtled to the rescue, he'd been beaten and seized by five knights and had been chained behind the buttery.[5]

The reader needs to keep this hint of the author's real concern in mind as the story proceeds to another of Queen Louisa's mad solutions to her country's problems. Distressed at the misery and rapacity of pirates and cutpurses, she arranges to make them guardians of the royal treasure, so that they can steal as much as they want. She also advances the social leveling begun in "Muriel" by marrying her newly adopted princes and princesses to various bourgeois. When she even marries Muriel to Vrokror, the last unmalleable residuum of reality falls before her inspired madness. Peace, justice, and order triumph as this story, like its predecessors, ends with a vision of harmony.

Gardner provides a penultimate paragraph this time that makes finally clear the sense in which Queen Louisa's accomplishments are to be understood in the real world:

> The palace was full of light—beyond the windows, thick darkness. Nothing was wrong; nothing could go wrong. It was a balanced kingdom, the only kingdom in the world where art reigned supreme. (p. 87)

But only humans create and understand art. Poor Trumpeter, after recalling the time when he had to be dragged forcibly away from the bed in which his beloved princess lay dead, and after witnessing the mad nuptials of her surrogates, retreats from the beings who can take comfort in such things: "When he reached the depths of the forest, he began to howl" (p. 87). That last word ought to catch one's attention; it is the same used to describe Trumpeter's perception of opera, one of the highest forms of art. The ironic echo hints at a "moral": he who mistakes art for howling, he whose savage breast cannot be soothed by art, is doomed to howl indeed in this painful world.

Art, then, is a divine madness, and Queen Louisa is its symbol. Like the queen, the artist is charged with transmuting into something rich, strange, and beautiful a world in which justice is "just ice" (p. 142), a world darkened by poverty, infidelity, war, class struggle—and the deaths of princesses. The reader who understands the aesthetic allegory in these stories will not dismiss their author as some flower child offering simple-minded solutions to the ills that flesh is heir to, for Gardner means to shape a parable of art's ability and responsibility to change, as a rueful Grendel puts it, "dry sticks into gold." Without that essential transmutation, life is in danger of being just what the first story's existentialist witch claims it is: miserable and meaningless.

Ship of State

Art's ability to remake the world, demonstrated in the Queen Louisa stories, must be matched by an ability to probe truth in all its complexity. Gardner engages that complexity impressively in the short novel that gives its title to the *King's Indian* collection. The author of this "celebration of all literature and life" (p. 316) on occasion intimated that he considered it one of his best works, and in multiplicity, resonance, and sheer intellectual audacity it justifies his pride. The narrator of "The King's Indian," Jonathan Upchurch, recalls his coming of age on an epic voyage of the whaler *Jerusalem*. Like the hero of every initiation story, the nineteen-year-old Upchurch must take painful lessons in distinguishing the real from the ideal and the illusory. He learns not only about the chicanery and duplicity of his fellow men but also about the illusions built into existence itself. His tale, in fact, is grounded in metaphysics; at sea in a craft he cannot pilot, he blithely reflects: "In landlessness alone lies the highest truth, shoreless, as indefinite as God!" (p. 212). This line, lifted almost verbatim from chapter 23 of *Moby-Dick*, tells the reader that Upchurch's voyage will take him away from security and stability (the land, in Melville's trope) into the oceanic mystery of existence itself, for Melville describes the sea, in the first chapter of his great novel, as an "image of the ungraspable phantom of life." But along with metaphysics, the author of "The King's Indian" takes an interest in ethics, politics, and aesthetics, and the reader will discover corresponding symbolic dimensions to the story. One recognizes in the *Jerusalem*, for example, the American ship of state and in Jonathan Upchurch an artist-hero who addresses himself to the complex relationship of truth and illusion in politics and art—and explores once again the question of the artist's responsibility to society.

74595

The plot of "The King's Indian" concerns a hoax, a deliberate creation of illusion, perpetrated by the *Jerusalem*'s owners, Tobias Cook and James T. Horner. On his return from a long voyage the commanding officer of the *Jerusalem*, Captain Dirge, learns that the vessel has in his absence been reported lost with all hands. Moreover, a painting has been salvaged from the wreck—a painting that proves to be identical to one hanging in the captain's cabin. The owners soon convince the credulous captain that the two paintings are "a single painting seen from different points in Time" (p. 286) and that on some different plane of existence or time he and his crew have in fact suffered shipwreck. The crucial painting—the owners have simply had it copied for their prank—is a portrait of the arch-magician Luther Flint, whom Dirge admires for his knowledge of the occult. Dirge makes the mistake of apprising Flint of what he thinks he has stumbled on and of his plans to make a voyage to the site of the alleged sinking. Flint is a complete charlatan, but according to one of his henchmen, the scoundrel "Swami Havananda," he has "hunted all his life for some holiness past magic" (p. 308). This same Swami Havananda, under the name of Wilkins, was the one charged with having the portrait of Flint copied and "salvaged." One of the perpetrators of the owners' hoax, he keeps his knowledge to himself—even when Flint enlists him in another, more vicious hoax. His search for the sacred notwithstanding, Flint murders the captain and his daughter, replacing the one with an automaton under his control and the other with his own daughter, Miranda. Gardner thus constructs a set of hoaxes within hoaxes and hoaxers hoaxed. Ironically, then, Jonathan Upchurch's penetration of veil after veil of the *Jerusalem*'s mysteries leads him and the reader from illusion to a reality that is insubstantial. It consists of the delusion of Luther Flint, the duplicity of his confederate, and the practical joke of the ship's owners.

But we are taken in if we see the owners as the ultimate hoaxers. They are, after all, the creation of a storyteller named Jonathan Upchurch, who is in turn the creation of a storyteller named

John Gardner. Fiction itself is the Ur-hoax. Gardner knows that a fundamental paradox of fiction is that it expresses truth through what is nominally falsehood. The imaginary thing—a ship called the *Jerusalem*, say—functions metaphorically or symbolically. It proves to be a microcosm, a little world made cunningly, or it proves to be the great world en route to the apocalyptic end foretold for it. "The world's a ship," says Melville, "on its passage out." The owners of such a ship, those at whose bidding it posts o'er the sea, begin to take on mythic attributes, to resemble parodic manichaean deities, "Beelzebub and Jaweh" (p. 197), who set the great human experiment of confusion and aspiration in motion.

The symbolism lends itself with greater consistency, however, to something less grandiose—the voyage of the American ship of state. Gardner's insistent, Whitmanesque capitalization of "Captain" elevates the vessel's master to the status of founding father or president (though surely not so credulous as Dirge, a number of the founding fathers took seriously to the mumbo jumbo of Freemasonry). The first idealistic dreamer, the archetypal Captain, charts a course extraordinary in the annals of nations. His virtuous daughter—like Liberty aboard the American ship of state— will sail with him, defying the superstitious proscription of women at sea. But this first, inspired Captain is succeeded by less high-minded leaders: crass politicians, opportunists, and "bunkum artists" like Flint and Wilkins. The female passenger becomes a pasteboard ideal, if not something worse, and the great mission of the voyage comes more and more to be compromised. The crew must be fleshed out with slaves, and the rendezvous with destiny south of the Vanishing Isles begins to be forgotten as business— especially the larcenous "commerce" with other ships—proves increasingly lucrative. In this circumstance, the simultaneous allegiance to high principles and high profits, one finds the quintessential American paradox, the curious mixture of idealism and materialism that Fitzgerald captured in *The Great Gatsby*. But sooner or later, Gardner suggests, this dual vision must falter. The crew of the *Jerusalem*, many of whom once believed in their special destiny, become disenchanted as the adventure wears on and high expectations wane. Billy More explains:

> What we wanted was to do something BIG—make use of big energy for a big purpose, and do it fast—big speed—and do it, like Jesus Christ himself, at a mighty big cost. But the bigness drained out, that's what happened, Johnny. The dream became merely the Captain's dream. Our purpose changed, as purposes will, like any other thing in Nature. The big success had been too long coming, and the cost was beginning to seem absurd—our freedom to be each his own man, not cogs in a machine which is doing some job we've got no use for. (pp. 288–289)

With such a disaffected crew, the ship faces rough sailing, just as disillusioned Americans face a dangerous political future. What happens aboard the *Jerusalem* is not, in other words, simple historical allegory, with events on the voyage in a one-to-one relation to events in the American past. Events on the voyage take on meaning according to a more complex and Janus-faced allegory, interpretation of which requires looking simultaneously into the history and into the future of the American nation. The mutiny, for example, functions both historically and prophetically. As a symbolic version of the American Civil War, it results in the freeing of the slaves but also in further bloodshed, further confusion. But it is also—and this is one of the many affinities between "The King's Indian" and *October Light*—an augury of the civil war to come and of the terrible political and social dislocations that will accompany it. In fact, the struggles among Wolff, Wilkins, Flint, Upchurch, and Ngugi are most understandable as a meditation on a future in which the nation may have to survive periods of fascism (the rule of the vicious second mate, Wolff) and anarchism (Wilkins' tenure) before peace can be restored. The register of all this turmoil, Jonathan Upchurch, is American man chastened by his experiences with political reality and illusion. But through his ingenuity and good faith Liberty finds redemption, the ship's poly-racial crew share in its preservation and navigation, and the voyage comes to clear democratic sailing at last.

In telling a sea-tale with nationalistic overtones, Gardner joins a distinguished company that includes Homer, Virgil, Camoëns, and Whitman. "The King's Indian" is in fact a composite of all the great sea stories, though for immediate precedent and inspiration Gardner looks to Coleridge, Poe, Melville, and Twain, all of whom authored famous examples of first-person narratives recounting symbolic voyages. Coleridge's "The Rime of the Ancient Mariner" provides the more superficial parallels: Gardner frames his tale like Coleridge's poem, with an aged "mariner" telling a bizarre story to an initially reluctant "guest." Like the Ancient Mariner, Upchurch survives horrible experiences in Antarctic regions with a crew described as "a company of deadmen" (p. 216), and as the first mariner learns to honor his fellow creatures (the albatross, the water-snakes), Upchurch learns to respect the harpooner James Ngugi and his black brethren. When a character refers to the harpooner as "Nigger Jim" (p. 318), we realize that Jonathan's ethical maturation also reenacts that of Huck Finn. Of course Ngugi, like his Indian colleague Kaskiwah, comes primarily from Melville; indeed, as the savage harpooners recall Daggoo, Tashtego, and Queequeg in *Moby-Dick*, the black slaves secreted in the *Jerusalem's* hold derive from Fedallah and the dark oriental stowaways aboard the *Pequod*. Gardner's narrator, finally, is another Ishmael who ships with a monomaniac, an Ahab tragically bent on piercing through to the forbidden heart of things.[6]

But Gardner borrows most heavily from Edgar Allan Poe's literary hoax, *The Narrative of Arthur Gordon Pym*. That the *Grampus*, the vessel on which Pym stowed away, is said to have been on the scene when the phantom *Jerusalem* went down is only Gardner's most obvious allusion, for he takes from *Pym* much of the outline of the voyage, numerous incidents, and even Poe's words and phrases. Chapter 4, for example, recycles Pym's drunken escapade aboard the *Ariel*. Like Poe's hero, Upchurch sails to disaster one October night in a boat valued at seventy-five dollars; he even departs from a wharf next to the defunct lumberyard of "Pankey & Son." The bloody mutiny aboard the *Jerusalem* reenacts, again in

Poe's words and phrases, the one in *Pym*—except that Gardner makes the axe-wielding cook Chinese instead of Negro. At the end Upchurch and the survivors of his crew hear the birds Pym encountered near the South Pole (crying *Tekeli-li*) and pass by the mysterious white figure he saw. Pym brushes the very secrets of existence at the climax of his narrative; Upchurch, at the climax of his, sails into the same locus "outside corpuscular experience" (p. 287).

The verbatim borrowings from Poe may trouble the reader familiar with the plagiarism scandal over Gardner's *The Life and Times of Chaucer* (1977).[7] Doubtless out of chagrin, Gardner never offered a satisfactory explanation of that deplorable incident, though he apologized repeatedly in public. Much of the Chaucer biography is necessarily impressionistic and fictive, and I suspect that he wrote it for the most part in the frame of mind he brings to his creative writing rather than that he brings to scholarship. One should remember, too, that by the mid-1970s Gardner probably thought of himself less and less as a scholar and more and more as a novelist—with the creative artist's right to appropriate useful material without acknowledgment. After all, creative artists from Chaucer himself to Shakespeare and from Handel to Mozart have always cheerfully plagiarized each other. Even Poe, an obsessive exposer of plagiarists, borrowed ideas from other writers.[8] The material from *Pym* in "The King's Indian," at any rate, is not theft but homage. "The King's Indian" brims with literary allusions because its author, like Eliot in *The Waste Land*, seeks to remind his reader of the extent to which the literary past breathes through the literary present.

Only the work of major artists finds its way into Gardner's allusive scheme. One looks in vain for allusions to, say, Longfellow's "The Building of the Ship" or Holmes's "Old Ironsides"—poems that might be expected to resonate with the novel's patriotic theme. At the same time that he refuses to pay homage to second-rate poets, however, Gardner creates in Luther Flint another avatar of the bad artist that stalks through his fiction. As builder of the Dirge automaton, Flint is the artificer who impiously usurps the divine prerogative by an attempt at literal creation. The epithet applied to Captain Ahab, "an ungodly, god-like man," describes Flint as well, for he fits the archetype defined by Professor Hunter in "The Ravages of Spring," by Bannadonna in Melville's "The Bell-Tower," by Wells's Dr. Moreau, and by Victor Frankenstein. Even if he originally seeks "some holiness past magic," his art is rendered corrupt by its means—the murder of Captain Dirge and his daughter—and trivial by its end—the fleecing of passing ships. As the naming of his daughter indicates, Flint is a degenerate Prospero, an artist-wizard whose Caliban—Wilkins—is no moral inferior. Miranda, an instrument shaped to her father's nefarious ends, is in a way his *chef d'oeuvre*, but such a masterpiece only demonstrates that artists like Flint produce at best a superficial and meretricious beauty.

A "spokesman for all criminal, all pseudo-artistic minds" (pp. 315–316), Flint comes off poorly in comparison with a real artist like Jonathan Upchurch—or John Gardner, who modeled for Herbert L. Fink's depiction of Upchurch (p. 209). Not only does Upchurch, as narrator, compose a story for the "guest" and the reader he represents, he also creates fictions for his fellow crewmen aboard the *Jerusalem*. With a resourcefulness worthy of Scheherazade, he prevents their dealing summarily with him by making up stories about himself. Gardner insists that the difference between the good and bad artist concerns the ends of artifice. Defining moral art as art that frames myths to live by, he depicts Flint and Upchurch as artists who literally die and live, respectively, by the fictions they create. Even in the afterlife, the setting in which the narrator actually spins his yarn, good art means continued life, whether life be construed as literary immortality or something more literal. In this venue Upchurch, waited on by an angel in a cozy public house, remains vital and animated, while Flint and his daughter, with "faces . . . gray as the faces of newly drained cadavers in the mortuary" (p. 294), lead the tenuous existence of miserable shades, beholden to an art greater than theirs for whatever meager substance they boast.

The proper task of the artist is at once to create illusion and to penetrate it, and the entire plot of "The King's Indian" demonstrates this fundamental aesthetic paradox as its narrator spins the web of baffling illusion his younger self, as protagonist, must unravel. In the deepening enigma of "Augusta Dirge," and in her gradual unmasking, one sees this double movement—knotting and unknotting—in concentrated form. The assumed name of Gardner's heroine conflates the first names of Arthur Gordon Pym's companions: Augusta derives from Augustus Barnard, Dirge from Dirk Peters. Perhaps as a reply to Leslie Fiedler's contention that Pym's companions are unconscious projections of homoerotic fantasy,[9] Gardner feminizes and unifies his protagonist's alter ego. Thus Upchurch's relationship with Augusta enacts what Jung called the encounter with and integration of the anima, the feminine component of the male psyche. More broadly, the anima is primal woman, and Gardner reminds us that woman has become "humanity's showpiece, transformed by nineteen centuries of pampering to a stage creation, tinseled puppet painted, taught speech by troubadours—championed by knights who knew her lovely and probably unfaithful—philosophized by painters and jewelers and poets" (p. 304). In his relationship with the captain's daughter, Jonathan progresses from idealization and romantic involvement to the discovery that she dissembles (about being a poet, for example) and the realization that she differs radically from what he has, along with his fellow Western man, taken her to be.

As he discovers the truth about Miranda, Jonathan discovers the truth about the ship in which they sail, its robot captain, the oracular Jeremiah (named, perhaps, for Jeremiah Reynolds, who jogged the imaginations of both Poe and Melville), and members of the crew like the odious Wilkins and the noble James Ngugi. His quest for the truth beneath appearances complements the novel's political theme, for political freedom depends in large measure on freedom from illusion. Consequently, much of the examination of varying claims regarding metaphysical reality bears ultimately on the political and historical ramifications of that reality. In the course of his maturation Jonathan passes through phases of transcendental complacency and growing existential doubt, and these reflect similar periods in the intellectual history of America. In between he broods on the vile institution of slavery and his complicity in it. His youthful, uncritical acceptance of the universe and his place in it coincides with the period of maximum deception by Augusta and reaches a climax just before certain revelations about her come to him. "I began to know things people don't know if they've never given up all private identity to a shoreless sea or a forest extending, arch on arch, the breadth of fifteen mountains. I began to comprehend time and space not by mind or will but by a process more mystical . . . . the whole universe was my soul's extension, my ultimate temporal-spatial location" (p. 267). In this phase he describes himself as "at one with all things living or inanimate" (p. 279). He begins to discover Augusta's duplicity at the same time that he realizes a personal culpability with regard to slavery, feeling "guilt cold and boundless as damnation" (p. 276). His world picture shifts: "No longer was I one with the wind, the sea, the motion of the ship. No longer were stars gone-out-long-since my ultimate skin. I was an object in a great bumping clutter of objects" (p. 277).

After such knowledge, what forgiveness? The rest of the story gauges the prospects for a return to some kind of confidence or trust in the universe, some "faith" not at odds with experience. Jonathan Upchurch has lost one kind of faith, and he is not alone. Mr. Knight, the first mate, has seen his faith eroded by science; he worries "that the world's mechanical" (p. 290). According to Billy More, much of the crew has lost faith in the purpose of the voyage. But given the circumstances of that voyage, the multiform crisis of faith aboard the *Jerusalem* is only to be expected. Originating in the faulty knowledge of the captain and in the bad faith of the owners, the voyage is undertaken to determine a question of free will—a line of inquiry virtually guaranteed to result in spiritual loss. The original Captain Dirge, talking himself into the fatal expedition, had wondered whether "what will be *must* be," whether "all our freedom is a ludicrous illusion" (p. 286). His answer lies partly in the conditions under which he undertakes his quest; his own freedom is compromised by the fact that when he thinks he is freely challenging fate, he has actually been manipulated by the *Jerusalem*'s owners. The final truth is some middle ground between freedom and determinism, as Melville intimates when, in chapter 47 of *Moby-Dick*, he says that chance, free will, and necessity interweave to shape our lives. (Jonathan Upchurch echoes Melville when he meets Augusta: "I saw the impishness as Augusta's line of *necessity*, the kindness as *free*, the perfunctory quality as the random stroke of *chance*"—p. 252.) But these components are not immutable. Knowledge augments freedom; lack of knowledge diminishes or cancels it. Thus Captain Dirge's tragedy was that he lacked knowledge. He placed his faith in Flint, the bad artist who, deluded and deceitful himself, fails signally to deliver the truth that makes one free.

Chance and necessity also constrain liberty, the political analogue of free will. Are the crew of this ship capable of self-determination? Gardner's task is to affirm artistically that the great democratic experiment is worth making, that the ship of state will not founder without captain, king, dictator, or god as a source of absolute authority. To do so he must recognize certain realities without abandoning altogether certain desirable ideals, and he accomplishes this end by means of a brilliantly ambiguous touch, the recurrent references to Nowhere. Nowhere, initially, yawns for the mariner who is mentally careless in the rigging. Jonathan would have taken "the step to Nowhere" (p. 238) his first time aloft were it not for the vigilance of Billy More (this scene, incidentally, borrows extensively from the passage in which Arthur Gordon Pym clings to a cliff, drops, and is caught by Dirk Peters). Jonathan's danger stems largely from a dazed conviction that taking the fatal step would enable him to mingle pleasurably with the inanimate universe—a pantheistic notion not at odds with the intellectual and literary inclinations of his day. But in the course of the novel the Nowhere motif begins to take on another significance. When the desire to take the Step to Nowhere is described as "a hunger to sink into the absolute freedom of suicide" (p. 237), we recognize a recurrent theme. Repeatedly in Gardner absolute freedom—anarchy—*is* suicide. The Nowhere motif, in other words, may ultimately have a political significance— a significance hinted at in the surname of the character who first names the phenomenon: Billy More.[10] For Nowhere is the literal translation of Utopia, the secular version of the City of God from which Jonathan's ship takes its name, and the word's recurrence throughout the book adumbrates an ambivalent attitude, on the part of the author, towards America's perennial Utopian aspirations. The built-in, etymological irony of the term for a perfect society reminds us that ideals, proverbially, cannot be attained. Gardner knows full well that the original Miranda's phrase, "O brave new world," has become in the modern period—thanks to Aldous Huxley—an ironic commentary on political millenarianism; nevertheless, he seems to realize that despite the snares of idealism Utopian ambitions are indispensable to the American Dream. Thus when, in the concluding paragraphs, the triumphant Jonathan fondly addresses a representative cross section of his fellow Americans—"you niggers, you Chinese Irish Mandalay Jews, you Anglo-Saxons with jackals' eyes"—he is high in the rigging of his symbolic ship, "teetering on Nowhere's rim" (p. 323).

"The King's Indian" ends with Gardner's symbolic affirmation of the future of America. Even Miranda is redeemed. As the *Jerusalem's* lone female passenger, she has been seen as Liberty compromised, but in that the story turns on who shall possess her and for what ends, she can also be seen as a personification, like Hart Crane's Pocahontas, of the American Land. She is claimed at last by Jonathan, "monarch of Nowhere" (p. 242), who salutes her and his liberated, poly-racial crew in a voice significantly described as "orbiculate." This word would seem to mean simply that his tone is "rounded" or "orotund." But the word literally means "like a circle," and if one recalls that the circle symbolizes faith, one discovers a final comment on the Nowhere theme. Billy More, counseling Jonathan on survival in the rigging, tells him he can avoid the final step to Nowhere by keeping his mind on his faith. At the close, perched once again on "Nowhere's rim," Jonathan speaks in an "orbiculate" voice—a voice full of faith, and at that moment he embodies the extraordinary balancing act that has always characterized the American political ethos.

To a large extent faith is the subject of not only this tale but of the collection as a whole. Faith is the chief casualty of the dark night of the soul examined in "Pastoral Care" and the other stories of "The Midnight Reader." All of the characters in the first two sections of *The King's Indian* perch on the rim of despair, but some of them—John Napper, Queen Louisa—discover grounds for optimism about their condition. "The King's Indian" is a sunnier tale than its predecessors; it celebrates the nation that produced its author at the same time that it celebrates its own highspirited and redemptive art. But art figures directly or indirectly in nearly all of these stories. Those in which art figures least—"Pastoral Care" and "The Warden"—are also the bleakest, and those in which it is most central—"John Napper Sailing Through the Universe" and "The King's Indian"—are the brightest. Art, then, properly functions as an antidote to despair. The author of *The King's Indian*, not content merely to document the world's "bitter reality," fashions "new and wonderful possibilities," forges hope, keeps the faith.

6

The Dying Fall
October Light

Blessed were the days before you
read a President's message. Blessed
are the young, for they do not read
the President's message. Blessed are
they who never read a newspaper, for
they shall see Nature, and through
her, God.

—Thoreau

When *October Light* appeared in 1976, few recognized it as an ob-
servance of the Bicentennial—perhaps because it did not conform
to the general vulgarity of that year-long festival of chauvinism.
Gardner expressed his own disgust at Bicentennial excess when a
character in his novel discovers a picture of the Boston Tea Party
on a matchbook cover. "Everywhere you looked, it was the Bicentennial. Did people have no fucking shame?"[1] Gardner celebrated
the nation's two-hundredth birthday more thoughtfully. He set
the action of his novel in the days just before the general election
of 1976 and peopled it with characters embodying not only the
forces that created the American nation but also those that—for
better or worse—were reshaping it. As Leonard C. Butts points
out, "Gardner uses an old Vermont farmer, James Page, to em-
body the values upon which America was founded."[2] Born on the
Fourth of July, the seventy-two-year-old Page has devoted a lifetime to the cultivation of those Yankee virtues traditionally associated with the American ethos: honesty, frugality, self-reliance.
But these virtues can harden in a nation as in a man into self-
righteousness, parsimony, and a general failure of compassion.
Page's heart, like the Vermont landscape in winter, has undergone

"locking." Narrow, opinionated, and embittered, he rails against labor unions, welfare, democrats, television, and women's liberation with a virulence familiar to anyone acquainted with aged patriots. His antagonist is his eighty-year-old sister and housemate, Sally Page Abbot. A television-watcher and Republican-baiter, Sally has been mildly radicalized, late in life, after finding herself obliged to depend on the grudging charity of the brother to whom, as a man, the ancestral farm had been left as a matter of course.[3] Sally's struggle for her rights recalls that of the Wife of Bath in a similar domestic situation, and the churlish James, like Dame Alisoun's Jankyn, soon resorts to violence: he takes his shotgun to her television. Later, brandishing a piece of firewood, he drives her to her room and locks her in. But when the door is unlocked, she refuses to come out, and a state of siege ensues.

Sally sustains herself during this "war" with a crate of apples, a bedpan, a box of tissues, and a "trashy novel" she finds on the floor. In the thinly veiled allegory of her novel, *The Smugglers of Lost Souls' Rock*, one sees the larger implications of Sally's contest with her brother. *Smugglers* is a parody of the kind of fiction Gardner despised, but at the same time that this particular production is held up to ridicule, it provides a historical and social context for the passions of James and Sally. As Sally begins to realize that characters in *Smugglers* resemble people in her own circle, the reader begins to apply the heavy-handed symbolism of the novel-within-a-novel to the more subtle thematic drift of the frame story. Sally recognizes her violent brother James, for example, in her novel's odious Captain Johann Fist. The captain's name, suggestive of his brutality, derives from that of the legendary scholar Faust, the type of Western man's indomitable drive towards ever greater power and knowledge. That drive ultimately came to be regarded as distinctively American, and Captain Fist embodies a historical force still vital in Americans like James Page. A reader of Hegel, Fist is convinced that he but serves the awesome and divinely guided dialectic of history itself. But he also embodies the excesses of the expansionist spirit. Exploiting, taming, conquering, expanding, building railroads, slaughtering Indians, and enslaving blacks, this kind of American goes through life convinced of his own rightness. This rightness he construes in terms at once patriotic and spiritual, for American expansionism, not to mention the American economic system and the prodigies it has wrought, has its roots in the Calvinist and Puritan beliefs that, according to Max Weber's classic study, *The Protestant Ethic and the Spirit of Capitalism*,[4] shaped the national ethos. "'So!' cried Sally Abbot . . . . The novel was all about Capitalism—about those pious, self-righteous and violent True Americans who'd staked out their claim and, for all their talk about 'Send me your poor' (or whatever the Statue of Liberty intoned), would let nobody else in on the pickings" (p. 146).

Fist captains the *Indomitable*, smuggling marijuana from Mexico to San Francisco. His ancestors, one imagines, were the colonial scofflaws whose defiance of British trade restrictions before the American Revolution culminated in the Boston Tea Party. Two centuries later the "tea" party continues on the other side of the continent tamed by the colonists' descendants. "What sport for the Sons of Liberty!" (pp. 43, 337), chortles a prospective buyer of Fist's wares. The crew of the *Indomitable*, as Fist himself notes, represent the forces that have contributed to the dominance of Western civilization in general and of America in particular. Mr. Nit, for example, represents technology, but his name suggests that technology may be civilization's parasite rather than its servant. Basically godless and amoral, he is nevertheless as distressed as certain atomic scientists at the possibility of getting blood on his hands. Sally, rather unfairly, sees Mr. Nit as her niece's husband, the atheist handyman Lewis Hicks. Another crew member, the "ministerial" Mr. Goodman, embodies the goodwill that Americans profess so readily. His name also recalls the smug assumptions of our Puritan fathers, who addressed each other as "goodman." This character, however, seems in fact to be a good man, a "humanist," though he does not question overmuch the morality of his livelihood. His Vermont counterpart is less clear; he may be associated with the decent Horace Abbot, Sally's late husband, or with the clergymen who come to the siege-breaking party organized by friends of Sally and James. Mr. Goodman rescues a would-be suicide, Peter Wagner, who is then impressed into service—like Billy Budd aboard another *Indomitable*. In Wagner (named for Faust's reluctant servant), Sally sees her nephew Richard Page, a real-life suicide. Whereas Wagner, who drops from the Golden Gate Bridge, has figuratively "come to the end of his rope" (p. 16), Richard Page, who hanged himself, had done so literally. The last crew member, a sexy creature named Jane, is the *Ewig-Weibliche*. "What was Guinevere to King Arthur's court, or the Virgin Mary to the Christian religion?" (p. 98), asks Captain Fist rhetorically. Jane also seems to be a younger version of Sally herself. Sally envies her sexual freedom and sees her own situation mirrored in Jane's reluctant association with the captain. But Sally also identifies with a group of black and Indian smugglers who compete with Fist. Santisillia, "the Indian," and Dancer, who crew the aptly named *Militant*, are also allegorical figures. Just as America's conception of itself has been challenged by her own minorities, so do the crew of the *Militant* challenge the *Indomitable* and all she represents. Sally the nascent feminist challenges her brother James in much the same spirit. *Smugglers*, then, allows Gardner to make resonant the tragicomic antagonism of the elderly couple on the Vermont farm. Theirs is the portentous conflict of the *Indomitable* and the *Militant* writ small.

Yet the frame story has a resonance all its own. It boasts a mythic dimension that complements the sociohistorical allegory of *Smugglers*. The myth behind the frame story is the one long applied by American writers to their native land. According to this venerable literary tradition, America is the new Eden in which man must once again make moral choices having enormous consequences. The frontiersman, the archetypal American, is the new Adam alone in a paradisal wilderness. His decisions about the land and the beings with which he shares it are the moral equivalent of those executed by the first Adam. According to some versions of the myth the Edenic possibilities of the new land are perpetual, and the American nation is the most shining promise of all to a humanity eager to right the wrongs that began in the original garden. But many see the fall reenacted on these shores. Faulkner's Ike McCaslin, for example, becomes convinced that the new covenant has been abrogated by men's insistence—and even the aboriginal Americans are guilty of these primal sins—on owning both land and their fellow men. Similarly Pynchon's Oedipa Maas, in *The Crying of Lot 49*, discovers to her chagrin what men like her former lover, the quasi-mythic tycoon Pierce Inverarity, have done to the once-pure American wilderness. Like Fitzgerald's Nick Carraway, she discovers the disparity between the Edenic American dream and the eminently postlapsarian American reality.

Gardner exploits the tradition masterfully, for *October Light*, set in autumn, is a story of the fall in more senses than one. The novel's warring couple are in fact an elderly Adam and Eve. In Eden, man's first parents may have been more siblings than spouses, but one need not get into the theological controversy over prelapsarian sexuality to suspect allegory in a story in which a woman consumes apples—and later attempts to undo her partner with apples. Even if Lane Walker, the minister, did not see James Page as the "old Adam" (p. 420), the reader would be inclined to make the connection for himself. Like the first man, James Page had two sons, and one, Richard, may have been responsible for the death of the other, Ethan, who fell from a ladder left out by his brother.[5] In his pocket, as if to remind himself of the Original mistake, James habitually carries a snake's skull, an emblem of mortality and of the evil that engendered it. But the real serpent in James' Eden is the television—"the filth of hell made visible in the world" (p. 3)—that has seduced Sally. Patriotism and piety have always gone hand in hand in the American Eden, and the programs of this foul seducer are appropiately characterized as "blasphemy and high treason" (p. 4).

Adam and Eve sinned in seeking knowledge, and it is in terms of knowledge and guilt that the author describes James Page's final epiphany. Like Adam and his progeny, Page suffers from some primal guilt that is an ineluctable part of his existence. He knows that he is himself responsible for the failure and ultimately for the suicide of his son Richard. But when he learns from a chance remark of Sally's that his son did not commit suicide merely to spite him, he realizes how groundless his lifelong misery has been. "Guilt. All this time he'd carried it, a burden that had bent his whole life double and when he caught it and held it in his two hands and opened them, there was nothing there." Yet beyond guilt—and hardly comforting—is knowledge: "Tears streamed down the old man's face, though what he felt did not even seem sorrow, seemed merely knowledge, knowledge of them all from inside, understanding of the waste" (p. 430).

When, in the end, Page discards his snake's skull and edges towards accepting television, one is tempted to think that Gardner is depicting the acceptance of evil in a fallen world. But Gardner is not engaging in Christian apologetics. Although he seems to view James' experience of crippling guilt as a kind of universal, something with which all men must grapple, he insists that the guilt— of James Page, at least—is essentially illusory. In allegorical terms, the old Adam is his own redeemer. No Christ, no "new Adam," is required, and Gardner reinforces the point by introducing a singularly inept and reluctant savior in *Smugglers*. In that production the Christ figure, a complement to the Adamic James Page, is the shanghaied Peter Wagner. When Mr. Goodman pulls the thirty-three-year-old would-be suicide from the water, Mr. Nit's disgusted comment is "Jesus" (p. 30)—a remark he makes four times, then changes to "Christ" (p. 31). Jane's initial comment is "Jesus Christ" (p. 32), and Mr. Goodman thinks the bedraggled Peter looks "like one of those pictures called *Descent from the Cross* (Mr. Goodman had once been a museum guard)" (p. 30). The crew loses no time in hailing Peter as their "captain" and "pilot"— both traditional iconography for Christ. Soon Peter imagines himself aboard a vessel called *The New Jerusalem* (p. 98). "And so now he had been chosen saviour of this groaning, floating little Eden.

Saviour, not leader, there was no mistaking that, 'Captain' him and 'sir' him as they might. Pride and damnation were their leader; agent: J. Faust" (p. 114).

One puzzles over just how this Christ's career is to be perceived. The attempted suicide might correspond to the Crucifixion, which took place when Christ was thirty-three, but Peter's subsequent experiences in the "underworld" last longer than the three days traditionally allotted to the harrowing of hell. Peter's dropping into the lives of the *Indomitable's* crew corresponds more closely to Christmas, or rather Epiphany, with Mr. Goodman and Mr. Nit as gaping magi. This Jesus receives his call aboard the *Indomitable*, which flees death and the forces of hell in the form of the ghastly Dr. Alkahest—a senile old man obsessed with marijuana—and the *Militant*. Ironically named for alchemy's "universal solvent," Dr. Alkahest is allegorically Death (pp. 39, 282)—the most universal "solvent" of all. The *Militant*, under the absentee leadership of the satanic "Dusky," first appears on the horizon as "darkness made visible" (p. 138), and Fist denounces its crew as "devils" (p. 145) and "Lucifer's legions" (p. 146). In this schema Peter's concussion—which puts him out for three days (p. 267)—is his crucifixion, and the sojourn on Lost Souls' Rock corresponds to Christ's last days on Earth, which culminate in the ascension.

Yet the conclusion is closer to apocalypse than ascension, for Peter Wagner's career is as much Christ's second coming as a symbolic reenactment of His first. Thus Santisillia refers to Lost Souls' Rock as another Patmos (p. 267), equating it with the island where Saint John the Divine had the vision recorded in Revelation. Thus, too, the entire crew of the *Indomitable*—en route to this Patmos—seem to be named John: Johann Fist, Jane, Jonathan Nit. The author does not mention Mr. Goodman's first name, but one doubts that it breaks the nominal pattern. When the general cataclysm occurs on the island, only the Christlike Peter and the still-religious Jane survive. One must, however, avoid pushing analysis of *Smugglers* too far and obscuring the satire on its pretentiousness, its ineptitude, and its ultimate emptiness. What is the rationale behind Christian allegory in a novel that so eloquently discovers the groundlessness of such things? Besides, one could as easily argue that the nihilistic Peter Wagner is in fact not Christ but Antichrist—falsely worshipped by a degenerate humanity and sharing their fate at the final reckoning. Gardner means for his readers to see that fictions like *Smugglers* are so laden with symbolism that ultimately they lack coherence. Such symbolism, intimidating readers and seducing critics, functions as a smokescreen for an author lacking any real message and therefore purveying a lot of false ones to disguise his moral bankruptcy and his artistic dishonesty.

The philosophical pretensions of *Smugglers*, in other words, go beyond the half-baked Christian allegory. But just as Peter Wagner, the parody-Christ who saves no one, comes off poorly in comparison with James Page, the old Adam who saves himself, so does the dark philosophizing at one level contrast sharply with the simple sanity eventually brought to bear in the frame story. The philosophical allusions woven through *Smugglers* are nowhere denser than in the scene in which Captain Fist is tried by his enemies and late friends, who have in effect joined forces. Captain Fist's own philosophical position seems less than clear, because it emerges in the welter of competing philosophies at his trial. Though he peppers his discourse with references to Hegel and Rousseau, Fist is most recognizable when, during that trial, he rhapsodizes on the glories of America and the free enterprise system in rhetoric resembling that of Nathan "Shagpoke" Whipple in West's *A Cool Million*. One glimpses the grounds on which Gardner himself would condemn Fist when Peter Wagner, interpreting the testimony of Santisillia, labels the captain an existentialist. Gardner always applies this term pejoratively, for reasons adumbrated in *On Moral Fiction*: "Whereas Sartre invoked 'the individual transcendent goal,' the future as negation of the repellent present (what Bluebeard, being Bluebeard, decided one dark night he would make of himself, a murderer by rule)," others "conceived a transcendent goal for humanity as a whole . . . a world ruled not by policemen but by moral choice, a world where every man's chief ambition was to be Christlike."[6] In affirming an ethics of individual choice, Gardner argues, Sartre and his followers are powerless to disaffirm the pernicious choices of the selfish or perverted. Thus Bluebeard, Fist, and their kind, convinced of an absence of absolute, preexistent moral guidelines, erect value systems the benefits of which accrue to them alone. By labeling as "existentialist" the selfishness of Fist, his representative capitalist, the author intimates his quarrel with the ideology of rugged individualism: "The only laws the Captain knows are the ones he made up" (p. 380).

Each of the witnesses in Fist's trial takes the stand more to propound his own metaphysics than to contribute to the workings of justice. Mr. Nit seems to be defending the determinist world view that his own involvement with technology makes congenial. Likewise, the speech of Peter Wagner merely mirrors the nihilism he embraces, whereas Dancer's fulminations, predictably, compound Marx and Islam. The task for a generation so philosophically confused is pronounced by Santisillia in a scene that anticipates the trial: "We were supposed to be talking about . . . justice for the future, how to make gods that exist" (p. 280). The question—how to establish moral standards or "gods that exist" and have some real meaning—is at the heart of all ethical philosophy, but the attempt to sort things out in *Smugglers* soon degenerates. Such a jumble of philosophies (earlier Plato, Bergson, and Spinoza have been invoked) figures in the trial scene and its anticipation during the waiting period on Lost Souls' Rock that the reader gets lost. His bafflement is reflected in that of the Mexican drug smugglers, who, though they do not understand English, compose the audience for the Americans' silly exercise in noncommunication and self-justification. One sees the Chaucerian influence on Gardner here, for the colloquy on Lost Souls' Rock resembles nothing so much as a Parliament of Fowls.

The scene functions nicely because Gardner means to show that books like *Smugglers* habitually raise all manner of serious questions without answering them. Such fiction has nothing to offer its readers beyond the dreary reiteration of despair and Angst. Gardner probably set out to write a story incorporating all of the worst features of contemporary fiction as he saw it: the sensational or schematic plot, the refusal to attempt affirmation, and—least forgivable—the failure to allow character to shape action. A novel in which no one develops or matures is a weak novel indeed, and perhaps the single greatest liability of *Smugglers* is that none of its characters changes in any way. Even the joining of one crew with the other is done *faute de mieux* rather than as a result of enlightenment on their parts.

For the most part, *Smugglers* succeeds brilliantly as polemical device, but one must admit that it is less than satisfactory on one count. Although one agrees readily enough that the novel-within-a-novel is pretentious twaddle, one wishes for a clearer satirical target—what Fielding gives his readers in *Shamela*, for example. Unfortunately, attempts at discovering possible targets lead to bafflement or indignation, for what major contemporary novelist is guilty of anything like *Smugglers*? The most likely target, according to Joe David Bellamy,[7] is Robert Stone's *Dog Soldiers*, winner of a National Book Award the year before the publication of *October Light*. But however strong his indignation at the recognition accorded this truly minor novel, I find it hard to believe that Gardner would have thought it important enough to lampoon. Other possibilities, though, are even less likely. The flying saucer at the end of *Smugglers* might lead one to think of Kurt Vonnegut, whose *Slaughterhouse-Five* balances various modern horrors against transcendental nonsense from the planet Tralfamadore. This butterfly, too, hardly required breaking on Gardner's satiric wheel. From hints Gardner drops in his critical writing and in interviews, one might also suspect a satire on Thomas Pynchon, whose *Gravity's Rainbow* ends apocalyptically. But if so the attack reveals only a failure to read Pynchon carefully. The apocalyptic conclusion of *Gravity's Rainbow* is hardly the kind of *deus ex machina* seen in *Smugglers*. Perhaps the likeliest candidate for Gardner's satire is

John Barth, prince of what Gardner calls the "smart-mouth" cynics. *The Floating Opera*, Barth's first novel, resembles *Smugglers* in its suicidal hero, Todd Andrews; its sexually casual heroine, another "Jane"; and its archetypal capitalist, Harrison Mack. The novels also share a tone of comic nihilism. Of course the search for a particular target is misguided if Gardner merely meant to create a perfect example of bad fiction by committing all the literary crimes he deplores among his contemporaries. If *Smugglers*, the resulting pastiche, avoids satirizing any particular book, it also avoids making its creator appear self-serving or ungracious—as Hemingway was made to appear by *The Torrents of Spring*, his parody of Sherwood Anderson. Nevertheless, the lack of a clear target risks leaving the reader (certain of some polemical intent) confused about Gardner's satiric purpose.

The big questions of political and metaphysical destiny—those dear to the hearts of authors producing novels like *Smugglers*—cannot be answered satisfactorily until they are posed in terms that take into account emotions like love, guilt, and compassion. For the *Indomitable* and the *Militant*, as for the United States of America, there can only be the kind of solution that the peaceful settlement of the war between James and Sally discovers. If men and women can learn to see into their hearts, recognize their own evil, and forgive themselves, then they can find the grounds for reconciliation with their fellows. James Page's self-knowledge is a remarkable thing in one of his years, yet Gardner makes the reader believe it and accept his humility and his change of heart. "No hero is ever righteous," Gardner once remarked in an interview; "a hero makes mistakes, recognizes them, says, 'I made a mistake,' and tries to do something about it." [8]

To be sure, the reconciliation between brother and sister—between factions only superficially polarized—will take one only so far towards imagining any millennial solution of the racial, political, and economic problems elaborated in *Smugglers*. Gardner therefore adds depth to the resolution of his novel's central conflict by introducing into the action two veteran civil rights activists—one actually a member of an oppressed minority. The Reverend Lane Walker and Father Rafael Hernandez live close to much of the conflict that shakes America—closer than James and Sally, however well-informed, can be. The clergymen provide Gardner with an important link between the two levels of his novel. Occupying a middle ground between the frame story and *Smugglers*, they make clearer the connections between the two that the difference in scale and narrative tone might obscure.

Both men, but especially Father Hernandez, pose an ideological threat to James Page, yet they represent what Page must come to accept. The forces of change proliferate in the old farmer's America, but these waves of a more just future—black, chicano, and feminist activism, the welfare state, even television—threaten to capsize the bark of Yankee integrity that he personifies. They threaten, in fact, the very ship of state, for James Page is ultimately America itself, beset by disaffected minorities, the third world, the intellectual and moral depredations of the mass media, and complacent democrats spending the country into bankruptcy. By the end of the novel, however, Page has a kind thought for Father Hernandez—quietly recognizing the other man's courage and decency—and concedes a modicum of tolerance not only to Sally's feminist position but even to the hated television, which he realizes will raise the general sophistication of the electorate during political campaigns and bring more truth to politics than was to be found in the days he remembers so fondly, when tame bears, talking horses, and other such flimflams shilled votes among hicks like—he suddenly realizes—himself. In James Page, then, one sees an older idea of America criticized, even threatened, but one that ultimately allows itself to be reshaped to the ends of justice, the ends the country was founded to serve.

In its attention to such questions and to the individual human beings who must address them *October Light* exemplifies all that is most attractive in Gardner's advocacy of "moral fiction." Rather than explicitly denouncing the kind of fiction typified by *Smugglers*, Gardner merely shows the reader that Sally's book affects her emotionally, and little analysis is required to see demoralization giving way to a certain moral slippage—in, for example, her incipient regret at having missed the kind of sexual freedom enjoyed by the heroine of the novel. Sally becomes "more wry, more wearily disgusted with the world" (p. 21). "Why . . . this ugly cynicism? It was an effect of the novel, she had to suppose. An unhealthy effect, no question about it!" (p. 38). As Sally finds it subtly demoralizing to start thinking about the "world" and the "universe," with their grim prospects, Gardner is indirectly insisting on the validity—indeed, the superiority—of a fiction of everyday life. In the frame story's domestic focus he reminds us that however terribly enlightened and Angst-ridden modern man is, however convinced of the groundlessness of all values, he still busies himself quite purposively from day to day trying to provide for himself and his family, educate his children, and minimize the dangers posed to himself and his loved ones by a perilous world. Only the most grievously stricken with what a John Barth character calls "cosmopsis," the cosmic view that defeats purposeful action, would deny that such behavior, however coldly deterministic the instincts in which it is rooted, tends automatically to confer on life a purpose largely indistinguishable from that formerly derived from teleological convictions about existence.

If Gardner chose to celebrate life's tenacity in the face of certain death, he did so out of heroic optimism, not blindness, for he refused, as an article of literary faith, to misrepresent the human condition. Though receptive to modern "idealist" philosophies (e.g., those of Collingwood, Bradley, and Brand Blanchard) and convinced that contemporary physics and chemistry make positivist biases about existence and reality less and less tenable, Gardner scrupulously declined to embrace mysticism, spiritualism, or other mythologies of transcendence. Even when he made the highest claims for his métier, he conceded its meaninglessness from the perspective of eternity: "Art is essentially serious and beneficial, a game played against chaos and death, against entropy. It is a tragic game, for those who have the wit to take it seriously, because our side must lose; a comic game—or so a troll might say—because only a clown with sawdust brains would take our side and eagerly join in."[9]

There is, then, a darker side to every Gardner novel—the side against which he must define whatever affirmation he attempts. In *The Resurrection* it is the protagonist's untimely and meaningless death, in *Nickel Mountain* it is the workings of dreadful chance, against which humanity seems so frail, and in *Grendel* it is the nihilist dragon, sayer of the eternal no. The darker side of *October Light* is the advanced age of the main characters, an aspect that links it to such novels as Muriel Spark's *Memento Mori* or Updike's *The Poorhouse Fair*, which also focus on autumnal lives. Gardner's characters will soon experience a winter more absolute than even their native Vermont's, and the reader senses that James and Sally, both affected by the imminent death of their friend Ed Thomas, terminate their war as much out of the realization that their own remaining time ought not to be squandered in bickering as out of any other form of enlightenment. From his hospital bed Ed reminds James that life, whatever its trials, is a rich and infinitely valuable thing. Though dying himself, Ed takes great comfort in contemplating the unfailing redemption of winter by spring, of death by the following cycle of life. He also takes advantage of his friend's embarrassed docility (for James's drunken rampage the night of the siege party may have caused Ed's heart attack) to remind him gently that change, whether of the technological or the social variety, has its positive as well as its negative side. The word "progress" is not, as James seems to think, a euphemism for "decline." Ed implies that what James in his mule-headedness takes for decline can just as easily be taken as evidence of some rich new dawn, a spring after winter, for Americans like James and himself.

The idea of a new beginning, one appropriate to the Bicentennial year in which the novel's action transpires, inheres also in its seasonal setting, for Halloween, according to Sir James George Frazer, was observed by primitive peoples as the beginning of the new year. The ancient Celts, who called this festival the Eve of

Samhain, kindled a new year's bonfire—an October Light, so to speak—and renewed hearth fires all over Ireland from its flames.[10] Some such renewal seems to take place in the characters of Gardner's novel, as in the country for which they stand. Other venerable Halloween traditions embellish the novel less obliquely; for example, as the spirits of the dead return to the hearth for nourishment and warmth on Halloween, the book is filled with evocations of the dead—both the characters' own personal dead and the nation's. American folk heroes like Ethan Allen, Parson Dewey, and Judge Sherbrooke are mentioned frequently, for they, particularly, would be abroad on this, the nation's two-hundredth Halloween. On the personal level there are the crowding memories of Sally's husband Horace and of James's wife Ariah, his sons Richard and Ethan, and his Uncle Ira—all dead. At least one real ghost also puts in an appearance: Sally sees it through her window during the storm that anticipates the human violence building indoors. But the most remarkable of the Halloween revenants is the bear that James Page encounters at the end. Bears, the author has noted, are sometimes thought to be "visitors from another world" (p. 13), indeed, from "the underworld" (p. 303). James, who "believed that his ghosts, insofar as they were real or had the power of things real, were allies in the grim, universal war" that he perceives as "the battle of spirit up through matter" (p. 14), encounters the ghost of his wife Ariah in the bear, for its reproach to him for shooting at it—"Oh James, James!" (p. 434)—is the one she often uttered.

The novel's climactic revelation concerns a fateful Halloween twenty years earlier, when Richard Page's prank resulted in the death of his Uncle Horace. Like his father, Richard would thereafter be haunted by an uncle's death. But the persistent focus on the season, past and present, suggests that Halloween is more to *October Light* than a source of mildly supernatural touches. Some attention to the actual dates on which the action occurs will be illuminating. These must be deduced from the novel's one concrete date, for Gardner specifies the day of the month only for the second day of the war between James and Sally, the day culminating, after the party designed to lure Sally out of her room, in James' accident and rampage. James deserts the party for Merton's Hideaway and cronies like Sam Frost, who grins at every observation, "making everything he said sound humorous—if you asked him the date and he told you 'Today is October the twenty-ninth,' he'd wink and give you a poke as he said it, as if the date had salacious implications" (p. 289). By means of this indirect dating, the reader can figure that the novel begins on the twenty-eighth, that the apple crate intended for James falls on Ginny on the thirtieth, and that Ginny's return from the hospital, Sally's emergence from her room, James' encounter with the bear, and the end of the book all occur on Halloween proper. Apparently a matter of importance, like the specificity regarding season and year, this careful dating makes *October Light* an analogue to another literary work with a Halloween setting—Joyce's "Clay." One of the stories in *Dubliners*, a book that anatomizes Ireland less charitably than Gardner anatomizes America, "Clay" concerns the pathetic Maria, a superannuated nursemaid invited by one of her former charges to spend Halloween at a family hearth. In her holiday outing, the spare and frail woman becomes symbolically one of the host of disembodied spirits that seek out sustenance and human warmth every Halloween. But Joyce makes her at once a witch ("when she laughed . . . the tip of her nose nearly met the tip of her chin")[11] and a picture of tragically wasted maternal instincts—a Virgin Mary manqué. Like Gardner, Joyce presents characters who personify his native land. Maria is the paradoxical mixture of piety and sterility that embodies Ireland itself. Meek, pure, even persecuted in a minor way for righteousness' sake (her host blows up when she tries to play peacemaker on behalf of his estranged brother), she is an ideal candidate for the blessings bestowed by Christ during the Sermon on the Mount—which happens to be the text for church services on the day after Halloween, All Saints'. Joyce, ever indirect, says nothing about the Sermon on the Mount, but he does emphasize Maria's role as a peacemaker and her other gentle qualities. Moreover, he makes a point of mentioning that she resets her alarm clock for early mass on the morning after her Halloween visit.

Gardner may expect his reader to make a similar connection and to carry it further. The liturgy for All Saints' Day includes not only the Sermon on the Mount but also a scene from the apocalypse. The one makes a fitting commentary on the frame story, the other on *Smugglers*. The frame story's characters and their dead include some that are poor in spirit, some that mourn, some that are meek, some that hunger and thirst after righteousness, some that are merciful, some that are pure in heart, some that are peacemakers, and some that are persecuted for righteousness' sake. One can, for example, number Lane Walker, Father Hernandez, and the others who come to the siege party among the peacemakers; the young people, Terence Parks and Margie Phelps, among the pure in heart; the feckless Richard Page among the poor in spirit; and so forth. But as in the Bible the point is not really to identify as blessed particular individuals or groups but rather to set up criteria that are inclusive. Thus characters whose ideologies vary widely may fall under the same rubric: like the clergymen, both Sally and James hunger and thirst for "righteousness"—and are persecuted for its sake. They are also "they that mourn": Sally for Horace, James for Ariah, Richard, and Ethan. In other words, the inclusiveness that accounts for the universal appeal of the Beatitudes accounts as well for the appeal, the genial humanity, of Gardner's novel.

The possibility of such indirect reference to the New Testament need not lay the frame story open to the complaint previously registered for the pretentious Christian symbolism of *Smugglers*, for the Sermon on the Mount is after all the most humanistic message in the Bible. But if the familiar verses from Matthew hint at a universal salvation, Revelation makes clear distinctions between the saved and the damned. The apocalyptic verses in the All Saints' text describe the masses of those sealed in their foreheads gazing up at a refulgent Lamb of God; consequently, in the parody-apocalypse that concludes *Smugglers*, Peter and Jane gaze up at a refulgent flying saucer and plead for salvation ("Save us! . . . Beam us up!" [p. 400]) as one disreputable companion after another is swallowed up in the general destruction. The naming of their Patmos—*Lost* Souls' Rock—hints at their fate at the same time that it provides another ironic glance at the liturgical calendar, since All Souls' Day follows All Saints'. The souls prayed for on All Souls' are those of the faithful departed—all others are numbered among what Thomas Pynchon would call the preterite, the passed over, the "lost."

But Gardner is the god that says "Depart from me ye accursed," and along with these desperate souls he consigns *Smugglers* itself—or rather the kind of fiction *Smugglers* represents—to the outer darkness. Salvation, in the form of self-knowledge and domestic tranquility, he reserves for decent folk like James Page and for the nation Page personifies—more believably, at last, than the squabblers of the *Indomitable* and the *Militant*—at the beginning of its third century. It was a remarkable inspiration that led the author to juxtapose his engaging Vermont world with the cynical and soul-weary world of *Smugglers*, which manages superficially to entertain—and thus to avoid the impatience of—the reader who readily perceives its inferiority to the frame narrative with its real people, real problems, and real values. As in *The Resurrection* and *Nickel Mountain*, Gardner focuses on the domestic scene and its redemptive aspects. He does not distort, and he does not sentimentalize, but he asserts that life, and the art that celebrates it, can be positive, hopeful, even redemptive. "I think basically what literature does," he remarked in an interview, "is not so much to apply new values, which is kind of what science does, as reassert traditional values which have worked and question traditional values when they seem to be risky."[12] One could ask for no more succinct description of what Gardner accomplishes in *October Light*.

7

Dealing with Dragons
The Children's Tales

Toto, I have a feeling we're not in Kan-
sas anymore.

—*The Wizard of Oz*

The proposition that major literature can include children's fiction receives strong support from Gardner's four books for young readers. Collections like *Dragon, Dragon and Other Tales* (1975), *Gudgekin the Thistle Girl and Other Tales* (1976), and *The King of the Hummingbirds and Other Tales* (1977) offer an extraordinary range of fabulation, humor, moral counsel, and entertainment. The novella *In the Suicide Mountains* does the same and more; it is that rare accomplishment, a book equally rewarding to children and adults. All of these fit into the tradition of children's literature as it has developed during the last three centuries. Gardner favors the dragons, giants, witches, clever or enchanted beasts, kings, queens, princes, princesses, knights, tailors, cobblers, millers, and resourceful cadet sons that have always been staples of children's stories and folktales. Though none of Gardner's stories is set in any recognizable locale, the feel is generally old-world, not new. Inherited from the major gallic, teutonic, and slavic sources of modern children's stories, his settings are the kingdoms and villages of fairy-tale Europe. This traditionalism extends also to plot features lamented by faint-hearted revisionists of the fairy tale. Though he tells humane, positive, and sweet-tempered stories, he does not go out of his way to make them bloodless, nonviolent, and sanitized. One encounters, therefore, the occasional decapitation or other fearsome development. Taking his cue from Bruno Bettelheim, he maintains that terror creeps into even the sunniest childhood and

that fiction can help the young deal with things they find frightening, things that cause the nightmares all children experience at
some point in their lives. Inasmuch as the fears of children resemble many of the fears of adults—sometimes, indeed, they are
identical—one should not be surprised to discover that Gardner's
fiction for children deals, in a simplified way, with the same themes
that figure in his adult fiction. In dragons, giants, witches, and the
like the young reader encounters fanciful versions of what the
adult reader encounters directly: dark existential truths, minatory
realities, *lachrymae rerum*. Only in *In the Suicide Mountains* must the
young reader grapple with adult subject matter unmediated by
fanciful allegory, for the dragon in this tale merely reifies what has
at the outset been introduced explicitly as the story's subject: the
desire to do away with oneself. But Gardner's young readers, like
their adult counterparts, learn that dragons of every kind can be
defeated by those who cultivate certain traits and values.

The antagonists in Gardner's uneven first collection, *Dragon,
Dragon*, come closest to being completely divorced from authentic
evil; nevertheless, the attentive reader will recognize among them
adumbrations of terrors that infest the real world. In the title story,
for example, the dragon that mocks every heroic or noble gesture
is clearly related to the dragon that elsewhere in Gardner threatens
to swallow humanity's every aspiration to purposeful existence—
the dragon of cosmic absurdity. In fact, absurdity on a smaller
scale figures importantly in this story. Since the idea of defeating a
dragon is absurd, the dragon must be defeated absurdly: it is dis-
patched, therefore, when the pretensions of its human enemies
reduce it to helpless laughter.

The dragon's chief adversaries are the three sons of a modest
cobbler. The first two, distinguished by cleverness and strength
respectively, fail to defeat the dragon because they disregard
the seemingly useless counsel of their wise father. The youngest
brother—the one whose character most nearly resembles that of
the unassuming father—succeeds because certain habits of honesty and conscience are most fully developed in him. But the story

has more to offer. Its young reader learns that poetry is a potent thing, even when it wears motley (a silly little verse is the dragon's undoing), and that making one's way in the world depends in large measure on proper deference to the wisdom and experience of one's elders.

Gardner enlivens his tales for children with humor as engaging as that found in his other work. As the dragon's demise demonstrates, he has a good sense of the kind of absurdity that children find delightful, but he also provides diversion for adult readers. Thus the dragon commits depredations that will make the young whoop (he "put frogs in people's drinking water") and the more sophisticated smile (he "changed house numbers around so that people crawled into bed with their neighbors' wives").[1] Old and young alike will be amused by the absent-minded wizard who accidentally changes the queen into a rosebush and cannot remember how to change her back.

The queen's husband also comes in for ribbing. With his ambivalent attitude towards authority and his healthy democratic sensibility, Gardner nearly always presents kings as more or less ridiculous, their ineptitude alternating with cowardice. The king in the second story, "The Tailor and the Giant," has a habit of disappearing into an alley whenever a battle is about to be joined with the ferocious giant; leaderless, his army of foolhardy conscripts suffers a terrible fate. The message of this story, which seems designed to allay the fears of the very shy and timid, is a little less clear than that of the first. One of the story's ironies is that the zeal of the conscripts comes to nought, while the quietism of a draft-dodging tailor results in not only the defeat of the giant and his minions but also the rescue of the captive armies. In the end the tailor sees his lack of military ardor vindicated, for he finds that the bold and violent entities all around him effectively destroy themselves and each other. The soldiers end up more terrified by what they had lacked the imagination to anticipate than the tailor ever was. Nevertheless, the tailor's triumph is not wholly the result of his meekness. He does have to face up to his fears, deal with the pangs of conscience (he feels bad when he dodges the draft and others must suffer in his place), and sally forth at last from his safe haven.

Gardner is not above a bit of irreverence with his tales. Though not quite subversive, they sometimes resemble the sort of thing a Saki character occasionally entertains children with, to the consternation of their mother. One wonders, for example, just how seriously to take "The Miller's Mule," which seems to deploy its standard fairy-tale features—the three hazards, the helpful counselor, the winning of riches and a princess—to no particular end. The mule of the title and a bored princess rather easily take advantage of the protagonist, a miller who fails signally to live up to his profession's reputation for cunning. The humor of the story is probably its strongest point, but it consists of little more than the miller's being persuaded to admit to any calumny on the part of the mule. When two creatures of fabled stubbornness—woman and mule—compete to have their way with the miller, and when the woman wins, a theme emerges that our feminist age will not take kindly to: a designing woman will stop at nothing.

The concluding story in this collection, "The Last Piece of Light," succeeds somewhat better, for its theme resembles that of "John Napper Sailing Through the Universe." Both stories concern the search for dwindling, enfeebled light, and both show art (Napper's painting, the Lady of the North Star's little poem) as the key to dispelling a symbolic darkness. "The Last Piece of Light," however, nearly has an unhappy ending because the heroine, Chimorra, cannot remember the magic verse. "It's an interesting poem," she remarks on first hearing it. "You think it's going to rhyme and then it doesn't" (pp. 61–62). More interested in analysis than in the kind of appreciation that leads easily to memorization, Chimorra is a fledgling literary critic, and when she subsequently forgets the verse, with terrible consequences for a world dependent on light, Gardner slyly hints that the world is taking a big chance when it makes critics the sole custodians of its art.

Gardner's second collection, *Gudgekin the Thistle Girl*, represents a major advance in his ability to deal entertainingly with serious subjects. Two of the tales, the title story and "The Griffin and the Wise Old Philosopher," offer a subsurface complexity normally found only in adult fiction. "Gudgekin the Thistle Girl," in fact, is one of Gardner's most satisfying tales, second only—among the children's fiction—to *In the Suicide Mountains*. It offers something substantial to both the small child and the young adolescent, and for this reason it might be useful in teaching the importance of re-reading. It starts by indirectly advising its young readers to be compassionate towards the misery of others and to be cheerful. The incentive to keep smiling is especially charming: "As she grew older she grew more and more beautiful, partly because she was always smiling and refused to pout, whatever the provocation; and soon she was as lovely as any princess."[2] But Gardner complicates this seemingly unexceptionable counsel; gradually he makes the reader uncomfortable with the poor little thistle-gatherer's excessive sweetness. She begins to be just a bit cloying. Though her consideration of others leads to a substantial reward (the queen of the fairies takes the thistle girl under her wing), Gudgekin's happiness remains tentative, incomplete. Real fulfillment depends, as the story develops, on Gudgekin's continuing to learn about the world and herself. Her infantile sweetness threatens to make her, like Candide, perpetually innocent, good-hearted, and taken advantage of. She learns, then, "the importance of self-respect" (p. 17), and with that phrase one discovers real psychological depth in this little *Bildungsmärchen*. The story addresses a serious subject indeed, for the lack of self-respect is a killer, especially among young women in a male-dominated society.

Gudgekin's education does not end with this lesson; learning it over-well, she rejects a prince who inadvertently makes fun of her name and her profession. Fortunately this lover saves her from her own inflexible pride, so that in the perennial battle of the sexes she has the good fortune to lose—and thus wins. Of the prospect of marriage with the handsome and clever prince who has circumvented her new-found and overblown pride, she says: "Oh, very well . . . . It's no worse than the thistles" (p. 20). Perhaps this ending, in which one laughs at the girl's reluctance to be happy, is Gardner's finest touch, for fostering the simplistic expectation of "living happily ever after" is the one thing for which fairy tales and other popular culture might legitimately be reproached. A character in *Freddy's Book* makes an apposite comment: "As a child, you loved books, but you came to understand that they were tricks and illusions. They told you love stories, but you looked at the world and you saw no such love—on the contrary, you saw people struggling to find the kind of lover they'd seen in books, and you saw the illusion destroying marriages."[3] In "Gudgekin the Thistle Girl," unlike most such tales, one senses that the heroine and her prince will have to work at getting along with each other. Each has an ego, and each must learn to take the other's feelings into account. A child who will one day get married can learn no better lesson from the stories to which he or she is exposed.

"The Griffin and the Wise Old Philospher" is a philosophical fable—or perhaps a mock-philosophical one. Certainly for children it is mock-philosophical, in the Lewis Carroll vein in which the absurdity provides the entertainment. But like Lewis Carroll (who introduced a griffin into *Alice's Adventures in Wonderland*), Gardner frequently proves to be playing with rather abstruse matters in his children's stories. In this one a griffin appears in a certain kingdom and generates confusion among its people. Witnessing only befuddlement among men, and not realizing that he is himself the cause of it, the griffin decides to spend more time among them to discover how they ever get anything done; his increased presence, of course, only complicates matters further. The frustration of the griffin and that of the men exacerbate and feed on each other. Like Henry II of England in a similar moment of exasperation, the king asks: "Who . . . will rid me of this damnable griffin?" (p. 28). But no violent barons come to his aid, for in these stories knights tend to be either foolish or cowardly. The king's choice of a "wise old philosopher" to deal with the nuisance proves inspired, because the griffin, trying to resolve his paradox, is himself a philosopher. With a shrewish wife and a conviction of his own essential ignorance, the human side of this philosophical agon seems to be a spiritual descendant of Socrates—but ironically his wife, only outwardly a Xantippe, is largely responsible for the line of reasoning that leads to a solution of the griffin problem.

The philosopher comes to realize that the problem is one of perception and definition. Men are confused by the griffin because they define a griffin as something "unreasonable" (p. 36), something that generates confusion. The philosopher decides that the griffin can be defined out of existence; thus when the king asks whether or not he has rid the kingdom of the griffin, he says: "What griffin?" (p. 39). The philosopher's breakthrough coincides with—and somehow, apparently, contributes to—the griffin's similar conclusion: the notion that men get things done is an illusion on his part. His problem solved, he leaves men in peace, ignoring them thereafter. The story thus plays with some rather refined scientific and metaphysical ideas about perception. According to Heisenberg's uncertainty principle, one cannot measure both the velocity and the location of a particle simultaneously. As one sees in the griffin's experience, the act of observing alters the thing observed. This Catch-22 of modern physics has its complement in the eighteenth-century metaphysics of Bishop Berkeley. Refuted in time-honored fashion by Dr. Thorpe in "The Ravages of Spring," Berkeley's theory maintains that external reality can be verified only through the senses and may not exist independently of them. The griffin falls into the solipsistic trap of this kind of reasoning when he persuades himself that human competence is merely an illusion on his part. But the reader, secure in his human knowledge of the griffin's error, would do well to examine his own assumptions about things illusory—things like griffins, for example. Gardner would have been aware of one of the best known myths concerning griffins, that of the one-eyed Arimaspians and their war with these fabulous creatures. One cannot help seeing this little story as a fable about the errors of the figuratively one-eyed—a fable, in short, about imagination.

Comparatively slight, the other two stories in this collection offer less humor and less astute psychological observation than either "Gudgekin" or "The Griffin and the Wise Old Philosopher." Nevertheless, they provide young minds with some worthwhile precepts. In "The Shape-Shifters of Shorm" a kingdom is troubled by the "annoying and alarming and unnatural" (p. 49) beings of the title. Though the troublesome Shape-Shifters are otherwise harmless, ridding the kingdom of them is thought to be imperative. What transpires is an ecological fable, for the killing of the Shape-Shifters involves also the killing of three innocents. Needlessly sanguinary, the tale is less satisfying than "The Sea Gulls," which completes the collection. This story, Gardner's shortest, teaches a simple lesson: one ought not to mortgage the future for the present, especially if one must lie and cheat into the bargain. Whatever the present danger, better to opt for the known good than to gamble it on a problematic resolution of an immediate problem. Three of the characters in the story embrace the opportunity to escape danger by being turned into sea gulls. A fourth, whose elementary sense of relative values tells her that to be a human is always better than to be a sea gull, is the only one who prospers.

Like the best children's fiction, Gardner's offers not only advice (make a habit of smiling, be kind and considerate, try to see the other person's point of view) but also symbolic treatment of things that may trouble children unconsciously. Children are, for example, sometimes perplexed or frightened by what they see of relations between the sexes, relations to which they must somehow graduate as they grow older. The subject of growing up and dealing with the opposite sex, handled with only middling success in the *Dragon, Dragon* collection, receives rather more intelligent attention in "Gudgekin the Thistle Girl" and in the title story of Gardner's 1977 collection, *The King of the Hummingbirds*, where the author achieves new heights of wit and charm and new depths of psychosexual meaning. Here, as in "Dragon, Dragon," Gardner recounts the success of a less-than-flamboyant cadet son. Where his ostensibly more gifted brothers fail to open the stuck garden gate and free the trapped princess, young Olaf succeeds because of a train of circumstances growing out of his single unique ability: he has the gift of always seeing the other person's side of things. As a result he has innumerable animal and human friends, all of whom suspend their mutual animosities to help him.

Gardner demonstrates a growing sophistication in his ability to address questions of sex indirectly, at a level beneath the threshold of infantile consciousness. But the sexual symbolism of a story like "The King of the Hummingbirds" is more directly accessible to an adult reader, especially one who recalls what a locked garden would mean to a medievalist whose very surname conspires with the allegory. The garden, often protected by walls and locks, traditionally represents woman. In *The Romance of the Rose*, a primary text for every Chaucerian, the hero desires a symbolic rose located at the heart of a garden patrolled by allegorical personages—Fair Welcome, Delight, Evil Tongue, Shame—who represent emotional or social aids and hindrances to the consummation of his love. The symbolism is unmistakable when, at the poem's climax, he reaches the rose and pokes his staff into the little grotto that shelters it. Equally unmistakable is the symbolism in Gardner's story, in which the gate to the garden will not open because of the dryness and hardness of a tiny thorn that has lodged in the lock. The lock must be lubricated with a viscous fluid, and when the wind from multitudinous hummingbird wings is instrumental in causing honey to bathe and soften that clitoral thorn, the suggestive collocation of birds and bees provides further support for a sexual reading of the story. The penetration thus effected is followed by the action of a plunger and by an orgasmic explosion. The princess, set free, can only say "Wow!"[4]

Stories like this one tell their young readers how one day they, too, can open some refractory gate, sexual or otherwise, if they have first cultivated certain pleasing habits of personality. The same theme is handled less suggestively in "The Pear Tree." This story is a little too hip to become a classic, but if one has systematically read through a goodly amount of traditional children's fiction, a tale that reads like something by Woody Allen can be very refreshing. "The Pear Tree" features a parody of William Blake, a princess who talks like a J. D. Salinger character, jiving black palace guards, and, as hero, a fat Jewish boy named Irving. The story turns on a test contrived by elves—Jewish elves—who know of the king's offer to marry his daughter to whoever brings her "a single perfect pear" (p. 36). Concealing the most beautiful pear tree in the world in a rose, the elves watch as one would-be suitor after another, frustrated at the disappearance of the tree, goes off in a huff. The successful suitor will be the one willing to go to the trouble to make a gift that ostensibly will do nothing for his suit. A poet almost succeeds but prefers to attitudinize over the rose with a highly derivative bit of verse. Only Irving thinks the princess might simply like the rose and takes it to her, having first to deal with a set of palace guards apparently recruited in Harlem. Behind all the absurdity is a fantasy about the instrumentality responsible for happy betrothals. The elves have no difficulty persuading themselves that the princess *ought* to marry a nice Jewish boy like Irving.

The other stories in the collection are equally delightful. "The Witch's Wish" bears some resemblance to *In the Suicide Mountains*, for it features characters who do not like the professions or circumstances in which they find themselves. The title character, in fact comes close to committing suicide, albeit inadvertently. The story's moral content is slight but pleasant: "Doing good nearly always makes people happy" (p. 30). Though less complex than, say, "Gudgekin" or "The King of the Hummingbirds," the story is one of the funniest that Gardner has written for children. One laughs out loud at the hilarious scene in which the witch and a frog have to watch their language around a trigger-happy and not very bright wishing pool surrounded by the tombstones to those who thoughtlessly complained, "I wish I were dead" (p. 26). The story also conveys an ecumenical message. The power of the witch's religious conversion is directly linked to the fact that she does not notice just what kind of church or synagogue she is in when she undergoes her conversion. The queen of the witches, by contrast, thinks the question of denomination tremendously important. Small wonder, the author hints, that the queen has been converted sixty-seven times—only to remain a witch.

The story that concludes this collection, "The Gnome and the Dragon," is a self-reflexive fiction remarkable for its daring but unlikely, I think, to entertain a child. For one thing, the story contravenes the traditional features of the fairy tale. The aspirant to half the kingdom and the hand of the princess does not succeed—because the aspirant, along with the princess he covets and her father the king, turns out to be a figment of the fevered imagination of the gnome of the title. The reader learns at the beginning that this gnome is a "great artist" (p. 47) who changes everything around him, creating all manner of extraordinary things and beings. The gnome cannot, however, handle one bit of recalcitrant reality: dragons. He cannot change them, and they terrify him. When the imaginary king offers an imaginary daughter to an imaginary billy goat if he will rid the country of dragons, one realizes that the whole story constitutes the gnome's elaborate strategy for dealing with his nemesis. He achieves the impossible by means of his imagination and his art. He is, of course, the same writer who once described himself in an interview as a "troll," and he is telling once again his familiar parable about art's responsibility to deal with those dragons of terrible reality. The story will probably baffle or frustrate any child who reads or hears it, for it really speaks directly to the adult who has read a good deal of Gardner's adult fiction. Nevertheless, it provides a bravura conclusion to this most entertaining of Gardner's collections for children.

The question of audience poses no problem in *In the Suicide Mountains*. Gardner's most substantial single tale for young readers is also his greatest success in terms of sustaining narrative interest at levels simultaneously accessible to both children and adults. Though in interviews he spoke of this work as aimed at children, one divines an intent to stimulate their parents as well.

In the children's tales considered hitherto, one finds themes that also figure in the adult fiction but not the fully-developed characters, significant actions, and narrative complexity required to sustain adult interest. A perfect hybrid, *In the Suicide Mountains* provides all of these without sacrificing the humor, fantasy, and comprehensibility that nearly always distinguish his other tales for children.

Both young and old will profit from the book's message: failure to reconcile the inner person with the role demanded of the outer can be harmful to one's psychological health. Gardner encourages his readers to accept the ways in which they are different and to realize that common behavioral models are not absolute prescriptions for human development. His three suicidal characters, Chudu the Goat's Son, Armida the Blacksmith's Daughter, and Prince Christopher the Sullen, are all racked by the divergence between what they want to be and what society or their families expect them to be. The decent-hearted Chudu, for example, is maddened by society's inability to see beyond his unprepossessing exterior; in the eyes of his biased neighbors, he will always be a spoiler of crops, a causer of accidents, a bringer of bad luck. The prince, similarly, loathes knight-errantry and relieves the tedium of the quest by playing his violin. Armida, who is tremendously strong and temperamentally heroic, tries desperately to be a simpering, vapid belle.

Gardner explained these characters further in an interview. "I laid out a scheme of why people commit suicide and of what things can be done to help them. I shaped it in the form of a tale. . . . I think what it says about suicide is true. It's as serious a book as I ever wrote, though it's couched in jokes and tales. Everything I know about suicide is in it, and I don't duck the ugly issues, the painful ones. One of the characters in the novel is a chemical suicidal, a person who by his constitution is that type; one of the characters is a sociopath, and one is a 'metaphysicalopath.' He just doesn't like the damn world."[5] At the same time all three, along with Richard Page in *October Light*, fit Freud's description of the suicide as one who, the superego preventing the infliction of violence on the sources of repression, is forced to visit the violence on himself.

Gardner knew his subject at first hand, as Stephen Singular reports:

> For years, during his marriage, his teaching career at San Francisco State, Southern Illinois University, and Bennington, and his long effort to establish himself as a novelist, Gardner was suicidal . . . . 'Whenever I thought I was going to leave the house and kill myself,' he says, 'there was always one thought in front of me: People who commit suicide pretty well doom their kids to commit suicide. There are times when you feel you ought to be dead, but I never feel that anyone else ought to be dead.'⁶

The last remark is interesting in the light of Freud's thesis about violence turning inward when it cannot be expressed against its real targets. Of course the reasons behind—and the targets of—such anger need not be people. Gardner may have felt like his characters in *Suicide*—crushed between what he wanted to be and what he had to be. After all, he went for some fifteen years defining himself as an artist, while the world defined him exclusively as a professor. He channeled enormous energies into his academic career (his list of scholarly publications is impressive by any standards), but he must always have felt that his time could be better spent on stories and novels.

Having survived his own suicidal tendencies, Gardner treats his characters with compassion and respect. He is careful to show that Chudu, however violent, is not vicious, that Prince Christopher, however romantic, is not effete, and that Armida, however strong, is not butch. Indeed, the author does a remarkable job of sustaining the reader's belief in the essential masculinity of a prince who prefers poetry and the violin to questing, and in the femininity of a maiden who can with equal dexterity pick up a horse or ride it after a dragon. As these details suggest, Gardner manages to instill a good deal of humor into his grim subject.

Chudu's violence, for example, is for the most part visited on a comical talking hat, and Prince Christopher at times looks like Gardner's own Chaucerian self-parody. His hilariously bad poem, "The Juggler and the Baron's Daughter," reminds one of nothing so much as Chaucer's jog-trot horror, "The Tale of Sir Thopas." Chaucer's fellow Canterbury pilgrims mercifully put an end to his ghastly rhyming, but Prince Christopher's hearers get the full treatment. The poem is so bad that even his horse is reduced to tears of smothered mirth.

No discussion of *In the Suicide Mountains* would be complete without some consideration of the four tales that interrupt the main narrative. In *The Forms of Fiction* Gardner and Dunlap point out that "the plot of a tale, unlike the plot of a short story, is loosely constructed; except in its simplest forms, the tale is more often than not discursive. The main story line may be interrupted by another tale or by several tales told by one character or in succession by a series of characters." They add that the interpolated tales commonly "serve to illuminate the situation in which one or more of the central characters find themselves."[7] The tales in *Suicide* bear out this generalization—even though, as noted on the copyright page, they "are adapted from traditional Russian fairy tales as collected by Aleksandr Afanas'ev, translated by Norbert Guterman." The first tale, about Vasily the Luckless, illustrates the proposition that things are not always what they seem: Vasily is not so luckless as he seems, nor Marco so rich, at least in the things that matter. The tale and its moral contribute to Gardner's story in that the abbot who tells it is in fact not what he seems: he is the notorious six-fingered man, an outlaw who impersonates the holy man he has murdered. The tale also mirrors the action of the frame story; the bogus abbot means to plant in the prince's subconscious the idea that one can survive an encounter with a dragon. He hopes thereby to rid himself of both prince and dragon, but ironically the hero will triumph over Old Koog with the assistance of a fair maid and a helpful third party—exactly as in "Vasily the Luckless."

The abbot's strange introductory remarks about digging down through illusion to the nuggets of truth—and realizing that even the nuggets are illusory—also have bearing on the frame story. The reader must go beyond the easy discovery that the abbot is not what he seems, for this character will ultimately prove neither abbot nor murderer. As he himself half realizes, the six-fingered man is inwardly regenerated by going through the motions of being a good man. At the end he will be "born again" as a miraculous babe (a conceit derived, perhaps, from Blake's "The Mental Traveller," which figures so importantly in *Grendel*). But the slate cannot be wiped completely clean when a man reforms. He will bear some mark of his former iniquity, and thus the miraculous babe lacks the appendage by which he was known in his former life. Psychoanalysis provides a term for what happens here: the hand has been "cathected" or charged with those fearsome libidinal energies that pose a threat to the healthy psyche. Psychologically, destruction of the hand brings peace to a troubled unconscious by placating the superego. The missing hand, in effect, is the hand that stole and murdered; the hand that healed the sick remains.

The abbot's brief second tale is more straightforward, less layered with irony. This, the familiar tale of the dancing princesses, illustrates the power of the man who, convinced he has nothing to lose, is willing to hazard all in a desperate undertaking—just as the six-fingered man wants Prince Christopher to do with the dragon. The tale again features a helpful counselor (the old woman), and its outcome, a doubly triumphant quest, foreshadows that of the frame story: as the impecunious nobleman solves the riddle of the dancing princesses and redresses his own fortunes, Prince Christopher defeats both the dragon and the six-fingered man. Both tales end with a royal wedding.

Between the defeat of the dragon and the defeat of the six-fingered man, and between the second and third interpolated tales, the arch-criminal makes some self-revealing remarks that provide further explanation of his subsequent reincarnation as the miraculous babe. Unaware that his guests have begun to suspect his true identity, he describes the six-fingered man—he is describing himself, of course—as "a master imitator," adept at all manner of disguise. "Surely he's imitated good men, from time to time, and accidentally picked up at least a touch of decent conscience. Imitate anything long enough—gaze at anything long enough with a careful eye—and you have a tendency to become it, or at least a tendency to respect it."[8] The speaker illustrates his point with a somewhat garbled account of Gardner's favorite message: life follows art. One of the central ironies in the book is the fact that the six-fingered man, *qua* abbot, has obviously become so ambivalent towards his own criminality that he in effect courts destruction by waiting too long to protect himself against the threat posed by the prince and his companions. He notes at one point that "the murderer, if he has any sensitivity at all, may become, in his own eyes, so thoroughly repugnant that he spends half his days and nights out at the edges of the cliffs, praying to God for the nerve to jump" (pp. 135–136). Ironically, then, the six-fingered man comes close to being the book's only successful suicide.

But habits, especially murderous ones, are hard to break, as one learns from the abbot's last tale, which concerns a miser who goes to extravagant lengths to avoid repaying a single kopeck. As the abbot approaches his end, his remarks become less ambiguous, and one can accept his interpretation of this tale more or less at face value. "It's easier to heal the sick or give blind men sight," he says, with obvious reference to himself, "than it is to part a miser from his kopeck—or a murderer from his knife" (p. 135). The abbot fails, however, to comment on the tale's happy ending. The miser suffers, but, along with the peasant he has cheated, he also grows richer. The frame story's climax, which follows, also leads to a happy ending—even for the doomed outlaw. Slain by Armida, Chudu, and Christopher, he is reborn, in the manner previously discussed, as the holy babe.

The babe inherits the six-fingered man's fondness for moralizing tales, along with his conviction—expressed more succinctly

now, as one would expect from someone less morally confused—
that "life follows art" (p. 157). This precept, in good fairy-tale fashion, makes an appearance three times in the story, pronounced by
the babe, by his former self the six-fingered man, and by Chudu
the Goat's Son, who attributes it vaguely to "the priests" (p. 11).
One notes that all who espouse this aesthetic credo are at least
nominally clerical: the priests, the abbot, and the babe who becomes an archbishop. Clearly, the sacerdotes who speak thus well
of art are not ordinary ones; they are what Stephen Dedalus called
priests of the eternal imagination—and John Gardner is one
of them.

The babe offers no exegesis of his allegory concerning the predations of Misery on two brothers, one rich but stingy and mean,
the other poor but decent. Misery afflicts them both in turn, but
the good brother defeats him twice, delivering himself and his
brother from the clutches of this nasty fellow. The story can be
taken as a lesson that men should, like the dwarf, the prince, and
the blacksmith's daughter, help each other in times of trouble or
danger. But the story's artful symmetry (each brother has a wife
who applies animal epithets to the rival brother and spits out the
window; one brother goes from being poor to being rich, the other
from being rich to being poor), also allows the reader to see the
brothers as two sides of a single personality—the six-fingered
man as criminal and saint, as vicious adult and innocent babe.
More importantly, the two sides are in the three heroes as well.
Each has a public self and a secret self, and as long as the two are
at odds, Misery preys on both. Misery—the desire to commit suicide—is defeated only through the integration and happy coexis-
tence of the two sides. The three heroes defeat the dragon, which
is in large measure the dragon of their own unhappiness, their
Misery, by giving free reign to their secret selves: the prince plays
the violin, the dwarf throws a tantrum, and Armida, who has
come up with the plan, rides the horse and wields the sword. The
victory over the six-fingered man results from a similar willingness to rise above stereotypes and let the secret self take over.

But the counsel to "be yourself" is relatively facile, like the abbot's shallow, Norman Vincent Peale-like interpretation of his own first tale: "A ripple of breath across the letter might in fact change all the writing. A little kick at the base of a tree might illuminate new golden options!" (p. 83). If Gardner's story did no more than promise that being true to oneself would result in fulfillment of the kind of romantic dreams critiqued in "Gudgekin the Thistle Girl" (love and marriage, social success and integration, "living happily ever after"), then it would ultimately be a step backward, however entertaining. But like such adult works as *Grendel* and *The King's Indian*, *In the Suicide Mountains* also celebrates a subtle vision of art and its power to make life rich, to defeat Misery, and even to reform the vicious. Thus Prince Christopher, reciting his poem or playing his violin, cheers himself up and postpones the deperate act he contemplates. His spirits also quicken whenever his host tells a tale; at the same time that they divert the three would-be suicides, subtly teaching them how to cope with their despair, the tales of the six-fingered man express his own deepening sense of moral regeneration.

The six-fingered man, master imitator and teller of moral tales, is a good artist, though a bad man. The paradox is not unique in Gardner's fiction (the Shaper, after all, is an adulterer, at least in his heart), but one senses that this character is particularly close to the writer who created him. In fact, one cannot help seeing something of an authorial self-portrait in this abbot who, though morally flawed himself, is no inconsiderable master of moral fiction, for *Suicide* dates from the period that saw the breaking up of Gardner's marriage of twenty-three years (it is the first of the books dedicated to Liz Rosenberg, who became his second wife); the committing of plagiarism in *The Life and Times of Chaucer*; and the publishing of "Redemption," a story that deals with the author's guilt at having, as a boy, killed his younger brother in a farming accident. One hopes that Gardner found art as regenerative in his personal life as it is in his fiction. For children as for adults, he wrote stories affirming that life is worth living. In the poetry, music, and fiction of *In the Suicide Mountains,* as in the magical little verses of "Dragon, Dragon" and "The Last Piece of Light"—not to mention the resourceful imagination celebrated in "The Gnome and the Dragon"—one sees the awesome power of art to deliver us from dragons, from darkness, from despair itself.

8

History as Fiction, Fiction as History
Freddy's Book

Demon est Deus inversus.

—Hermes Trismegistus

To appreciate fully the conceit behind *Freddy's Book*, one must keep in mind that it follows *On Moral Fiction*. In their contemptuous response to the critical book, some reviewers implied—so poor Gardner must have thought—that only a monster would impose thus on the world. Slyly, then, and without rancor, Gardner replied with the story of a gentle monster who writes moral fiction and takes the long view of human affairs. But the eight-foot-tall Freddy Agaard appears monstrous only because he dwells among twentieth-century pygmies. In an earlier age Freddy's stature would have made him a warrior and a hero, a man, indeed, like the eight-foot-tall Lars-Goren Bergquist, the character through which Freddy projects himself into the past. Our age would view a Lars-Goren, or for that matter an Achilles or Hercules, as a freak. It may similarly misvalue its writer of moral fiction.

In dividing *Freddy's Book* into two parts, Gardner risks irritating or at least puzzling some readers. Even those who understand and respect the convention of the narrative that frames or introduces another narrative—familiar in Boccaccio, Chaucer, Conrad, and James—may wonder at Gardner's unwillingness to return, at the end of the novel, to Freddy, his father, and their guest. But Gardner does not return to Freddy and the professors for much the same reason that James, at the end of *The Turn of the Screw*, does not return to his circle of ghost story amateurs. To do so would spoil the main tale. Each author wants to preserve and enhance certain effects: as the reader comes away from the James story with the chills unattenuated, he comes away from Freddy's story with an understanding of an exemplary moment in history, an understanding that would only suffer in a return to the petty squabbling of rival historians. If Gardner, devoting fully a quarter of his novel to Professor Winesap's preliminary narrative, introduces his main tale with less economy than James, he ultimately manages a much more sophisticated modification of meaning in that tale. The length of the prologue, in other words, allows Gardner to set up and explore the terms by which one judges Freddy's fictive approach to history—for both Freddy's story and the account that introduces it address basic questions concerning the truth of fiction and the fiction of history.

The imaginative writer who sets his story in the past can handle history in a number of ways. Ford Madox Ford, for example, aims at an impressionistic rendering of the historical actuality. In the preface to *A Little Less Than Gods*, a novel set in the Napoleonic period, Ford says "the novelist is there to give you a sense of vicarious experience."[1] By contrast Shaw, in *Saint Joan*, seeks to render the moment in the past when his own age came into being. He notes in the fifteenth century the emergence of all the currents that have shaped the modern world: nationalism, freethinking, "total war," and the concentration of power in secular hands. Gardner synthesizes the approaches to history of Ford and Shaw. Freddy Agaard's narrative, *King Gustav and the Devil*, renders the atmosphere of Renaissance Sweden at the same time that it reveals, in that age's politics and philosophical temper, the modern world in embryo. Though his father does not seem to think much of the historian Barbara Tuchman, Freddy looks to the past and finds, as she does, a "distant mirror" of the present.

Analysis of Gardner's novel, then, should begin with a consideration of the inconclusive discussion of historical methodology that runs through the prologue. For information on this debate, the reader depends on Professor Winesap, who tries to report his conversations with old Agaard faithfully; he tries, that is, to write an accurate "history" of his visit. But his account provides instead an object lesson in the elusiveness of historical objectivity. To the extent that he succeeds in being even-handed, the reader remains confused about whether he ought to endorse Winesap's "soft" history—psychoanalyzing historical figures and interpreting productions of the popular mind like myths and fairy tales—or Agaard's "hard" history of facts and demanding research. At the same time that he manages a certain objectivity regarding professional issues, Winesap fails signally to be objective about himself and Agaard personally. Unwittingly, Winesap slants his account, tending to portray himself as open-minded and forbearing, his rival as graceless and nearly senile. Winesap does not handle the first-person narration well enough to make the "I" appealing and thus fails to mask the self-serving intention. Even if the reader does not notice Winesap's disingenuousness, he finds his bluff-and-hearty act every bit as disagreeable as the nastiness ascribed to Agaard. The reader remains, then, without even personal clues with which to decide between the professional positions represented by the two.

In *King Gustav and the Devil*, a novelist resolves the differences of the rival historians and relieves the confusion of the reader. This narrative reveals that art, which allows imagination to discover meaning in the superficies of facts, provides a surprisingly reliable and satisfying mode of historical discourse. In writing the book, Freddy seems to have taken into account the positions of both his father and Professor Winesap with regard to the theory of history. The book combines exhaustive research—it is filled with factual material about the rise to power of Sweden's first great king, Gustav Vasa—with acute analysis of the personalities involved: the opportunistic Vasa, the world-weary Brask, the upright Lars-Goren Bergquist. Freddy also considers the role of popular culture in history. He brings in Bernt Notke's widely loved sculpture, *St. George and the Dragon*, and looks at folk-beliefs about witches, satanism, and the supernatural generally. Freddy improves on the methodology of his father when he allows into the historical equation an imaginative construct like the struggle with the Devil; he improves on the methodology of Professor Winesap when he moves from history to fiction rather than from fiction to history. Thus where Winesap, an eyewitness, produces unreliable and confusing history in his account of what takes place during his visit to the Agaard home, Freddy merely imagines himself an eyewitness and produces, with great success, an account of events much more remote and complex. The artist, Gardner implies, is the ultimate historian.

Freddy has taken an interest in Winesap's work before he meets him, and Winesap's gift of the paper on "Jack and the Beanstalk" evidently persuades Freddy to allow his father's guest to see the manuscript he has produced. The scholar gives his paper to Freddy with the notion that since "Jack and the Beanstalk" contains, among other themes, a fantasy of Oedipal revolt, the boy will see himself, however large, as playing Jack to his nasty father's "flesh-eating giant."[2] But when Freddy reciprocates, later that night, Jack Winesap ironically becomes the "Jack" of the fairy tale himself, cowering as the giant approaches his place of refuge. In Freddy's manuscript, moreover, this latter-day visitor to the giant's lair finds a treasure comparable to that won by his cousin in the folktale. That historian and novelist exchange manuscripts complementary to each other compounds the irony and adds to the sense of layered significance that unifies the two parts of Gardner's novel. Winesap, in his paper, had described "Jack and the Beanstalk" and its analogues as fantasies of revolution against giant England on the part of the politically diminutive Welsh; Freddy, in his novel, makes the outwitting of giant Denmark by politically diminutive Sweden the historical setting for the story of how the comparatively tiny Lars-Goren outwits and defeats the Devil.

When, early in Freddy's novel, the narrator remarks that "one had no chance against the Devil" (p. 80), the reader recognizes a favorite Gardner theme. Freddy's book, like *Grendel*, concerns the molding of a Christlike hero, a Beowulf or St. George, who defeats the supposedly invincible monster. Dragon, world-rim-walker, or Devil, the enemy remains the same—that which, in the affairs of men, leads to strife, bloodshed, faction, war, and all the other things that make life itself seem evil. Freddy's Devil sows all of these, not to mention distrust, dishonesty, guilt, and doubt, so that spiritual certitude on the one hand, and political order and freedom on the other, seem impossible. Yet Sweden attains the dream with the leadership of heroes who challenge the Devil in all his guises.

He who challenges the Devil allies himself with the Devil's divine opponent. But to Gardner both God and the Devil are simply forces for good and evil projected from the mind of man onto the stage of the world. Lars-Goren, ostensibly an exemplary Christian, is more comfortable with "a world of spirit—vaguely, God" (p. 83)—than with the orthodox description of divinity. Scarcely less heterodox with regard to Satan, he comes to recognize the real diabolical enemy in his own creeping suspicion that "the world makes no sense . . . no sense whatsoever. Suppose good is evil and evil is good, or that nothing is either good or evil" (p. 150). He fears that the cynical nihilism, the despair, of Bishop Brask will swallow him too. Lars-Goren defends himself by nurturing a sense of responsibility to his family and his people, and by refusing to surrender his instinctive yearning for justice. In his triumph over the Devil, he defeats not the agent of evil but the *idea* of such an agent, for the evil comes from within and must be dealt with there. Lars-Goren's victory means that he will no longer allow himself the moral and psychological convenience of thinking that evil comes from outside and has a mind of its own. Like Lars-Goren, man must understand that he alone bears the responsibility for the evil in the world. The only evil for which man is not ultimately responsible—unless he actively promotes it—is death. But against death man has an ally: the powerful instinct by which life preserves and perpetuates itself. The Devil senses this vital power as Lars-Goren stalks him: "It was as if, for an instant, all existence had become one same thing, at the center of it a will, a blind force more selfish than the Devil himself, indomitable, too primitive for language, a creature of awesome stupidity, wild with ambition" (p. 244). The language here echoes that with which, in *Grendel*, Gardner describes those emblems of thrusting nature, the ram and the goat. Lars-Goren, like Beowulf, becomes an instrument of the life-force that triumphs over death.

Lars-Goren draws his strength in large measure from his pastoral origins, from which he derives his knowledge of the good: home, family, peace, harmony. Such wholesome values and sensible priorities help him mentally and spiritually to survive his season in the precincts of corrupt, urban power—and to resist Bishop Brask's assertion that the pastoral Eden exists only at the sufferance of the cities: "Cities are where the wealth is, and the power that makes your little hideaway safe or not safe. And what are the cities but hotbeds of rivalry and cunning, fear and exploitation? It's the old story—Abraham and Lot: Abraham up there with his sheep in the mountains, Lot struggling to stay honest down in Sodom and Gomorrah" (pp. 214–215). Though the career of Lars-Goren demonstrates that decency inculcated with rural origins can move unscathed into and out of those centers of vice and corruption, the novel ends portentously with a reference to "the yellow light of cities" (p. 246)—the evil that remains after the demise of the Devil.

The novel's representative urban man, Bishop Brask, wallows continuously in doubts, cynicism, self-loathing, and despair. He even dies at a moment of existential paralysis. If sterility reproduced itself, one could say that Brask descends directly from Chaucer's Pardoner, for at one point the narrator describes him as "gesturing like a man selling relics to a man with no faith in them" (p. 220). One can, however, affirm the spiritual kinship of these two studies in corruption and Angst. Brask refers to himself sexually as *"eunuchus ex nativitate"* (p. 208), a phrase he takes from the Gospel of Saint Matthew (19:12). This condition underlies the sterility of his values, his actions, and his counsel. The scriptural commentary of Rupertus Tuitiensis, adduced by Robert P. Miller to explain the sterility of Chaucer's Pardoner, applies to Bishop Brask as well: "The eunuch who may not enter into the church of the Lord, who does not produce seed in Israel, and who ought to be cursed because he has not produced seed in Israel, is the man who, though able to edify his neighbor with his words, has kept silent, or who, though he has known good and useful things, loves idle and vain ones."[3] Bishop Brask prides himself on his mastery of rhetoric, but he deploys language to narrow and even vicious ends. Though here, too, he resembles the Pardoner, one hears other literary echoes when he declares: "I live on rhetoric, like a spider on its threads" (p. 206). For Blake, in *The Marriage of Heaven and Hell*, spiders represent the fruits of misguided metaphysics and rhetoric, and Swift, wading into the ancients-and-moderns controversy with *The Battle of the Books*, makes the spider a type of the degenerate modern. Where the bee, the type of the ancient, produces sweetness and light by means of honey and beeswax, the spider produces only cobwebs and flybane. One need not listen long to the rhetoric of Bishop Brask, vestigially another of Gardner's "bad artists," to know him for just the kind of arachnid modern that this author, like Swift before him, considers most destructive.

Brask is not, however, the only abuser of language. An important theme of the novel concerns the proper ends of writing and speaking. Gardner imagines the moment in history when propaganda—the deliberate slanting of language for frequently unworthy ends—comes into being and complicates forever the task of charting, in Matthew Arnold's phrase, "that huge Mississippi of falsehood called *history*." Much of the success attained by Gustav Vasa, discoverer of propaganda, derives from his inspired manipulation of the word, first in his speech to the miners at Dalarna (he imitates the techniques of Mark Antony in a similar situation), then in his subversion of the newly invented printing press to immediate political ends. Soon, taking their cue from Gustav, everyone is busily propagandizing, pouring out tracts and counter-tracts. Even that sly military man, Behrend von Melen, takes to scribbling.

If in the beginning was the Word, Gardner hints, then the Original Sin was a sin against the Word. As original sinner, Gustav Vasa is the political Adam who, seduced by the Devil, falls and bequeaths a terrible legacy of guilt and sin on all who would govern after him. Poised between Lars-Goren and the Devil, his two chief counselors, Gustav is a representative human soul, influenced now by virtue, now by vice. The allegory resembles that of *Dr. Faustus*, in which the Good Angel and the Bad Angel vie for the soul of the protagonist, or *Othello*, in which the protagonist hesitates between the angelic Desdemona and the satanic Iago. Indeed, Gardner invites the second comparison when he slips an allusion to *Othello* into the thoughts of Professor Winesap, who, resisting the appeal of Professor Agaard's Brask-like negativism, says to himself: "Sorry, Iago, I'm dining with my wife!" (p. 16).

But if Gustav resembles Othello, he does so chiefly as a political figure and leader of men. Like *The Wreckage of Agathon* and "The King's Indian," and to a certain extent like *Grendel* and *October Light*, *Freddy's Book* works most coherently as political allegory, for in this novel Gardner describes the evolution of the modern totalitarian state and its dictatorial creators. In the steps of Orwell, Koestler, and the Shakespeare of *Julius Caesar*, Gardner creates for his readers the texture of political intrigue, the fate of political naïveté, and the seductions of power. In Gustav Vasa, a George Washington who becomes a Josef Stalin, readers encounter a gifted leader in all his ambivalence—both the charisma and what Max Weber calls its "routinization." Indeed, along with the brilliant leadership, the ruthlessness, and the instincts for political infighting that make Gustav the liberator of his countrymen, Gardner reveals the inevitable paranoia, corruption, and delusion that make him their enslaver as well. In the subversion of the press, in the interest in eugenics, in the proliferating executions ("he was ordering the execution of his enemies, real and imagined"—p. 233),

in the insane and perverted idealism, and in the paranoid per-
secution of the ideologically impure, one begins to recognize the
lineaments of the ruthless totalitarian strong man, the twentieth
century's most familiar political type. Like the Communist ideo-
logues of our time, who think to change human nature along with
human institutions, King Gustav comes to believe that he can
eradicate not only his enemies but also evil itself: "It crossed
Gustav's mind that sooner or later, he must drive his friend the
Devil out of Sweden" (p. 120). Again, completing plans for frus-
trating a conspiracy against himself, he looks forward to challenging the enemy worthy of his genius: "I'll wipe them off the slate!—
and then, gentlemen . . . then we drive the Devil under the
ground!" (p. 184). When, however, he dispatches Lars-Goren and
Bishop Brask on their mission against the Devil, he reveals a certain schizoid cunning. He tells these two, a known troublemaker
and a potential one, to "go to the Devil" in more senses than one,
for the mission is as likely to be their death sentence as the Devil's.
Like Lenin taking advantage of the mutual antagonism among
Mensheviks, Social Revolutionaries, and Czarist counterrevolu-
tionaries, Gustav allows the mighty forces in opposition around
him to weaken each other.

But Gardner never suggests that methods other than Gustav's
could have forged, out of a beaten and disaffected people, a nation
that would dominate most of northern Europe for more than a
century. In his vulpine cleverness, however, Gustav relies on more
than the mailed fist and the fortuitous rivalry among foreign enemies. Recognizing the power of art as a moral force, he sends
Bernt Notke's sculpture of St. George and the Dragon, which
every patriot understands to represent Sweden and her enemies,
on a tour of the provinces. This inspired gesture reminds one of
the Soviets' encouragement of filmmakers like Eisenstein, Pudov-
kin, and Dovzhenko, whose work became a powerful weapon
against reaction and counterrevolution. Though the Soviets eventually made the mistake of dictating the subject matter and even
the style of socialist art, and persecuting artists with too much in-

tegrity, the first phase of state support was wisely unrestrictive. Similarly, Gustav creates no state art; he merely capitalizes on the impact of Notke's guilelessly inspirational work. Gardner refers to the sculpture repeatedly, for it is an example of the moral art, with its "models of virtue," that he espouses. Introduced in the historical prologue, Notke's sculpture represents more than Sweden and its enemies, as both the Devil and Lars-Goren realize. The Devil sees the sculpture exhibited in Härnösand, where the people view it with rapt veneration. "Suddenly hot all over," he realizes how powerfully such art counters his own baleful influence. "'Very well,' he thought, 'say the dragon refers to myself, and the knight has vanquished me.' He blinked, then flew up onto a crossbeam to think the matter through. 'Why should this hopeful little fantasy alarm me? Am I dead because a silly piece of wood is dead?' He cocked his head thoughtfully. 'No,' he decided" (p. 192). Though he also dismisses the idea that a hero capable of defeating him might be at hand, his bravado rings false. Lars-Goren, too, sees extra meaning in the sculpture: "It did not seem to Lars-Goren that the monster below the belly of the violently trembling horse could be described as, simply, 'foreigners,' as the common interpretation maintained. It was evil itself; death, oblivion, every conceivable form of human loss. The knight, killing the dragon, showed no faintest trace of pleasure, much less pride—not even interest" (pp. 147–148). The dispassionate look on the face of St. George suggests that he serves an idea greater than himself and looks into some truth that far transcends the evil he casually dispatches. Unable to see that truth himself, and unable to distinguish someone who does see it from someone whose mental blankness superficially resembles the hero's Olympian *apathein*, the Devil mistakes Bishop Brask, in a moment of moral paralysis, for a would-be St. George. "It was as if the man's mind had gone as blank as the face of Bernt Notke's carved statue, decadent art in all its curls and swirls—ten thousand careful knife-cuts and a face more empty of emotion than the face of the world's first carved-stone god" (p. 245). The Devil errs fatally in judging both the statue and the man who momentarily recalls its principal figure.

The heroic knight carved by Bernt Notke actually prefigures Lars-Goren, of course. But the blankness of the knight's expression—a typical feature in most representations of this subject— links Lars-Goren's son Erik to St. George as well. When Erik removes his helmet after a bit of impromptu training for knightly combat, "his face showed nothing, no shame, no pride, no fear— nothing whatsoever" (p. 144). A family servant declares him "brave and good-hearted as a saint" (p. 145). In introducing Erik and his aspirations, Gardner hints at the emergence of a line of heroes, a self-sustaining heroic ideal. But he also hints at a moral distinction between father and son, who thus resemble another pair of related heroes. Lancelot, morally compromised by the affair with Guinevere, falls short of the ideal attained by his son, the stainless Galahad, and Lars-Goran and Erik seem to follow the same pattern. A product of his age, Lars-Goren grapples too late with certain superstitions; he accepts, for example, the burning of witches as a matter of course. Since his more sensitive son despises the practice, a family crisis develops. "When I become lord here," Erik declares, "there'll be no more burning of witches," whereupon his father replies: "In that case . . . I must see that you never become lord here" (p. 140). While gazing at the sculpture, however, Lars-Goren realizes that his cruelty to witches scarcely differs from the cruelty of those who massacred the patriots of Sten Sture's party and burned their bodies on Södermalm hill. Lars-Goren then has his epiphany about the rightness of Erik's stand, and he accepts his son's accession. "His son met his eyes, but his face now showed nothing, as blank as the face of the knight staring straight into the sun" (p. 148).

The suggestion that the moral knight directs his gaze at the sun echoes a reference by old Sven Agaard to "rude heads that stare asquint at the sun" (p. 14). Old Agaard's memory changes Sir Thomas Browne's original phrase slightly. Browne wrote, in *Religio Medici*, of "vulgar heads that stare asquint at the truth." Knowledge of the original version of the phrase helps one to an under-standing of just what the truly heroic man contemplates. The hero stares directly—not "asquint"—into truth that is solar in its inten-sity, truth that is difficult indeed to look at without flinching. Lars-Goren must face a truth his son seems already to know: that evil subsists not in some diabolical entity but in stupidity, superstition, and prejudice—moral failings from which even men who abhor injustice are not exempt. Lars-Goren must, in other words, face the evil in himself.

One should remember that Sir Thomas Browne, no less decent and tolerant a man than Lars-Goren, once testified for the prose-cution at a witch trial. Lars-Goren's complicity in the burning of a witch seems to be a crucial part of the moral realism that governs Gardner's shaping of character. For credibility as a moral exem-plar, Lars-Goren must not be perfect. He must err and then re-deem himself. But when the ghost of the woman whose burning he has approved confronts him with his injustice, one fears that, doubting his own pretensions to being a just man, he will slip like Bishop Brask into cynical anomie. If, as the dead woman claims, the Devil is "a Nothing—mere stench and black air" (p. 266), then the responsibility for the evil of her burning lies squarely with Lars-Goren. "So this is the Devil!," he thinks miserably, "So this is existence!" (p. 229). To compound the burden, his companion, Bishop Brask, readily accepts the witch's assertion—perhaps the most insidious of all the thoughts that rob the heart of the will to persevere—that existence itself is evil. Yet despite the existential confusion all around him, despite the abundance of evidence that all aspirations to virtue, heroism, and the "dream of justice" lack meaning in a godless universe, Lars-Goren refuses to give up the moral quest. He knows "that all human beings make mistakes, that knowledge is progressive, if it exists at all" (p. 230), and he dares to hope. The outcome of the great struggle that follows re-veals the inadequacy of the old witch's knowledge. Though evil has no source other than life, life itself is far less evil than good. One wonders from the first, of course, just how far to trust this ghost, for the Devil may have sent her with information calculated to instill a false confidence (the adversary is "mere stench and black air") and to bleed off reserves of energy and moral will (" the evil is life itself"—p. 231). To the extent that, living or dead, she is the product of her own misery, envy, and misfortune, she has been enslaved by just those sources of evil that Gardner's Devil stands for. Thus, allegorically, she *is* the Devil's minion, while at another level she is the projection of the doubt, despair, and exhaustion of the two questers. Her appearance to Lars-Goren's wife after the slaying of the Devil suggests that she has all along been the Devil's familiar and is thus in a position to know of his passing as soon as it occurs, but the tone of her message suggests that Lars-Goren's heroism has freed her from her own guilt and from the rest-disturbing hatred she feels, even in death, for those whose injustice condemned her.

The idea here is a recurrent one in Gardner, one that seems to go back to his involvement in the death of his brother Gilbert. As early as "The Old Men" one sees Gardner concerned with "objectification of guilt," and characters from Henry Soames, in *Nickel Mountain*, to James Page, in *October Light*, must wrestle with guilt that threatens to paralyze and destroy them. Gardner sees guilt as the virtually unavoidable corollary to the trial and error by which human life develops. The guilt, visited on one arbitrarily, figures among the accidents of life. Even in small things, it lies in wait to take its toll. Jack Winesap, for example, visits Professor Agaard and his son partly out of a vague sense of guilt, perhaps the result of his having failed to recognize the name of a once-famous historian: "Try as I might, I could make no sense of this guilt I was feeling, but there was no mistaking that it was guilt. It did not seem to me, though perhaps I was mistaken, that it was anything so simple as my not having recognized his name" (p. 13). In his visit to the man he has wronged in this slight manner, he gradually becomes aware that old Agaard, too, suffers from guilt, and of a rather greater magnitude.

Merely outlasting such guilt and achieving some kind of self-forgiveness and recognition "that all human beings make mistakes, that knowledge is progressive," is in Gardner's eyes heroic. Lars-Goren must shoulder the terrible guilt of what he comes to realize was his appalling injustice to the old woman, and his victory over his own debilitating doubt recapitulates, in an explicitly heroic mode, the victory of James Page, who drove his son to suicide, and the victory of Henry Soames, who thinks himself responsible for the death of Simon Bale. Some readers of *Nickel Mountain*, incidentally, take the title of the chapter in which Bale appears, "The Devil," to refer to the sinister Bale himself. But in fact the title refers to that which battens onto poor Henry Soames when he thinks himself responsible for Bale's death. The Devil in *Nickel Mountain* is guilt, and one can at least partially interpret the Devil of *Freddy's Book* the same way. Early in the story, wooing Gustav Vasa, the Devil seems conjured out of Gustav's emotion at having survived the massacre in which so many of his kinsmen have perished. This emotion, often described by concentration camp survivors, is guilt. But when another kinsman survives the death for which Gustav would have been guilty indeed, the king, like his equally guilty and miserable subject the witch (another survivor of multiple family deaths), feels a lifting of the burden and becomes capable of exercising his better nature. Where the witch, redeemed, reports Lars-Goren's victory proudly to his wife, the king destroys a death warrant, deciding on a trial: " 'Let the Riksdag decide,' he thought" (p. 246). He even begins to dream of granting a certain degree of freedom of the press to his people.

As in *Grendel*, the hero's triumph has eschatological overtones: Lars-Goren is a savior, a Christ who frees men from the guilt of Original Sin by his apocalyptic struggle with what the author of Revelation calls "the dragon, that old serpent, which is the Devil" (20:2). This theme, along with the novel's setting, recalls Ingmar Bergman's film *The Seventh Seal*. There the knight returns to Sweden for an apocalyptic struggle with Death. Like Lars-Goren he encounters social chaos, witch-burning, and, in his heart, existential doubt. All of the horrors that afflict his native land stem from the ubiquity of Death, for plague stalks everyone, high and low. Bergman's Death strongly resembles Gardner's Devil, inasmuch as each projects allegorically the forces of superstition, doubt, guilt, and despair that have always beset humanity. Bergman cannot, any more than Gardner, offer his audience a message of Christian hope, and he can go only so far in countering the great antagonist against whom he pits his knight. One cannot defeat Death, though one can sometimes circumvent him, as the knight does when he becomes a decoy to enable a little family of strolling players to escape. Gardner's decision to make his hero's immediate antagonist the Devil instead of Death allows more latitude for affirmation, for where one cannot hope truly to vanquish death—as James Chandler discovers in *The Resurrection*—one can rise above the fear of Death and thwart that fear's rabble of demonic offspring: the superstition, dread, and ghastly uncertainty that generate the world's evil.

But in all this talk of the Devil, where is God? God seems conspicuously absent, his place seemingly usurped by the dark forces of chaos. Bergman's knight, grappling with guilt in the confessional, discovers only Death, that guileful sacerdote, behind the grille. Gardner's Lars-Goren, by the same token, takes on a Devil whose words, bafflingly, are those of God. "*I repent me that I ever made man*" (p.245), says the Devil, echoing the Almighty in the sixth chapter of Genesis: "And it repented the Lord that he had made man on earth. . . . And the Lord said . . . it repenteth me that I have made them." (One recalls a similar distancing of the message from orthodox Christianity in the scriptural echoes of *Grendel's* nihilistic dragon.) Both Gardner and Bergman understand that human beings must assume the responsibilities traditionally ascribed to God: the ensuring of justice, the protecting of the weak and innocent, and the driving back of encroaching chaos. In the last analysis God and the Devil, or rather the good and evil they represent, exist within the heart of man. Through secular faith, hope, charity, and courage, man allies himself with this god within; through hatred, fear, ignorance, and despair, he allies himself with this god's antagonist.

But beyond the battleground of good and evil in man's heart lies the external universe, which operates impersonally and often capriciously. Gardner dramatizes the role of chance in human affairs by means of the Lapp shaman and his three stones dancing towards the line on an agitated drumhead. The stones, white, gray, and black, dance out the fates of the three characters their colorings suggest: Lars-Goren, Bishop Brask, and the Devil. The narrator has suggested the broader meaning of the climactic action much earlier in the story:

> From time to time in the history of the world, there comes some great moment, sometimes a moment which will afterward be celebrated or mourned for centuries, at other times— perhaps more often—a moment that slides by unnoticed by most of humanity, like a jagged rock below the surface of the sea, unobserved by the ship that slips past it, missing it by inches. At the time of this story, the world was teetering on the rim of such a moment. Immense forces hung in almost perfect balance: the tap of a child's finger might swing things either way. (p. 68)

Thus at the crucial moment of Lars-Goren and Bishop Brask's encounter with the Devil, the child who watches the shaman interferes with the divination: "Abruptly, impishly, the child reached out and struck the drum. The gray stone leaped eastward, as if by will" (p. 243). As the stones fall out, so goes the book's climactic struggle between the Devil and his adversaries; hence Brask dies soon after the child bounces the gray stone from the drumhead.

The shaman's ritual, then, charts the deterministic forces of the external universe. But after chance (the randomly-dancing stones), compounded by caprice (the act of the child), makes its contribution to the outcome of the great struggle, two stones, representing Lars-Goren and the Devil, remain. And just here, Gardner insists, the individual will can prevail. When the Devil destroys Brask (the bishop's last nihilistic mouthings give him away), Lars-Goren seizes the opportunity and cuts the Devil's throat. Unlike, say, the characters of Thomas Hardy or Theodore Dreiser, who suffer in a similarly conceived universe, those of John Gardner retain enough free will to make a difference. Fate often spares the undoomed man.

Gardner's surrogate storyteller also survives the vagaries of chance. Because of the aleatory mutation of some chromosome, or because of a stray gamma ray's striking some little trigger in the anterior lobe of the pituitary gland, Freddy Agaard grew up a monster; indeed, he grew up a potential Grendel if one credits old Agaard's description of his son's violent temper, the results of which Jack Winesap mentions seeing. But Freddy rises above the affliction visited on him by a capricious universe. He becomes an artist, and he reminds the reader of his presence at the end of his story. The child who participates in the shaman's divination ritual thinks that "people should be told" of an event as momentous as the killing of the Devil, but the shaman explains that "for centuries and centuries no one will believe it, and then all at once it will be so obvious that only a fool would take the trouble to write it down" (p. 246). One hears in the remark Freddy's modesty, and behind that the disarming wit of John Gardner. Collectively, they are the "fool" who takes the trouble to tell a story that will be honored only by those who, having learned to distrust the received wisdom of an age contemptuous of moral art, will listen to the message of *Freddy's Book*: that human heroism can outface any evil. The struggle with evil—now heroic, now cowardly—generates the history that is the ultimate concern of *Freddy's Book*. If the penultimate paragraph, which hints at the imminence of war with Russia, refers to our age as well as Lars-Goren's, then we shall sorely need both heroes and moral conviction to come through, for the evil that twentieth-century man grapples with is the threat that history itself will come to an end.

9

Theme and Variations
The Art of Living

Mon métier et mon art, c'est vivre.

—Montaigne

The stories in *The Art of Living*, to quote from the flyleaf, "probe the mysterious and profound relation between art and life." The relation proves multifarious. In "Nimram," the first story, Gardner introduces the collection's master theme—that life itself can be art, at least up to a point. Thereafter he subjects that theme to a variety of refinements and complications. In "Redemption," for example, he develops the conventional idea that the artist transmutes his suffering into his art. In "Stillness" art represents the stay against life's confusion. In "The Music Lover" and "Come on Back" art comforts the bereaved. In "Trumpeter" and "The Library Horror" the ambiguous relations between art and insanity receive attention. In "Vlemk the Box-Painter" art improves on reality, and in "The Joy of the Just" it tempers revenge. These themes overlap from story to story, and in the title piece, "The Art of Living," Gardner draws them all together. Thus in contrast to the form of *The King's Indian* (arranged in linear progression from less to more affirmational stories, from "midnight to dawn"), the form of *The Art of Living* is that of a set of variations on the theme of art— literature, music, painting, dance, even cooking—and its relation to life and its problems: disease, guilt, depression, injustice, insanity, death, and the perennially absconding ideal.

A set of variations requires an announcement of the theme. Gardner provides this announcement in "Nimram," the story of a world-famous conductor who meets and befriends a terminally ill sixteen-year-old girl on a transcontinental flight. As if to encourage the reader to recognize the musical form of the collection as a whole, the author contrives to make music—from seemingly casual allusion to structural principle—especially important to this first story. Nimram's life, for example, is so orderly and satisfying that it resembles a work of musical art. His wife even "interprets" him the way he interprets scores. Moreover, the very structure of the story approximates the tonic-dominant-tonic progression familiar in music. It begins in a sunny but shallow major key (Nimram's good fortune, successes, and happy marriage), shifts to minor-key discord (Anne Curtis and her affliction), and concludes in a return to the tonic and consonance (the conductor and the girl united in the performance of Mahler's Fifth Symphony).

Like most celebrities, Nimram prefers anonymity in his private life and answers evasively when the girl sitting next to him asks about his profession. "Are you a gambler, then?" she asks half seriously. "I guess we're pretty much all of us gamblers," observes Nimram. "I know," she replies. "Winners and losers."[1] This exchange has the effect of suddenly focusing one of the story's central concerns: the role of chance in life. "Supremely lucky" (p. 8), a man for whom luck is "the single most notable fact of his life" (p. 13), Nimram has never questioned his "notorious good fortune" (p. 18). Even his first name fits the pattern. Benjamin, according to the Oxford edition of the King James Bible, means a son "of the right hand, i.e. fortunate." Though he is not intended as a picture of complacency like Jack Winesap in *Freddy's Book*, Nimram has been successful and lucky so long that he seldom thinks of ill-fortune and its toll. In Anne Curtis he meets one of the losers in the lottery of life that he seems always and effortlessly to win.

In life one is at the mercy of chance. Disease, like the lightning that killed the Vienna Quartet, strikes at random. Art, by contrast, is perfectly orderly, and Gardner suggests that music—specifically the performance of Mahler's Fifth Symphony that Anne hears Nimram conduct—can help the doomed girl come to terms with her fate. Because soaring is a traditional image for the creation or experience of art ("my adventurous song, / That with no middle

flight intends to soar," says Milton in the opening of *Paradise Lost*),
Gardner describes the story's climactic orchestral performance
metaphorically as a flight, the complement to the real flight Nimram and the girl have just experienced together. He likens the
sprawling orchestra to an enormous aircraft; the conductor, who
pauses over the score "like a man reading dials and gauges of infinite complexity" (p. 26), becomes the pilot who takes it aloft on
wings of song.

The two flights are life and art. The first struggles through the
mortal aether; the other sails through the empyrean. In the flight
from Los Angeles to Chicago Nimram acquires from Anne Curtis
an awareness of mortal contingency that can only make him a
more sensitive musician—even if, at the same time, such knowledge must also qualify the ultimate significance of his art. In their
second, metaphorical flight together he provides an experience
that allows the dying girl some respite from the terrible truth with
which she lives. Listening to Mahler, she can believe that her imminent death, the end of her life's flight, will be only the beginning of another flight like the one she now experiences: "trans-
port" to a more orderly existence. If the Reaper pictured in Mary
Azarian's illustration takes her as pleasurably as the "vast sweep
of music" that rolls over her "as smooth and sharp-edged as an
enormous scythe" (p. 26), she has nothing to fear from him.

In art, moreover, the dead live. Poised to begin the Mahler, Nimram's musicians seem "the breathless dead of the whole world's
history, awaiting the impossible," and Gardner likens them, as
they begin to play, to "all of humanity, living and dead . . . come
together for one grand onslaught" (p. 26). The conceit recalls Robert Browning's "Abt Vogler," in which a musician imagines both
unborn "presences" and "the wonderful dead" in the musical edi-
fice he builds. Browning may also be behind the choice of musical allusions in the story. The two most prominently mentioned
works in "Nimram" are Brahms' First and Mahler's Fifth Sym-
phonies, in C-minor and C-sharp minor respectively, and Gardner
means, I think, for his readers to recall the famous conclusion of

Browning's poem, in which Abt Vogler realizes that his remote, thrilling modulations must end in a return to the tonic of quotidian reality. Having been carried out of life to the mystical heights of art, the musician resigns himself to "the C Major of this life." The realm explored musically by Abt Vogler was an article of faith for Browning. Gardner's narrator, one feels, would also like to believe, but unfortunately he lives in an age in which "the C Major of this life" has taken on a sinister, existential meaning. Nevertheless, he spares Anne Curtis the return to unaesthetic reality. She will die now hopeful that the dead, sentient or not, inhabit the same realm of order and beauty that she has experienced in music.

Though art cannot cure a terminal illness, it can minister to a troubled heart, and in "Redemption," the story that follows "Nimram," Gardner gauges art's power to effect this kind of healing. The story concerns an incident in the author's childhood, for like Jack Hawthorne Gardner as a boy accidentally killed his younger brother and for years wrestled with misery and guilt. The story is important because Jack's guilt seems a pure distillate of the guilt that figures so prominently in Gardner's fiction. The struggle with guilt in "The Old Men," in *Nickel Mountain*, in *October Light*, in *Freddy's Book*, and in *Mickelsson's Ghosts* would seem to derive from the experience that gave rise to "Redemption." But one must avoid assuming that a work of fiction, however autobiographical in inception, presents a completely unaltered account of past events.

> My fiction is usually autobiographical, but in a distant almost unrecognizable way. Once in a while, as in the story "Redemption," I write pretty close to what happened. But I fictionalized that too—which worries me in fact. When you get to an event that close to real life and you change the characters, you run the risk of your sister, or your mother or father thinking: 'You don't understand me. That wasn't what I was thinking.' I *know* that's not what they were thinking, but I need searchlights on a piece, so I have to change characters, make them more ap-

propriate to the fictional idea, the *real* subject, which isn't just history.[2]

In "Redemption," then, fictional rather than historical purposes determine the characters. The father, mother, and sister become "searchlights" to illuminate the main character, Jack Hawthorne, and the central theme, guilt and redemption.

The story concerns guilt and redemption in the conventional religious sense only tangentially, in the struggle of Jack's father and mother to retain their faith. Jack, however, drifts towards an agnosticism that, in sundering guilt from its theological rationale, makes his misery greater than ever. One suspects that for Gardner, owing to the harrowing experience recounted in this story, the myth of primal guilt was a powerful one, not to be dismissed along with the fairy tale of Adam and Eve and their disobedience. Christianity, then, responds to something truly universal when it makes guilt central to its world picture, and secular man, no less than religious man, must come up with strategies for redemption. In this story, therefore, Gardner examines the redemptiveness of art. It is not a panacea, since it can only work over a long period of time, but the author makes clear that Jack's recovery from despair begins with his immersion in music and takes on real commitment when, listening to his teacher try out a new horn, he experiences the power of art as an epiphany.

The horn teacher, old Yegudkin, is indispensable to the story, for his ill fortune is meant to be compared to Jack's. Without him, Jack's guilt would appear isolated, a matter not of universal experience but of private obsession. The old man, having survived the Bolshevik terror, has seen horror on a vast and terrible scale. He has witnessed one of the atrocities so common to the history of mankind, especially in the twentieth century. Such atrocities generate guilt that must rest on the collective shoulders of humanity, whatever the immediate culpability of a Lenin, a Stalin, or a Hitler. Thus in the accidental death of little David Hawthorne and in the genocide witnessed by Yegudkin the story includes both the random and the calculated horrors that force many in the twentieth century—including artists—to despair. But old Yegudkin is a testimonial to the human spirit, the human instinct to survive and endure. Unlike another of his pupils, Taggert Hodge of *The Sunlight Dialogues*, young Jack learns from him that one can rise above personal misfortune. He learns, too, that art can defeat despair and redeem life. His discovery at the end that he must not expect to attain the mastery of his teacher, though ostensibly a fresh cause of grief, will lead him to a healthy determination either to prove his teacher wrong or—like John Gardner—to aim at excellence in another field of art. Perhaps, like his creator, he will turn again to the making up of stories that had once been his solitary diversion. He will know about pain and guilt, and he will have a conviction about the proper ends of art that will make very good capital for a young artist.

If, on the other hand, Jack Hawthorne were to abandon art altogether, he would find himself, within a few years, in the position of Joan Orrick in "Stillness." In this story, the next variation on the theme of art and life, one again recognizes biographical details. Gardner includes an account of what appears to be his own courtship of Joan Patterson when he was a college student in the midwest, first at DePauw, then at Washington University in St. Louis. Joan Orrick remembers meeting her husband Martin when she was a young piano student, already working professionally, and he was a brash, ambitious undergraduate. He would drive down from Indiana on his motorcycle to visit her in St. Louis. Like John Gardner, his youthful nickname was "Buddy." Like Gardner too, he becomes a novelist, a scholar, and a judge for the Neustadt Books-Abroad Prize. But as with "Redemption," Gardner alters his characters. Joan Orrick, for example, seems no longer involved in music, and as Gardner told Stephen Singular, his first wife's continuing interest in composition was a source of friction between them.[3] The author allows little sympathy, at any rate, for Joan and Martin Orrick, and one hopes that their ennui represents a heightening of the spiritual and emotional state of their real-life

counterparts. Though the narrator makes no mention of an imminent breakup, such as occurred in Gardner's own marriage, one
doubts that these two numb, tired people can stay together much
longer.

The story unfolds from the woman's point of view. On a brief
visit with her husband to St. Louis a quarter of a century after
their courtship, Joan grieves to see the decay of the once-vibrant
inner city. She imagines meeting herself as she was when she
lived there as a fifteen-year-old. For the younger self such an encounter would have been seeing into the future, but by the end
of the story Joan realizes bitterly that one does not need second
sight: "Sooner or later everyone, of course, knows the future"
(p. 64). One must read closely to understand Joan's unhappiness,
for ostensibly she and Martin have little to complain of. They obviously do not lack for money or material possessions, and she
imagines her present self telling her former self: "We're happy"
(p. 51). Yet she takes painkillers and tranquilizers for some vague
affliction—evidently neurasthenia—that has led her doctor to suggest a psychiatrist or prayer. She is the kind of emotional basket-
case bred in great numbers in the suburbs and memorably etched
in Part II of *The Waste Land*, "The Game of Chess."

Emotionally and psychologically, she has fallen victim to the
same decline and deterioration she notices all around her. "Despair," as Gardner says in *Mickelsson's Ghosts*, "was simply a part
of the natural entropic process."[4] She broods over things swallowed by time—from a bustling St. Louis to relatives now dead.
She also wonders what became of Pete and Jacqui Duggers, the
dancers she had once worked for. Pete Duggers, a tap dancer, had
the knack of capping virtuosic acceleration with a sudden repose.
"You see?," he would say, "Stillness! That's the magic!" (p. 55).
This thaumaturgic stillness, the story's central trope, suggests
the "momentary stay against confusion" that art, according to Robert Frost, strives to achieve. Joan's recollection of Pete Duggers's
counterentropic stillness masks an unconscious yearning to arrest
the flux that carries her and all things towards oblivion. "It came

to her suddenly, for no apparent reason, that Pete Duggers had looked like the hero of her favorite childhood book, Mr. Mixie-dough, in the story of the whole world's slipping into darkness" (p. 61). When her children were growing up, she had been unable to locate a copy of the book (one recognizes the plot of Gardner's own children's story, "The Last Piece of Light"); it, too, has slipped into darkness.

Duggers and Mr. Mixiedough are types of the artist, and Joan's problem is that she is no longer an artist herself. She seems to have abandoned her musical calling, and this betrayal of art lies at the heart of her present anomie. The story ends, ironically, in a stillness that has little in common with aesthetic stasis. With Martin asleep beside her, Joan lies waiting for her Demerol to take effect, drifting on a tide stronger than any drug towards a stillness more profound than the one with which Pete Duggers liked to end a dance. It is, of course, the stillness that follows the dance of life.

Some artists, in contradistinction to the author of "Stillness," would insist that art, far from arresting the flux or otherwise countering entropy, should hold the mirror up to a reality they perceive as existential. If chance rules the universe, then art, too, must be aleatory. "The Music Lover," Gardner's next story, should please anyone who deplores the experimental music occasionally included in classical concerts to improve and educate ears prejudiced in favor of melody and harmony. It concerns the encounter of Professor Alfred Klingman, the elderly music lover of the title, with some music of this type and with the composer responsible for it. The composer's program, intended to achieve the traditional goal of artistic iconoclasm, "épater les bourgeois," miscarries because the bourgeois, typified by the minister's wife sitting near Professor Klingman, care chiefly about preserving decorum. At a program in which someone saws a cello in two, the bourgeois prove loathe to let on that they miss the aesthetic point. The story resembles "The Emperor's New Clothes," for of all those present, only one naive and childlike old man responds honestly and appropriately to what happens on stage.

The composer, a sinister figure, is another of Gardner's bad artists, and the author gives him no name, as if to comment on his lack of humanity. Because such artists are by nature confused, Gardner allows his character only a limited coherence, so that one follows his rambling apologia to Professor Klingman with difficulty. The composer manages, though, to expose his warped and diseased understanding of those big words he professes to despise yet nevertheless bandies earnestly: Beauty, Reality, Art. He makes clear, too, that he deplores the shabbiness of reality. Experience does not live up to expectation, and reality forever fails to outstrip imagination: "'So this,' I thought, 'is a fire. This is what it's like to have a house on fire. Is this all there is to it?'" (p. 74). He fails to understand and make appropriate use of the instinct for ideality that makes him human. Baffled and outraged that the world offers no reality commensurate with the sublime emotions generated by art, especially poetry and music, he embraces an aesthetic of truth-in-art. "I've searched the globe for some firm reality that could give me the shadow of a hint that our musical intuitions are not madness" (p. 76). Convinced that to compose in the old sublime mode is to falsify, he decides to produce art that will faithfully reflect the dreariness and triteness of reality. He becomes in effect a *merdiste*, rubbing his audience's collective nose in what he has discovered. Thus like Grendel or Luther Flint the composer locks himself in what for Gardner's more enlightened artists—John Napper, Vlemk the Box-Painter—is only a phase, a way station on the road to a more responsible artistic creed. "The great artist, whatever the form he chooses," Gardner declares in *On Moral Fiction*, "breaks through the limited reality around him and makes a new one." [5]

The musical artist routinely achieves this kind of breakthrough because he works in an essentially abstract medium, one in which "imitation of nature" figures only peripherally, in program music or in settings of texts. But Gardner's captious composer debases himself and his art. He composes not music but noise, and he provides a sensitive listener like Professor Klingman not pleasure but pain. That the composer should also be a pianist, like the woman with whom Professor Klingman had once shared his pleasure in music, compounds the insult to the old man. Though the detail of the dead wife risks sentimentality, it enables Gardner to hint at a realm of experience that does not belie the emotions generated by music. Young, solitary, and self-centered, the composer does not know, as Professor Klingman does (and is about to explain as the story concludes), what losing a loved one can mean. Nor does he know the solace to be had from communing with one's dead through the art that had once been shared. One cannot, in "reality," come close to the dead, however one might wish to. But one can do so in the way that Professor Klingman does. The composer claims to have been as disappointed at the feelings attending the death of a friend as by his other experiences, but the boast only reveals the stunting of his capacity for friendship. One suspects, at any rate, that if he had been in the habit of attending concerts with someone he had loved and lost to death, he would not despise the emotions that music can summon. Nor would he compose as he now does.

This story differs from Gardner's earlier treatments of the bad artist theme in that it centers on music rather than on literature or painting. Indeed, given the difficulty of conceptualizing music in moral or ontological terms, one finds all the more remarkable the fact that fully half of the stories in *The Art of Living* concern music to a greater or lesser extent. In addition to "The Music Lover" one notes "Nimram," "Redemption," "Stillness," and "Come on Back." As might be expected in a collection whose form—the theme and variations—is itself musical, Gardner makes music his new front in the war between affirmation and denial, the war for moral art.

The collection pivots, however, around two unmusical tales in which insanity becomes a metaphor for art. "Trumpeter," discussed with the other Queen Louisa stories in chapter 5, is a fantasy about "the only kingdom in the world where art reigned supreme" (p. 87). Its queen, the supreme artist, is utterly mad, but her art transforms the lives of all her people. In "The Library Horror," on the other hand, the author explores a more ambiguous artistic insanity. In this story, as in "The Ravages of Spring" (in *The King's Indian*), Gardner adopts the manner of Edgar Allan Poe to tell a grotesquely comic tale of mental dissolution. As Poe recurs obsessively to the image of living entombment, Winfred, this story's narrator, mentions his notion that his crowded library resembles a "crypt": "One feels, in our library, buried in books, entombed" (p. 91). Such, in fact, is his eventual fate, though not in the usual sense.

Like the narrator of "The Tell-Tale Heart," Winfred gradually reveals his mental instability. When, in his library, he starts encountering the great characters of literature, seeing Becky Sharp seducing Raskolnikov and Captain Ahab disputing with Dr. Johnson, the story shifts into an Alice-in-Wonderland mode, at once droll and unsettling. At first one assumes that Winfred is describing his encounters with literary characters figuratively. Every lover of literature has met these inhabitants of the library and found them vivid, living personages. But the sane reader distinguishes between imaginary characters and real human beings with whom he can interact. When Winfred explains that he has suffered a mortal wound from the Greek hero Achilles, one begins to realize how things stand. He has mentioned his genetic predisposition to insanity and his conviction that modern physics undercuts commonsense assumptions about reality. Inspired by the proposition that characters in good fiction are really no different from real people (inasmuch as they are governed by the same laws of character and psychological motivation that obtain in the real world), he finds it easy to take the next step: conflating the phenomenal world and the imaginary world.

Because he thinks he is bleeding to death and because his sanity is slipping, Winfred tells the reader repeatedly that his "time is limited" (pp. 89, 90, 91, 95), but he fails to understand the last and most ironic restriction on the time at his disposal. Like the denizens of his library, he is *himself* a fictional character, and he has only until the end of a story by John Gardner to have his say. Thus at the end, as time really does run out, Winfred meets triple oblivion: he lapses into complete madness, perishes of his wounds (at least in his fevered imagination), and sinks into the void at the bottom of page 100. Yet paradoxically, in joining those other shades in the bookshelves, Winfred has become immortal; the reader can encounter him in his own library whenever he wishes.

Though Gardner would not disagree with Winfred's formulations regarding character and fiction, he means to distance himself from Winfred's fallacy, the notion that somehow fiction is superior to life. Thus he makes all the characters Winfred meets smaller than life. Even Achilles, to Winfred's puzzlement, is only five feet tall. The point is that a literary character, from the Wife of Bath to Falstaff to Becky Sharp, is still just a simulacrum, bulking less than any human being in the flesh. The measure of Winfred's lunacy is his preference for books over his wife's charms, for fantasy over life and love. He has retreated into a world remote from the responsibilities of real life. Unable to respond to his wife or to visit his institutionalized father, he finds himself attempting to deal with them as fictional characters. He reasons that since fictional characters can have as much reality as live human beings, he can shape the lives of his beautiful, neglected wife and his allegedly insane father by writing about a love affair between them: "If a fictional character, namely Achilles, can make blood run down my chest . . . then a living character, or two such characters—my father and my wife—can be made to live forever, simply by being put into a fiction" (p. 96). What sounds like unselfishness, however, is merely an infantile fantasy of wish fulfillment: he wishes that the two troublesome human beings in his life could divert each other so that he need not have anything to do with them.

Winfred, immersed in the kind of art enshrined in his library, neglects the "art of living," and not by accident do stories correcting his heresy bracket "The Library Horror." Both "Trumpeter" and "The Joy of the Just" concern lives in which order and justice prevail—lives edging, without the sacrifice of vital qualities, towards the condition of art. In "Trumpeter," in fact, Queen Louisa actually arrives at that condition; she converts her life and her kingdom into pure art. In "The Joy of the Just," by contrast, Gardner presents a more realistic fable. He suggests that one can, without lapsing into madness or fantasy, extract at least a modicum of justice from the world.

"The Joy of the Just" takes its title from Proverbs 21:15. According to the scripture-quoting Aunt Ella Reikert, who goes to great lengths to chastize a dissembling preacher, "it is a joy to the just to do judgment . . . and destruction shall be to the workers of iniquity" (p. 110). She slightly misquotes the original, which reads "*but* destruction shall be to the workers of iniquity" (emphasis added). The word "but" hints at a qualification, the possibility that the doer of judgment runs the fisk of faltering, miscalculating, "working iniquity"—and paying a high spiritual price. Thus one encounters the real drama of this story in Aunt Ella's motives, for in her obsessive campaign for justice she runs the risk of losing charity.

But the story's comedic spirit precludes any character's managing much in the way of real villainy. It takes place in one of Gardner's bucolic farming communities (this one in southern Illinois), and the reader never doubts the essential good will of all concerned. Though she tricks the preacher out of his horse and sends the poor animal to the knacker, and though she contributes indirectly to the burning down of the church, Aunt Ella never falters in her affection for the rather appealing preacher and his wife. This affection, along with the sense that her animus could never descend to anything so base as hatred, keeps the reader on Aunt Ella's side, in spite of her excesses. She seems pleased that her "correction" actually brings the ministerial couple closer together. The preacher's willingness to lie to protect his wife also strikes the reader as a venial sin. But such a sin, unchecked, can corrupt the soul; soon the preacher proves willing to try to sell a poor old woman—whom he and his wife have already wronged once—what he knows to be a worthless horse.

The other characters function chiefly as foils to Aunt Ella. Darthamae, her niece, counsels restraint, while Leon, Darthamae's husband, quotes the gospel of forbearance at her: "The meek shall inherit the earth" (p. 103). When he invokes this famous promise from the Sermon on the Mount a second time, one suspects, as in *October Light*, a more extensive subtext from the Gospel According to Saint Matthew, and indeed, looking up "Blessed are the meek: for they shall inherit the earth," one finds that it immediately precedes "Blessed are they which do hunger and thirst after righteousness: for they shall be filled" (Matt. 5:5–6). It is the "last word," and a champion scripture-quoter like Aunt Ella would know it. But she has had her satisfaction, and Leon does not require correction. She passes up the opportunity to outquote him for the first and only time in the story.

The preacher does not get off so easily. When he reproaches Aunt Ella for her "childish" behavior, she responds tartly: "Of such is the kingdom of heaven" (p. 135). She hints that the preacher will have little claim to heaven unless he, too, become as a little child. In growing up one tends to lose the childlike conviction that wrongs should be corrected; one begins to accept the world's many compromises. But Aunt Ella's insistence on simple justice, her conviction that right is right and wrong is wrong, makes her the story's archetypal innocent, its Christian *qua* "little child." At the end she reminds those present that she has not acted from wrath: "It was for his correction, out of pure charity. Bless him" (p. 135). She has regularly applied the "bless him" formula to another little child, her grandnephew, and now for the first time she extends it to the preacher. It is indeed a joy to the just to do judgment, if they lose not charity.

Aunt Ella's plot against the minister unfolds as a three-act comedy: "The old gypsy pea trick" (p. 117), the spiked grape juice, the staged hit-and-run. She is a life-artist, and "The Joy of the Just" is the most straightforward treatment of the art-of-living theme that figures lyrically in "Nimram," shifts to the fabulous in "Trumpeter," and culminates in the title story. Before the recapitulation of this and other themes in the last story, however, Gardner executes two more variations of life's relation to formal art: "Vlemk the Box-Painter" and "Come on Back." Both focus on the question of art's contribution to the human community, the society at large. The longest fiction in *The Art of Living*, "Vlemk the Box-Painter" runs to novella length, but unlike the title novella in *The King's Indian*, it neither concludes nor gives its name to the volume. Gardner's diffidence on this point might suggest that he hesitated to claim as much for this story as for its counterpart in the earlier collection; on the other hand he did not publish "The King's Indian" separately, as he did "Vlemk." The story that can most profitably be compared with "Vlemk," however, is another from the earlier collection: "John Napper Sailing Through the Universe." Both concern an artist who attempts faithfully to reproduce physical reality, only to find himself "gazing . . . into the abyss" (p. 170). But one would err to dismiss "Vlemk" as "John Napper" warmed over. Gardner evidently felt the need to treat the subject of the artist's emotional and psychological health at greater length than he had done earlier. The extra length also enables him to explore more fully the effects of the protagonist's art on the social milieu. One notes, too, that the mode of realistic memoir in which "John Napper" is written gives way to the mode of fable or parable in "Vlemk." Thus Gardner makes the same transition his artists make—from realism to fantasy, or rather from reality to the inner vision that transforms reality.

One may wonder why Gardner gives his hero such an odd profession. Why a box-painter? Vlemk's boxes—people buy them as presents—may never actually contain anything. A painter of vacuity, he produces art that would seem to exemplify Oscar Wilde's dictum that all art is essentially useless. But one may argue that art counters the "comic futility" (p. 150) of the universe. In such a futile universe (Italo Calvino, a favorite of Gardner's, would call it "cosmicomic"), man exists in a perennial predicament, a permanent fix. To be in this kind of trouble is to be, in Vlemk's own favorite phrase, "in a box" existentially. Art exists to decorate this box, and Vlemk is thus the archetypal artist.

The portrait of the princess that is at once Vlemk's glory and his folly is the proverbial "speaking likeness" made literal. That the picture's first words take away Vlemk's powers of speech reminds the reader of another commonplace: an artist's work does his talking for him. When Vlemk falls mute, one understands that a painter who records reality so slavishly has, in effect, nothing of his own to say. He regains the ability to speak when he improves the portrait according to the dictates of a personal vision. The picture's continuing to talk after its alteration argues that Vlemk still has departed not a whit from reality. But now the reality is the one he has created.

He has also created himself, for his intimacy with the painting, the fact that they are always together until he takes it to the woman he loves, suggests a psychological component, a projection of the anima with which he must come to terms as part of his psychological maturation. But the anima exists in a variety of forms, and Vlemk also projects her in his flattering portrait of the barmaid. "He'd lifted her breasts a little, tightened her skin, raised a sagging eyebrow, increased the visibility of her dimple. In short, he'd made her beautiful, and he'd done it all so cunningly that no one but an artist could have told you where the truth left off and the falsehood began." The point here is that the portrait lies only temporarily, because the barmaid grows "increasingly similar to the fraudulent painting, smiling as she served her customers, looking at strangers with the eyes of an innocent, standing so erect, in her foolish pride, that her breasts were almost exactly where Vlemk had placed them" (p. 161). She has been transformed by a painting. She goes from harridan to cheerful pinup, and by the end of the story she has graduated from prostitute to married woman.

In painting the princess, Vlemk does exactly the opposite of what he does in painting the barmaid. The barmaid sees an ideal and grows into it, her sagging eyebrow rising to the level of the painted one; the princess sees the truth about herself and despairs, so that the drooping eyelid of a painted likeness merely accelerates the decline of its counterpart in the living face. In various paintings of the princess Vlemk promotes her every velleity to the status of confirmed character trait. Miserably, the princess fulfills every painted prophecy: "The Princess Looking Bored," "The Princess Considers Revenge," "The Dream of Debauchery," "The Princess Gives Way to Wrath," and so forth.

The unhappy princess and the king her father enable Gardner to realize the theme of art's effect on society with great economy. As Vlemk proceeds through the stages of his artistic development—meticulous craftsman, unsparing naturalist, despondent dauber, soulless calendar-realist—the princess registers the effects. Her moral and physical health seems related in an almost magical way to Vlemk's art, for she reacts to it even when she has not seen it. When he is just a good painter, at the beginning, she is lovely but rather heartless; after his unsparing portrait of her, followed by the terrible "Reality boxes" (p. 172), he visits her and wonders at her incipient physical decline. At this time the reader learns of her father the king's mysterious malady. The king, visibly dying, fears that his daughter will fall victim to the disease that wastes him, and he intuits the existence of a curse somehow associated with Vlemk. "Beg him to remove the curse," pleads the king. "Otherwise we're doomed" (p. 200). The curse, of which Vlemk remains ignorant, is the curse of bad art. But if the sickness in the royal family and in the kingdom for which it stands stems from the failure of Vlemk and his fellow artists to do their duty, the society deserves part of the blame for failing to honor its artists properly. The trio of embittered or impotent artists at the tavern— ex-poet, ex-violinist, would-be axe-murderer—illustrates the status of the artist in this society, which honors only artisans like the bell caster, the gargoyle carver, and the stained-glass-window maker. The story's hero, the only real artist who practices, falls slave to a flawed and deadly aesthetic which eats away at the society symbolically in the persons of its monarch and his daughter. Once he fights his way free of that debilitating aesthetic, Vlemk lifts the curse on the royal family and the curse on himself. When he marries the princess, now queen, insuring the prestige of at least one artist, he completes the undoing of the vicious circle in which bad art, despised artists, and a sick society feed on each other.

Vlemk's early career in a way resembles that of the doomed Charley Hughes in the collection's penultimate story, "Come on Back." The story is a reminiscence—virtually a memoir—of Remsen, New York, the village of Welsh immigrants Gardner visited as a child. As in "Redemption" and "Stillness," he may have changed certain details of character to suit the demands of art. Though he gives the main character his own childhood nickname of "Buddy," he mentions no brothers and sisters and changes the name of the maternal side of his family from Jones to Hughes. The first-person narration, another contrast with "Redemption," enhances the air of memoir. Of course memoirs, like fiction, depend on experiences that the writer selects and arranges for presentation; hence a purely factual memoir exists only in the realm of the Platonic ideal. A story like this one reveals the thinness of the line between fictional and autobiographical writing. But to arrange the past into patterns, fictions even, constitutes an "art of living" not necessarily limited to writers. Ordinary people like Charley Hughes or his grandnephew Buddy also need fictions of the past. The more consciously—and honestly—one converts the past into art, the more likely one is to achieve a life that is orderly and fulfilling, like some great novel, rather than slapdash or disorganized or false, like second-rate fiction.

Gardner's account of a boy's visit to his Welsh relatives bears a strong resemblance to another Welsh meditation on childhood, Dylan Thomas's "Fern Hill." Like that great poem, "Come on Back" realizes the magical, idyllic quality of the places where one knew childhood pastimes and childhood innocence. It also resembles the poem in the moving tension that exists between the mature consciousness of its narrator and the innocence of the child-protagonist; rendering the sensibility of the child in the voice of the adult the child will become, the narrator evokes the gradual complication of innocence by experience. In "Fern Hill" Thomas reveals by degrees the sinister dominance of the initially parental or avuncular figure of Time. In Gardner's story the problems of the adult world impinge on the protagonist with the same incremental subtlety: he begins to comprehend unsuspected family tensions, from his father's resentment of the mother-in-law he has had to take in to the misery of his great-uncle Charley, who must also depend on the charity of relatives. "Come on Back," like "Fern Hill," culminates in the knowledge of death.

Uncle Charley dies by his own hand, defeated by guilt at his proving a burden to his relatives and by an inability to reconcile the promise of his art—singing—with the shabby reality of his life. Charley is a failed artist, a one-time great singer forever wed to the vision of his art. No thinker, he has never understood the fundamental, irremediable distinction between his orderly, transcendent art and his flawed, imperfect life. Condemned to live in the sphere of the imperfect and soon constrained to give up his art (like Joan Orrick, the collection's other lapsed artist), he can only drift miserably until the accumulated weight of his sorrows carries him under. His participation in a Welsh sing—apparently for the first time in years—sends him to the river. The child does not fully understand his great-uncle's fate, but one suspects that he will remember it if he later attempts some version of the calling, so fraught with peril, that Charley had to give up.

Gardner too, like Charley Hughes, wrestled with guilt and suicidal despair, but he also struggled more successfully to define the precise relations between art and life. Gardner's fiction, especially stories like "Come on Back," convince one that an art of living really exists. With poignant irony, Charley's Welsh brethren, better adjusted than their poor kinsman, turn to song, the art that Charley had tried to live in, to assuage their grief. For them, such art makes life's pain more bearable and life itself more livable. But though they embrace the art of living, they do not, like Winfred in "The Library Horror," make the mistake of attempting to repudiate life by retreating into art altogether. Nor, like Charley, do they give up on life when it proves incorrigibly unaesthetic. The boy who sings with them at the end, if he grows up to be a writer like John Gardner, will have learned from Charley's fate something about the ultimate moral criterion of art: it must enhance life.

The proper balance between life and the art that enhances it concerns Gardner most directly in "The Art of Living," the story that concludes the collection by recapitulating, like stretto in a fugue, the subjects of the preceding stories. In this story art bears on death, insanity, war, and the desire for revenge. How, Gardner asks, can art help man deal with the kind of senseless, unjust violence the world does to him? The story's hero, a middle-aged cook named Arnold Deller, teeters on the verge of a nervous breakdown as a result of his son's death in Vietnam. To survive emotionally, Deller must find a way to bring his humble art—cooking—to bear on his grief and on the suppressed violence in his heart. That violence has its emblem in the dragon—Gardner's usual symbol of evil—tattooed on Deller's arm, and thus Deller's story concerns the touch-and-go process by which the practice of his art enables him to tame the dragon, to make it a symbol, as in Chinese mythology, of evil subdued and controlled.[6]

The cook's son, Rinehart, had written to his father about eating Imperial Dog in Vietnam, and the cook has become obsessed with the idea of making this dish in the restaurant where he works, even though he must defy the restaurant's manager to do so. Everyone in the story, including Finnegan the narrator, views Deller as somewhat cracked, but by now readers should know that a certain kind of craziness is often Gardner's conceit for the daring of the moral artist. One even senses a connection between Deller and his creator, for each sets himself a formidable task. The cook risks losing his job, for his project disgusts not only the restaurant's manager but also its proprietor. Gardner, by the same token, risks losing the reader, for he refuses to soften the ugly business of stealing and butchering the black dog called for in Deller's recipe. Through the impassioned remarks of his main character, however, Gardner reminds the reader that the instincts brought into play in catching and killing the dog are much the same as those involved in more respectable methods of securing meat—only less refined. These instincts, like those instrumental in making war, are ultimately responsible for the survival of individuals and species. Fortunately, since civilized life requires the taming and harnessing of such instincts, a means exists to convert or channel them to the ends of culture. "That's the Art of Living. Not just instinct; something you do on purpose. Art!" (p. 286). To function properly, art must not completely obscure or mask the instincts it sublimates. Deller realizes that his fellow Americans understand what goes on in a slaughterhouse no more than they understand what goes on in Vietnam: "How do you feel about the packaged, drugged-up meat at your supermarket, or airplanes dropping bombs from so high up they don't know there's people down there?" (p. 305). Thus he orchestrates a primal experience for the small group of draft-age youths who constitute the town's somewhat effete motorcycle gang. Inveigling them into bringing him the black dog he needs, he turns the Scavengers into hunters. The bikers, hunting the dog and witnessing its slaughter, learn something about the mechanisms by which the world sets its table, and by extension something about the savagery that has swallowed Rinehart Deller on the other side of the world. They also inch closer to maturity, for as hunters they undergo a kind of atavistic training for the breadwinner roles they must eventually assume if they are to become an integral part of the society in which they have hitherto lived peripherally, even parasitically.

But Deller's real genius shows when he converts the primal experience into a civilized one: a ritual feast at which the four disaffected and hirsute adolescents become nothing less than refined dinner guests. Though none realizes the extent of their eminent metamorphosis, they are also on their way to becoming husbands, for they share the meal with four nubile girls, the daughters of the cook and the manager. Present too, at least in the imaginations of the diners, are the shades of Rinehart Deller and the "thousand thousand Asians" (p. 310) he has joined in death. Arnold Deller had learned long ago, as a soldier in Paris at the end of

World War II, "that food made peace between nations" (p. 272), and in this bizarre ceremony, this heteroclite work of art, he reconciles himself to his son's death and to the people who killed him. The meal is also sacramental, with overtones of Passover and the Christian Eucharist. The dog they consume is a symbol of the sacrificed Rinehart, whose name derives from *rein Herz*, "pure heart." Those present number eleven: the cook, the cook's helper, old man Dellapicallo, and the eight boys and girls. The manager, who refuses to partake and stalks off, is the Judas who rounds out the apostolic twelve.

Finnegan, the narrator, will take this scene with him when his turn comes to follow Rinehart overseas. One critic complained that Gardner leaves the narrator's present unaccounted for, but in fact the narrator gives the reader to understand that since the events in the story he has himself experienced the various primal lessons of war, that more elaborate form of the hunt. He has survived mentally and emotionally, one feels, largely as a result of the sense of community he takes with him to Vietnam—a sense of community fostered in moments such as those he tells about in Dellapicallo's restaurant. The story recalls the 1978 film *The Deer Hunter*, whose director, Michael Cimino, works the healing magic of art on the emotional trauma of Vietnam by bracketing scenes of stomach-churning violence and horror with ceremonies of community, human solidarity, and ritual.

Behind Finnegan, the literary artist, and behind Deller, the culinary artist, is John Gardner, relating or reconciling the "art of living" to the primitive instincts that are the human reality. Like Deller he is at least a little crazy to think that a plot to cook Imperial Dog is the stuff of art. But the hidden agenda of art—Deller's or Gardner's—is the necessity to integrate every truth, however ugly or even unlikely—into the higher vision. If the moment of communion around the table with which the story ends moves the reader—and surely it does—then Gardner, like Deller, has succeeded. "The Art of Living," at any rate, proves the most daring variation on the theme of the collection to which it gives its name.

The collection's title, *The Art of Living*, seems to invite Empsonian analysis of its ambiguity. It refers to life that aspires to the condition of art at the same time that it refers to the art that the living look at, listen to, read, or even eat. Between these two poles of interpretation, the stories of *The Art of Living* reveal a spectrum or—to retain the musical metaphor—a scale of intermediate positions. Off the scale at one end is death, and off the scale at the other end is the nasty, brutish, and sometimes overlong life (or death-in-life) that lacks art. In between, all is music.

10

No Man Is an Island
Mickelsson's Ghosts

You shall love your crooked neighbour
With your crooked heart.

—Auden

In *Mickelsson's Ghosts* Gardner handles with greatest fidelity the world's teeming confusion, its fallen state, its entropic decline, its subjugation by mortality and decay. These existential afflictions, coupled with the absence of some transcendent ideal to alleviate them, dictate the spiritual prostration of modern man, painfully rehearsed by Gardner's hero, the guilt-ridden, self-loathing, ethically earnest but confused Peter Mickelsson. The author, through Mickelsson, addresses himself to a question as old as Western philosophy: what, given the existential facts, constitutes ethical bedrock? Does the good exist as a criterion of right action? All of the classroom discussions that Gardner reproduces in such careful detail concern this question, as do all of Mickelsson's musings on Luther, Nietzsche, and his own previous philosophical contributions. Gardner suggests that the good seems to shift or perhaps to evolve. It is gauged, at any rate, by the community, which, though fallible, may also be evolving in tandem. The author allows one to conclude, in fact, that community not only charts the evolution of the good, it *is* the good.

But however central the philosophy, one should recognize the novel's conventional gothic features, too. What is the secret of the old house? Who killed Professor Warren and why? What does old Doc Bauer know? Gardner draws the gothic and philosophical elements together in masterful fashion, revealing the affinity of even the most primitive mystery story with serious epistemological questions. In dressing up his philosophical novel in the trappings of the mystery thriller, Gardner follows a tradition at least as old as Sophocles. For Gardner as for the author of *Oedipus Rex*, the greatest mystery inheres in character. In *Mickelsson's Ghosts*, as in the story of Oedipus, the mystery proves ancillary, though organically related, to the protagonist's self-discovery. Thus the most salient features of Gardner's mystery—the poisoned spring, the identity of Professor Warren's murderer, the motivations of the Susquehanna townspeople—lead invariably back to Peter Mickelsson's struggle with himself. Gardner knows, like Sophocles, that knowledge of the microcosm, the self, tends to promote knowledge of the macrocosm, the universe. Oedipus, tested and chastened by an orderly universe, affirms the justice of his fate, but Mickelsson seeks answers to his questions and reasons for his sufferings in a universe in which order is an ancient myth. Both men, however, learn a hard lesson about appearance and reality, and both find themselves mired in guilt.

Mickelsson's guilt deepens daily. It racks him for every species of omission and commission, from the killing of the black dog with his walking stick to the shameful failure to help Jessica Stark or the suicidal Michael Nugent. He forgives himself nothing, becoming fatalistic as fresh occasions for self-loathing present themselves: involvement with a teen-aged prostitute, acts of grand larceny and second-degree murder. These and other sources of guilt are among the "ghosts" that he must exorcise or learn to live with.

Through the agency of an unexpected ally Mickelsson comes to terms with all of his ghosts. The ally is the human community from which he never quite manages to sunder himself absolutely. At first, stupidly, he attempts to repudiate all of the communities of which he is a part: his marriage and family, his university colleagues, his students, his Pennsylvania neighbors. "It was community that kept one well and sane; that was the message of the book Michael Nugent had forced on him. Community was what he'd lost, leaving Providence, and what he'd fled, leaving Binghampton."[1] Mickelsson opts for isolation, in unwitting fulfillment of Nietzsche's prescription in *Twilight of the Idols*: "To live alone one must be a beast or a god, says Aristotle. Leaving out the third case: one must be both—a philosopher." [2] Like Nietzsche's philosopher, Mickelsson lives alone and in a solitude as miserable as that of Nietzsche himself. Indeed, as Mickelsson realizes, he resembles the great German philosopher in a number of ways. In addition to sharing a profession, both men descend from Lutheran ministers; hence they share an obsession with Martin Luther, chief architect of protestant Christianity. Both men end up at the feet of a woman, and both descend into madness. But where Nietzsche went literally insane, possibly from syphilis, Mickelsson arrives at a state of benign lunacy, the necessary condition, as Gardner often suggests in his fiction, for responding to the world positively.

A typical Gardner hero, Mickelsson suffers the ills of the modern age without giving up hope. But if Mickelsson's chief virtue is his refusal to surrender completely to the undertow of despair, his chief failing is his foolish flight from community. All alone, he turns more and more of his energies to the restoration of the old house he buys in a decaying corner of Pennsylvania. With just enough planning required to make the physical work directed and consuming, the labor on the house is, as he himself realizes, a kind of therapy for his debilitated mental and emotional state. But like its new owner the house cannot simply be made over, renewed cosmetically. Its ghosts remain through all of the restoration, and beneath its foundations bubbles the polluted spring, whose exhalations coat the joists with pure poison. Like Howards End, in the Forster novel of that title, or like Gilbert Osmond's Florentine villa in *Portrait of a Lady*, Mickelsson's house becomes an important symbol. Run-down and ghost-ridden, it is Mickelsson himself, for he, too, has ghosts and polluted foundations that—never to be exorcised or restored—must be accommodated or neutralized.

The revelation about the polluted spring beneath the Susquehanna house is foreshadowed by the repetition of a piece of Lutheran doctrine that runs in Mickelsson's mind: "Action was a problem" because "every movement of the spirit was poisoned at the source" (p. 402). The phrase figures again when, convinced that his terrible guilt disqualifies him as a moral philosopher, Mickelsson finds himself unable to complete a new book on ethics: "His advice to the world would be poisoned at the source" (p. 474). Though a "non-theist," he is at a point in his life where such a proposition seems overwhelmingly true. Whatever he does, he either fails to achieve the desired end or makes things worse. His attempt at saving Donnie Matthews's unborn baby, for example, results only in the death of the fat man and his own deeper immersion in guilt.

Ironically, Mickelsson's assault on the fat man is also a symbolic attack on Luther and his values. Indeed, for a terrifying moment one morning, Mickelsson mistakes the fat man for Martin Luther in the flesh. As Freud pointed out, miserliness expresses anal fixation, and with his money hoard the fat man is a symbol of the constipated Luther, whose anality Norman O. Brown—cited in Gardner's Acknowledgments—discusses in a famous chapter of *Life Against Death*. Unfortunately, the death of the fat man does not end Mickelsson's obsession with Luther and his oddly compelling world view. Luther is another paradigm of the philosopher who struggles with the fallen world and ends in madness, and as with Nietzsche, Mickelssons intuits an affinity. "He began to see, to his horror, more and more similarities between his own personality and Luther's" (p. 337). Mickelsson's inner drama—in a way it is the inner drama of every Gardner hero—is the struggle with the "excremental vision" for which the grossly scatological Luther had a profound tropism. Luther remains Mickelsson's *bête noire*, a figure as repellent and fascinating to Gardner's hero as Jean-Paul Sartre is to Gardner himself.

A world view such as Luther's fosters a conservative outlook, a conviction that meliorism in all its forms is an impious or at best misguided attempt to deny the Fall. Consequently, Mickelsson's resistance to Luther and his ideas tends to manifest itself in support for certain liberal-environmental causes. Though the positions he adopts—against the slaughter of whales, against nuclear power—are perfectly respectable, the reader may wonder at Gardner's willingness to allow his novel even fleetingly to seem like protest fiction. However forceful such fiction may appear at the contemporary moment, it fades with removal of the grounds for protest. In *On Moral Fiction* Gardner terms work of this kind "propaganda" and "moralistic art." Though fiction so conceived seems briefly important, it becomes "dated and thus trivial" beside "the true artist's celebration of the permanently moral."[3] But Gardner's criticism of this kind of literature need not mean that current social issues should remain wholly off limits to the serious writer. If one's novel takes place in the present, it may well touch on contemporary issues; it does so legitimately as long as the issues contribute organically to a theme or themes that will not date.

None of the social issues that exercise Mickelsson becomes a "message," something with which the author means to confront complacent readers. Though he is something of a radical on environmental issues, and though his position on abortion evolves in the course of the novel from "pro-life" to "pro-choice," Mickelsson has a professional reputation as a conservative. One reviewer of his book on medical ethics called it "a shrill pitch to the philosophical right" (p. 191; the phrase parodies John Barth's blast at *On Moral Fiction*). The hero's political and social positions are hardly doctrinaire, in other words, and the reader does not feel challenged to adopt this or that cause.

Mickelsson's Ghosts meets Gardner's own standards for good fiction, for the causes Mickelsson feels strongest about prove directly related to the novel's larger, less ephemeral philosophical questions. The problem of toxic waste disposal provides a good example. A danger to the community of Susquehanna at large, toxic wastes pose an especially obvious threat to that community's new citizen. "He, Mickelsson, had fled from the world's complexity to what he'd hoped might be Eden, and he'd found the place polluted, decaying" (p. 174). This passage appears early in the novel, long before Mickelsson knows about the secret waste dumps and the poisoned spring beneath his house, but the reference to Eden hints at the symbolic import of the decay and pollution he will discover. As he comes to recognize the magnitude and proximity of the poisoning, he comes to recognize also that it stands for more than the problem of one man or even one community: decay and pollution are the universal heritage. Microcosm and macrocosm, Mickelsson's house is not only himself but also the world; regardless of efforts at restoration, it will always stand over a spring poisoned by mortality and entropy.

The lesson learned, Mickelsson advances beyond his flirtation with a particularly shallow form of liberalism, the kind whose adherents remain perennially guilty of an unexamined conviction that Eden can be established or restored, that man is innately virtuous or perfectible. But in learning the truth about the human condition, Mickelsson does not retreat into despondent quietism. He is nudged, by people like Susquehanna's sheriff, Tacky Tinklepaugh, towards a more responsible and realistic liberalism, whereby one can still hope to neutralize or circumvent or rise above the poisoned spring at the heart of existence. Much water runs under the earth, and some of it remains pure, especially in Susquehanna, that "well-watered land" (p. 458). "Poisoned springs can be sealed off," remarks the sheriff. "I imagine your neighbors would be glad to pitch in. And they'd probably help lay in pipe from somewhere else" (p. 569). In community, in other words, lies the hope for Mickelsson's house and all that it symbolizes.

Mickelsson's sympathy with liberal causes grows out of his search, as a philosopher, for that which one predicates an ethics on: the good or the ideal. Charting this quest exhaustively, Gardner risks losing the reader, but he amply rewards the patience he demands. In the classroom discussions and in Mickelsson's desultory musings and summaries of his own previous work in ethics, the reader encounters nothing less than the entire philosophical history of the attempt to define the good, from Platonic idealism to contemporary sociobiological theory. But what, for Mickelsson, is the efficacy of this quest for the good, and what is the value of the boon secured? To answer these questions, one must examine several important scenes and sequences, including Mickelsson's long, confessional talk with Jessica Stark early in the novel, the debate he sustains through the fall semester with two of his philosophy students, and—most importantly—the pattern formed by his experiences over a number of crucial months.

In the long conversation with Jessica, the one in which he chronicles his failed marriage, Mickelsson sketches in the course of his quest and his career. In his dissertation, which became his first book, he had "showed in great detail how Nietzsche—and Nietzsche's deep-down hatred of Martin Luther—lies behind every contemporary philosophical leaf and flower" (p. 74), especially Freudian psychology, existentialism, and their ethically suspect congeners. In his second, more widely known book Mickelsson had struggled towards a postexistentialist ethics. If "the life of an organism constitutes its standard of values," he had reasoned, then "what promotes and enhances the organism's life is 'good' and what threatens its life is 'evil'" (p. 78). But where other thinkers (he mentions the quasi-fascist writer Ayn Rand and the sociobiologist Edward O. Wilson) gauge the enhancement of or threat to life in terms of individuals, Mickelsson has inclined towards a conception of survival values as they pertain to whole species—a position that carries with it the corollary that what might be good for the many might not be good for the one. He intimates, in this conversation, that human beings, like other social organisms, may be biologically programmed to admire and perhaps even to seek self-sacrifice in the interests of the community or the species. He is close, here, to the wisdom that Gardner finally endorses. Unable to rise above his own ego, however, he remains a kind of temporary philosophical hypocrite, cut off from the enlightenment that would obviate much of his subsequent confusion and suffering.

In the classroom and in the echoing corridors of his mind, Mickelsson continues this discussion through the remainder of the novel. With his students, for example, he ponders the existence of the ideal that would validate ethical reasoning. If the ideal exists, is it static and immutable, as Plato affirmed, or constantly evolving in a manner implicit in the arguments of philosopher-scientists like Aristotle, Darwin, and the contemporary Lloyd Motz? This split is dramatized in classroom debates between the nihilistic Michael Nugent and a bright student named Allan Blassenheim, with Mickelsson playing a Socratic devil's advocate. Though Mickelsson strongly doubts his efficacy as a teacher, he nevertheless gently guides his students to a recognition of the modern consensus that the ideal is chimerical. He pauses, though, over Blassenheim's suggestion, not unrelated to arguments Mickelsson himself has made in print, that organisms survive to the extent that they grow or evolve towards—or otherwise comply with—a set of "built-in standards" (p. 96) in reality. An ontological extension of the merely ontogenetic blueprints in DNA, such standards would constitute an ideal, something uniting metaphysics with physical science. Blassenheim illustrates this proposition with reference to the shadow structures of reality expressed in "mathematics . . . or chemical formulas." Even "the number *two*," he points out, "was up there for millions of years before anybody thought of it, right? It's built into . . . the structure of things" (p. 98). But Mickelsson resists, more out of a sense of duty than conviction, Blassenheim's suggestion that perceptual shortcomings preclude recognition of an ideal such as he postulates.

Gardner never quite allows his hero to accept Blassenheim's point intellectually, for Mickelsson needs to be liberated from his intellectual cul-de-sac. Mickelsson's mental, emotional, and physical survival depend not on some philosophical breakthrough but on experience. What he experiences—and the reader is invited to perceive—is an elementary philosophical lesson in the distinctions between appearance and reality. Blassenheim's argument about the possibility of an invisible ideal, of unperceived "moral absolutes . . . built into Nature" (pp. 281–282) and waiting to be discovered like the number two, receives support from a number of perceptual failures on Mickelsson's part. His colleague Lawler, for example, appears to be a slightly eccentric but otherwise estimable teacher and scholar, admirably concerned about a suicidal student. In reality he is a psychopath. Michael Nugent appears to have committed suicide; actually, he has been murdered by Lawler. Brenda Winburn, another of Mickelsson's students, appears bored in class; she eventually tells him that class, for her, had been deeply rewarding, "like *church* or something" (p. 575). Jessica Stark, finally, appears self-confident and in charge of her life; she is in fact "living on the edge" only a little more successfully than Mickelsson himself.

A corollary to the deceptiveness of appearance is the possible unreliability of reason. Though Mickelsson fails to notice his own errors of perception, or at least to understand their meaning, he stands almost too willing to doubt reason. It seems fallible at best, an elaborate pseudodox at worst. Mickelsson and his class consider the possibility that those who reason most effectively, like philosophers and other intellectuals, are ill-equipped to grasp truths that more practical humanity grasps intuitively. Blassenheim, once again, takes this point to its "logical" conclusion and so underscores one of the novel's central lessons. When Mickelsson asks him: "Where *is* it, if not from reason, that we get these value assertions . . . we're in some sense right to make?", Blassenheim invokes "the wisdom of the whole community . . . tested over time" (p. 185).

The assertion elicits an answering chord in Mickelsson, an "easy lay" for such propositions—"not that, in real life, he knew any community he did not hate" (p. 185). Ever a dialectician, he perpends the possible grounds for optimism about the collective wisdom of the community in the current popularity of

alternative . . . reality options . . . . The Western way of thinking had held its own since the pre-Socratics. Could it be because lately the community had expanded . . . ? Perhaps, to take the optimistic view, human beings instinctively widened their horizons, at least in certain situations, to take in views held by strangers. Perhaps, in accord with a principle he'd explored in the one book he was at all well known for, on medical ethics—the ultimately Platonic idea that justice and reason give

advantage in the battle for survival—people were programmed
by Nature to make an effort, if they were given sufficient time
to rise above their fears, to find merit in the opinions of people
not like them superficially, that is, culturally. Or was it, to take
the darker view, that people of the Western tradition were turning from their tradition in disgust, jettisoning the community
and the 'reality' it cherished, because the tradition had led to
the kinds of things his son was concerned about, greed, bes-
tiality, fascistic rectitude? (pp. 486–487)

One notes here the obsessive swing between the one and the
zero, the inability to resolve the question addressed. This inability
partially reflects a loyalty in Mickelsson, and in his creator John
Gardner, to Nietzsche's dictum that certainty is immoral. But it is
also meant to bring both Mickelsson and the reader to the point of
disgusted frustration, the point at which one realizes that such
tergiversation (to use the Kierkegaardian word) is profoundly debilitating. The same tendency to postpone resolution, to vacillate
between equally cogent alternatives, is seen in Mickelsson's equiv-
ocal stance on abortion. The lapidary sequence of the graduate
student's report on this subject, a brilliant set piece of philosophical discourse, ends in frustration for all present. "All Professor
Mickelsson's saying," one student concludes lamely, "is that if
abortion's too casual it's dehumanizing. A society where people
can kill people 'on demand,' so they don't have to go through the
embarrassment of explaining why, is a crappy society" (p. 222).
Subsequently, however, he waffles on even this point: "He'd been
a fool . . . in his class, arguing against abortion on demand"
(pp. 469–470).

In repeatedly going through the same dialectical motions, Mickelsson risks, as he realizes, more than the moral paralysis of a
pathological open-mindedness. When Nietzsche says "*this* is your
eternal life" (pp. 326, 337), he means not only to dismiss the dream
of an afterlife but also, Mickelsson thinks, to suggest that one's lot
in eternity may somehow be to repeat, infinitely, one's life as it has
been lived. Caleb and Theodosia Sprague, the ghosts in Mickels-

son's house, illustrate the horror of such a fate. The Spragues were not man and wife but brother and sister—or rather they were both. They had had a child incestuously, and when the child fell ill the brother, unwilling to reveal their shame, had refused to call in medical help. When the child died, the sister had killed the brother in revenge. Like the damned in hell, said to be condemned to infinite repetition of the characteristic vice or folly, the Spragues are doomed to their violent and destructive emotions—guilt, fear, anger—for eternity. As Gardner explained in an interview on National Public Radio's "All Things Considered," "that anger, that situation, sort of hangs on in the house, going on over and over and over again—all of which ties in with a lot of scary ideas in Friedrich Nietzsche, including the doctrine of eternal recurrence, which would argue that everything in the world is always happening, over and over and over and over and over."[4]

One can imagine the horror of such a doctrine to a man who finds himself repeatedly going over the same ground, whether in moral philosophy or in his emotional life. To escape the treadmill, Mickelsson reflects, one must become Nietzsche's *Übermensch.* "There were indeed supermen: men who . . . had given up thought long ago: men who simply acted" (p. 476). His father, dead within the year, had led such a life, and he thinks now that his father was a prototype of the *Übermensch.* Unfortunately, Mickelsson forgets that he has already experimented with the subordination of cognitive to conative, the abandonment of thought in favor of unreflective action. For months, working with his hands to restore his house or to build things in his workshop, he has tried to act like his father, only to discover the sterility of the conative ideal. Yet the example of the father holds the key to Mickelsson's deliverance. The philosopher always thinks of his father with respect and harks back to his boyhood happiness with something more than shallow nostalgia. The father had worked not for himself but for his wife and family; as a farmer he had been a caretaker—a pastor—of animals, the earth, and other human beings. Thus when Mickelsson reproaches himself for failing Michael Nugent, who he thinks has committed suicide, his guilty thoughts turn to his father: "Theoretically their professions were similar, farmer and teacher, *Pastores*. The sheep look up" (p. 394). The image of the sheep looking up, which figures three times in the novel, comes from Milton's "Lycidas," where it evokes the plight of those neglected by a corrupt clergy. In *Mickelsson's Ghosts* it hints at an eventual destination for the moral odyssey of the hero, who must face his own pastoral responsibilities at the same time that he accepts the pastoral offices of his neighbors. Gardner's novel culminates, again like "Lycidas," in a promise of resurrection. Mickelsson realizes that rebirth requires his rejoining the human race; he must start looking out for other people—Nugent, Brenda Winburn, Jessica Stark—and letting other people—Tim Booker, the Lepatofskys—look out for him. He discovers the truth of John Donne's famous meditation: no man is an island.

Community, then, is the novel's *summum bonum*, and its central action culminates in Mickelsson's registering the twin facts that he needs community and that community needs him. When the individual seeks isolation, he dooms himself and weakens the one force that can save him. He strays, so to speak, from those "built-in standards" Blassenheim describes. Thus the novel's climax comes when Mickelsson, knowing that the crazed Lawler will shortly kill him, calls from his heart for help—calls, that is, for what he has failed, hitherto, to give Nugent or Jessica. The moment of Mickelsson's extremity is one that figures in folk tales: in the moment of need one stands or falls according to one's prior moral investment in that moment. If, like Androcles, one has previously done the lion a kindness, one collects the debt and goes free. Though Mickelsson has generally failed his fellow man (even the aid to Donnie Matthews is tainted by a certain self-interest), he has done one or two selfless things, and the little girl whose fondness for the troll doll he once remembered hears his soul's cry and miraculously overcomes her muteness to deliver him.

The complement to his dramatic, telepathic rescue by the little girl is the Susquehanna community's forbearance with regard to his act of violence against the fat man. The sheriff and the other townspeople seem to know well enough who caused the fat man to die, but they decline to arrest Mickelsson. They feel that his absence will diminish their fragile community. They had, after all, declined to arrest the fat man too, though they had known him for a bank robber. One has the impression that the alcoholic sheriff, Tacky Tinklepaugh, routinely makes a variety of ethical distinctions of the type that Mickelsson is supposedly better qualified to make: "People take care of each other, when they're living right on the edge—they better anyway" (p. 569).

But the return of a doll hardly balances the assault on the fat man, the failure to come to the aid of Jessica Stark, or Mickelsson's other lapses and misdeeds. The disparity between the pluses and minuses in his moral account book suggests ironically that Martin Luther was right: salvation comes not through merit but through grace. One of the first things Mickelsson does when a neighbor looks in on him after his ordeal is to object grumpily: "I don't trust good works" (p. 571), and shortly, like Luther, he is saying to one of his incorporeal visitants, "Go away, devil" (p. 580). At the same time he comes to a final understanding of Luther's most implacable critic, Friedrich Nietzsche, who "had, in his final great madness, debased himself, throwing himself down, to no avail, before Cosima Wagner, admitting at last, symbolically, however, futilely, the necessity of what he'd dismissed from his system, amazing grace" (p. 578).

Yet the grace that saves Mickelsson comes to him as a community's "good works." Indeed, his distrust of good works is belied by his own readiness to do what he can for the hapless Brenda Winburn. Ironically, then, Mickelsson fails to understand that his experience constitutes not the victory of Luther over Nietzsche but the accommodation of the two. One expects the misjudgment, however, because complete enlightenment would violate the precept, Luther's own Catch-22, that is one of the novel's major premises: "Every movement of the spirit" is "poisoned at the source"

(p. 402). Remaining true to his own understanding of the world's imperfection, its fallen reality, Gardner refuses to allow his hero to circumvent the flaw at the heart of his ideational life. But this side of angelic understanding, Mickelsson knows well enough how much he owes to the community that has refused to write him off. Perhaps he knows as well that community is not invariably wholesome. Like everything else in the sublunary world, it is subject to decay or perversion, and one sees the ideal of community in an altogether different light in the Church of the Latter-Day Saints. Regimented and joyless, "Utah's vast army of locked-together minds" (p. 245) represents community gone cancerous, and indeed the house once occupied by its founder, Joseph Smith, now breeds cancers literally. With their moronic certainty, their "fascistic rectitude," the Mormons cheapen the profound ethical questions with which Mickelsson struggles. From the founder with his tablets of the law to the pride in being chosen people to the premium placed on unity and cohesion, the Mormons parody the Jews and their ancient ideal of a religious community. But in a world in which "all people were Jews" (p. 432)—in which, that is, all people are alienated, feeling themselves banished from some primal, nurturing community—the Mormons achieve only a cheap, ugly substitute for the lost ideal.

Not by accident, then, does Mickelsson's education in the rewards and responsibilities of community include romantic involvement with a Jewish woman. Herself the victim of another perverted community, the clannish and bigoted Marxists of her sociology department, Jessica Stark represents an advance in Gardner's characterization of women, just as Mickelsson's relations with her (and with Donnie Matthews) represent an advance in Gardner's ability and willingness to deal with sexual love. The extraordinary thing about Jessica is that she surprises not only Peter Mickelsson but also the reader and perhaps the writer as well. At first one registers her half-consciously as a pleasant erotic fantasy, the kind of character that in the hands of a lesser novelist would be shallow and only superficially credible. But just as Mickelsson finds his erotic fantasies coming true, he and the reader begin to realize this woman's human complexity.

She has a tragic past, having lost two children and a husband to death, and her tremendous suffering remains as a constant reproach to the hero's selfishness. Here, one feels, is *real* suffering, yet Mickelsson cannot rise above his own misery to worry about or sympathize with another's. When Mickelsson walks in on her making love to Tillson, the hunchbacked chairman of the philosophy department, he reacts at first with confusion and numbness. Only gradually does he begin to realize the constellation of motive and circumstance behind what he has witnessed. Whether she has betrayed Mickelsson with Tillson or the other way around, the lapse is thematically essential, for it helps Mickelsson, who has exploited Donnie Matthews and committed robbery and perhaps murder, to see that he is not alone in his errors, his omissions, his crimes, and his guilt. When he understands that others have their private sorrows and guilt yet go on functioning, he begins to see that he, too, might recover some kind of normal life. Learning empathy, Mickelsson must understand that, just as he teaches, every person's ethical choice must be made with reference to his or her own life necessities, pending the further evolution of a consensus regarding the ideal.

Inevitably, making these choices, one makes mistakes, generates guilt. At the end, Mickelsson's donning of the red huntsman's coat—its color at once emblematic of the sin that destroys and the love that redeems—reveals his understanding of and reconciliation to this principle. Hero and heroine, locked in coition, are surrounded by not only the ghosts that have figured hitherto but also the ghosts of numerous animals and birds, for they are in the room with all the guests' coats, so many of which have cost the lives of animals. Meanwhile, bones and blood fall from the sky, mute evidence of further carnage somewhere. The phenomenon of falls, "frog falls, blood falls, falls of bricks, cookies in plastic bags" (p. 486), has figured repeatedly in Mickelsson's thoughts. This one demonstrates that existence consists simultaneously of the ineluctably sanguinary and the irrepressibly miraculous. Both the bloodletting and the miracles have their place in Mickelsson's story.

In the passion of a philosopher, and in the mechanics of rebirth and renewal, we have come full circle from this author's first published novel, *The Resurrection*. In that work, Gardner writes of a philosopher's literal death and displaces the resurrection to the dead man's survivors and to the larger world of nature; in *Mickelsson's Ghosts* he treats a figurative death, the prostration of the main character, and is thus enabled to effect a resurrection of the moribund hero himself. The progression is significant, for Gardner continually sought to widen the grounds of affirmation, to bring under cultivation more and more of the twentieth century's moral wasteland. From novel to novel, therefore, he confronts and redeems more and more of the world's agony, aiming at what one of his characters calls "the sublime as the artistic conquest of the horrible" (p. 208). Like his friend Nicholas Vergette, the sculptor, he knew about the abyss over which he worked. But like Nietzsche he knew, too, that too much staring into the depths makes one a creature of the abyss. Moral art, according to Gardner, involves "flooring the ancient abyss" or, in the crucial metaphor of *Mickelsson's Ghosts*, sealing off the poisoned spring. One does not deny or forget the horror, but neither does one surrender to it.

Mindful of ultimate realities, then, Gardner insisted on the validity of his moral vision. His genius lay in an ability to find grounds for affirmation in a doubt-wracked age, to promote optimism without falsifying or misrepresenting the human condition. That Einstein, as Mickelsson notes, "refused to consider any theory of the universe that ruled out God" (p. 447) would have struck Gardner not as an argument for the existence of God but as an argument for the toleration, even promotion, of benign fictions. The author did not, however, advocate the knowing promotion of untruth, his respect for benign fictions notwithstanding; indeed, Einstein's successors have found less and less evidence of God in the universe they probe. But the scientist is time's fool. His work invariably becomes obsolete, and he remains forever at the mercy of a better-informed future. The artist, by contrast, is time's darling, potentially redeeming the future with every act of the imagination. If a being so powerful envisions a numinous universe and realizes it memorably in art, then all men may yet discover themselves children of the God thus created.

Notes

1. "Flooring the Ancient Abyss"

1. John Gardner, *Poems* (Northridge, California: Lord John Press, 1978), pp. 22–25.

2. *John Gardner: A Bibliographical Profile* (Carbondale: Southern Illinois Univ. Pr., 1980), p. xv. I am indebted to this fine book for most of the biographical and bibliographical information in this chapter, including the information about the printing histories of Gardner's books.

3. Stephen Singular, "The Sound and Fury Over Fiction," *New York Times Magazine*, 8 July 1979, p. 34.

4. C. E. Frazer Clark, Jr., "John Gardner," in *Conversations with Writers*, I (Detroit: Gale Research, 1978), 103.

5. John Gardner, "The Old Men," *DA* (1959), p. 1757 (State University of Iowa).

6. 16 July 1966, p. 25.

7. 21 Sept. 1970, p. 102.

8. Barry Baldwin, rev. of *The Wreckage of Agathon*, by John Gardner, *Library Journal*, 95 (Aug. 1970), 2716.

9. 97 (1 Sept. 1972), 2751.

10. June 1982, p. 70.

11. 25 July 1982, Sec. H, p. 8, col. 4.

12. Singular, p. 39.

13. *The Crack-Up*, ed. Edmund Wilson (New York: New Directions, 1945), p. 69.

14. *In Bluebeard's Castle* (New Haven: Yale Univ. Pr., 1971), pp. 136, 137.

15. Don Edwards and Carol Polsgrove, "A Conversation with John Gardner," *Atlantic Monthly*, May 1977, p. 43.

16. John Gardner, *On Moral Fiction* (New York: Basic Books, 1978), p. 82.

17. Edwards and Polsgrove, p. 44.

18. 8 May 1978, p. 26.

19. 16 Apr. 1978, p. 10.

20. 226 (22 Apr. 1978), 462.

21. 103 (1 Apr. 1978), 753.

22. Singular, p. 15. The source of the remarks quoted is not indicated; apparently they were solicited by Singular. For more on the controversy, see "A Writers' Forum on Moral Fiction," *fiction international*, No. 12 (1980), pp. 5–25, in which a number of writers comment on *On Moral Fiction* or simply "on moral fiction—however they might care to define it." From brief sentences to several paragraphs, the twenty-seven respondents reveal mainly what a wide variety of opinions and attitudes a phrase like "moral fiction" can generate. Barth and Updike each contribute a brief paragraph, in which they add little to what they say in the Singular article (Updike does, however, admit to a certain esteem for "anyone who can coin a phrase that becomes current, like 'objective correlative' or 'the me generation'").

23. "How Is Fiction Doing?", *New York Times Book Review*, 14 Dec. 1980, p. 3.

24. Gardner, *On Moral Fiction*, p. 19. See also p. 137.

25. Joe David Bellamy and Pat Ensworth, "John Gardner," in *The New Fiction: Interviews with Innovative American Writers*, ed. Bellamy (Urbana: Univ. of Illinois Pr., 1974), p. 180.

26. John Barth, "The Literature of Replenishment," *Atlantic Monthly*, Jan. 1980, pp. 65–71.

27. Singular, p. 36.

2. Et in Arcadia Ego

1. Although it was the fifth of Gardner's works to be published, *Nickel Mountain* is one of the author's earliest works, as he himself has pointed out in interviews. See Joe David Bellamy, *The New Fiction: Interviews with Innovative American Writers* (Urbana: Univ. of Illinois Pr., 1974), p. 191.

2. I am indebted here to William Empson's idea of pastoral as a "process of putting the complex into the simple." *Some Versions of Pastoral* (New York: New Directions, 1935), p. 23.

3. John Gardner, *The Resurrection* (New York: Ballantine, 1974), p. 133. Hereafter cited parenthetically.

4. John Gardner, *Nickel Mountain* (New York: Knopf, 1973), p. 179. Hereafter cited parenthetically.

5. John Gardner, *The Wreckage of Agathon* (New York: Harper, 1970), p. 86. Hereafter cited parenthetically.

3. Artists Divine and Otherwise

1. Joe David Bellamy and Pat Ensworth, "John Gardner," in *The New Fiction: Interviews with Innovative American Writers*, ed. Bellamy (Urbana: Univ. of Illinois Pr., 1974), p. 179.

2. Susan Strehle, "John Gardner's Novels: Affirmation and the Alien," *Critique*, 18, No. 2 (1976), 94.

3. John Gardner, *Grendel* (New York: Knopf, 1971), p. 8. Hereafter cited parenthetically.

4. Stephen Singular, "The Sound and Fury Over Fiction," *New York Times Magazine*, 8 July 1979, p. 34.

5. Marshall L. Harvey, "Where Philosophy and Fiction Meet: An Interview with John Gardner," *Chicago Review*, 29, No. 4 (Spring 1978), 75.

6. Bellamy and Ensworth, p. 173.

7. Craig J. Stromme, "The Twelve Chapters of *Grendel*," *Critique*, 20, No. 1 (1978), 83–92.

8. John Gardner, *The Construction of Christian Poetry in Old English* (Carbondale: Southern Illinois Univ. Pr., 1975), pp. 83–84.

9. See Christopher Butler, "Numerological Thought," in *Silent Poetry: Essays in Numerological Analysis*, ed. Alistair Fowler (New York: Barnes & Noble, 1970), p. 20.

10. William Michael Rossetti, ed., *The Poetical Works of William Blake, Lyrical and Miscellaneous* (London: George Bell and Sons, 1874), p. 184n.

11. Sir James George Frazer, *The New Golden Bough*, ed. Theodor Gaster (New York: Criterion Books, 1959), pp. 606–609.

12. As Helen B. Ellis and Warren U. Ober point out in "*Grendel* and Blake: The Contraries of Existence," in *John Gardner: Critical Perspectives*, ed. Robert A. Morace and Kathryn VanSpanckeren (Carbondale: Southern Illinois Univ. Pr., 1982), p. 53, Gardner's language in these passages comes from Blake's *The Marriage of Heaven and Hell*. Unlike Blake's speaker, Grendel fails to see that his void is the result of perceptual habits. Blake's speaker discovers that the "nether void" with which he has been affrighted is an illusion, and once freed from that illusion he finds himself on a pleasant moonlit bank listening to a harper. The fact that Grendel makes no such discovery leads Michael Ackland to a nihilistic reading of the novel in "Blakean Sources in John Gardner's *Grendel*," *Critique*, 23, No. 1 (1981), 57–66. Ackland, however, does not consider the unreliability of the narrator. Gardner's reader is expected to remember Blake's harper, who is instrumental in refuting the Puritan's idea of hell, and relate him to Gardner's, who offers an alternative to our modern hell of nihilism and despair.

13. Carl Gustav Jung, *The Archetypes and the Collective Unconscious*, Vol. IX, part I of *The Collected Works of C. G. Jung*, trans. R. F. C. Hull, 2d ed. (Princeton: Princeton Univ. Pr., 1968), p. 255.

14. Jung, p. 266.

15. Harvey, p. 82.

16. Quoted in Singular, p. 15.

17. *The Famous History of the Life of King Henry VIII*, in *The Complete Works of William Shakespeare*, ed. Hardin Craig (Chicago: Scott, Foresman, 1961), p. 1293.

18. For the argument that both *Grendel* and *Beowulf* "present a dichotomy which binds Grendel and Unferth on one hand and Beowulf and the poet/Shaper on the other," see Norma L. Hutman, "Even Monsters Have Mothers: A Study of *Beowulf* and John Gardner's *Grendel*," *Mosaic*, 9 (Fall 1975), 22–23.

4. Paradise Lost

1. John Gardner, *The Sunlight Dialogues* (New York: Knopf, 1972), p. 3. Hereafter cited parenthetically.

2. John Gardner, *Mickelsson's Ghosts* (New York: Knopf, 1982), p. 329.

3. Joe David Bellamy and Pat Ensworth, "John Gardner," in *The New Fiction: Interviews with Innovative American Writers*, ed. Bellamy (Urbana: Univ. of Illinois Pr., 1974), p. 173.

4. Paul F. Ferguson, John R. Maier, Frank McConnell, and Sara Matthiessen, "John Gardner: The Art of Fiction LXXIII," *Paris Review*, 21 (Spring 1979), 62.

5. Bellamy and Ensworth, p. 188.

6. Ferguson, Maier, McConnell, and Matthiessen, p. 42.

7. For a fuller discussion of the dialogues and of Gardner's borrowings from A. Leo Oppenheim's *Ancient Mesopotamia: Portrait of a Dead Civilization*, see Greg Morris, "A Babylonian in Batavia: Mesopotamian Literature and Lore in *The Sunlight Dialogues*," in *John Gardner: Critical Perspectives*, ed. Robert A. Morace and Kathryn VanSpanckeren (Carbondale: Southern Illinois Univ. Pr., 1982), pp. 28–45. Morris is helpful, too, on the novel's parallels with *Gilgamesh*. See also John R. Maier, "Mesopotamian Names in *The Sunlight Dialogues*: Or MAMA Makes It to Batavia, New York," *Literary Onomastics Studies*, 4 (1977), 33–48.

8. Bellamy and Ensworth, p. 188.

9. Ferguson, Maier, McConnell, and Matthiessen, p. 54.

10. "John Gardner's Order and Disorder: *Grendel* and *The Sunlight Dialogues*," *Critique*, 18, No. 2 (1976), 104.

11. Carl Gustav Jung, *Psychological Types*, Vol. VI of *The Collected Works of C. G. Jung*, trans. H. G. Baynes, rev. R. F. C. Hull, 2d ed. (Princeton: Princeton Univ. Pr., 1968), pp. 330–486.

12. I am indebted in what follows to Northrop Frye, *Fearful Symmetry: A Study of William Blake* (Princeton: Princeton Univ. Pr., 1947).

13. Bellamy and Ensworth, p. 188.

14. "Challenging the Literary Naysayers," *Horizon*, 21 (July 1978), 36.

15. Quoted in T. S. Eliot, *Collected Poems 1909–1962* (London: Faber and Faber, 1963), p. 86.

5. From Angst to Affirmation

1. John Gardner, *The King's Indian Stories and Tales* (New York: Knopf, 1974), p. 179. Hereafter cited parenthetically.

2. Paul F. Ferguson, John R. Maier, Frank McConnell, and Sara Matthiessen, "John Gardner: The Art of Fiction LXXIII," *Paris Review*, 21 (Spring 1979), 59.

3. Marshall L. Harvey, "Where Philosophy and Fiction Meet: An Interview with John Gardner," *Chicago Review*, 29, No. 4 (Spring 1978), 81.

4. John Gardner and Lennis Dunlap, *The Forms of Fiction* (New York: Random, 1962), p. 30.

5. John Gardner, *The Art of Living and Other Stories* (New York: Knopf, 1981), p. 79.

6. Like Ishmael, he is also a sometime schoolteacher. For more on the allusions and parallels to Melville and Poe, as well as to Robert Louis Stevenson, Charles Brockden Brown, Jack London, Joseph Conrad, and others, see Donald J. Greiner's fine article, "Sailing Through *The King's Indian* with John Gardner and His Friends," in *John Gardner: Critical Perspectives*, ed. Robert A. Morace and Kathryn VanSpanckeren (Carbondale: Southern Illinois Univ. Pr., 1982), pp. 76–88.

7. See Sumner Ferris's expose in *Speculum*, 52 (Oct. 1977), 970–974.

8. See Daniel Hoffman, *Poe Poe Poe Poe Poe Poe Poe* (London: Robson Books, 1973), pp. 97–99.

9. Leslie A. Fiedler, *Love and Death in the American Novel*, 2d ed. (New York: Stein and Day, 1966), pp. 394–400.

10. Gardner originally planned to name this character Tom More. See the page of Gardner's notes for this tale reproduced in John M.

Howell, *John Gardner: A Bibliographical Profile* (Carbondale: Southern Illinois Univ. Pr., 1980), p. 117.

6. The Dying Fall

1. John Gardner, *October Light* (New York: Knopf, 1976), p. 60. Hereafter cited parenthetically.

2. Leonard C. Butts, "Locking and Unlocking: Nature as Moral Center in John Gardner's *October Light*," *Critique*, 22, No. 2 (1980), 48.

3. James leaves the farm to Sally in his will; however, if she is no longer living, it goes not to Ginny, his daughter, but to her *husband*.

4. Trans. Talcott Parsons (New York: Scribner's, 1958).

5. This detail is a thinly disguised version of a mishap in Gardner's own youth. Gardner's identification with Grendel *qua* Cain was adduced in chapter 3. The Cain who wrote *October Light* dedicated it to his father. See also the discussion of Gardner's suicidal tendencies in chapter 7.

6. John Gardner, *On Moral Fiction* (New York: Basic Books, 1978), p. 26.

7. Private communication.

8. Joe David Bellamy and Pat Ensworth, "John Gardner," in *The New Fiction: Interviews with Innovative American Writers*, ed. Bellamy (Urbana: Univ. of Illinois Pr., 1974), pp. 185–186.

9. Gardner, *On Moral Fiction*, p. 6.

10. *The New Golden Bough*, ed. Theodor H. Gaster (New York: Criterion Books, 1959), pp. 617–618.

11. James Joyce, *Dubliners* (New York: Viking, 1968), p. 101.

12. C. E. Frazer Clark, Jr., "John Gardner," in *Conversations with Writers*, I (Detroit: Gale, 1977), 94.

7. Dealing with Dragons

1. John Gardner, *Dragon, Dragon and Other Tales* (New York: Knopf, 1975), p. 3. Hereafter cited parenthetically.

2. John Gardner, *Gudgekin the Thistle Girl and Other Tales* (New York: Knopf, 1976), p. 49. Hereafter cited parenthetically.

3. John Gardner, *Freddy's Book* (New York: Knopf, 1980), p. 236.

4. John Gardner, *The King of the Hummingbirds and Other Tales* (New York: Knopf, 1977), p. 15. Hereafter cited parenthetically.

5. Marshall L. Harvey, "Where Philosophy and Fiction Meet: An Interview with John Gardner," *Chicago Review*, 29, No. 4 (Spring 1978), 86–87.
6. Stephen Singular, "The Sound and Fury Over Fiction," *New York Times Magazine*, 8 July 1979, p. 34.
7. John Gardner and Lennis Dunlap, *The Forms of Fiction* (New York: Random, 1962), pp. 30–31.
8. John Gardner, *In the Suicide Mountains* (New York: Knopf, 1977), p. 127. Hereafter cited parenthetically.

8. History as Fiction, Fiction as History

1. Ford Madox Ford, "To Rene Katherine Clarissa" [Dedication], *A Little Less Than Gods* (London: Duckworth, 1928), p. viii.
2. John Gardner, *Freddy's Book* (New York: Knopf, 1980), p. 55. Hereafter cited parenthetically.
3. Rupertus Tuitiensis, *De Trinitate et operibus ejus. In Deuteronomia*, I, xxii (*PL*, CLXVII, col. 941–942); translated and quoted in Robert P. Miller, "Chaucer's Pardoner and the Scriptural Eunuch," in *Chaucer Criticism*, ed. Richard Schoeck and Jerome Taylor (Notre Dame, Ind.: Univ. of Notre Dame Pr., 1960), p. 225.

9. Theme and Variations

1. John Gardner, *The Art of Living and Other Stories* (New York: Knopf, 1981), p. 15. Hereafter cited parenthetically.
2. Paul F. Ferguson, John R. Maier, Frank McConnell, and Sara Matthiessen, "John Gardner: The Art of Fiction LXXIII," *Paris Review*, 21 (Spring 1979), 58.
3. Stephen Singular, "The Sound and Fury Over Fiction," *New York Times Magazine*, 8 July 1979, p. 34.
4. (New York: Knopf, 1982), p. 523.
5. (New York: Basic Books, 1978), p. 173.
6. J. E. Cirlot, *A Dictionary of Symbols*, trans. Jack Sage (New York: Philosophical Library, 1962), p. 83. "The generic dragon of China symbolizes the mastering and sublimation of wickedness," says Cirlot, citing Paul Diel, *Le Symbolisme dans la mythologie grecque* (Paris, 1952).

10. No Man Is an Island

1. John Gardner, *Mickelsson's Ghosts* (New York: Knopf, 1982), p. 236. Hereafter cited parenthetically.

2. *The Portable Nietzsche*, trans. Walter Kaufmann (New York: Viking, 1954), p. 467.

3. (New York: Basic Books, 1978), pp. 77, 78.

4. Aired 15 July 1982.

Selected Bibliography

Works by John Gardner

"The Old Men." Diss. State Univ. of Iowa, 1958.

The Forms of Fiction. Ed. John Gardner and Lennis Dunlap. New York: Random, 1962.

The Complete Works of the Gawain-Poet in a Modern English Version with a Critical Introduction. Chicago: Univ. of Chicago Pr., 1965.

The Resurrection. New York: New American Library, 1966. Gardner made many changes for the Ballantine edition, 1974. See Howell's *Bibliographical Profile*.

Le Morte Darthur Notes. Lincoln: Cliff's Notes, 1967.

The Gawain-Poet Notes. Lincoln: Cliff's Notes, 1967.

The Wreckage of Agathon. New York: Harper, 1970.

Grendel. New York: Knopf, 1971.

The Alliterative Morte Arthure The Owl and the Nightingale And Five Other Middle English Poems in a Modernized Version with Comments on the Poems and Notes. Carbondale: Southern Illinois Univ. Pr., 1971.

The Sunlight Dialogues. New York: Knopf, 1972.

Jason and Medeia. New York: Knopf, 1973.

Nickel Mountain. New York: Knopf, 1973.

The Construction of the Wakefield Cycle. Carbondale: Southern Illinois Univ. Pr., 1974.

The King's Indian Stories and Tales. New York: Knopf, 1974.

The Construction of Christian Poetry in Old English. Carbondale: Southern Illinois Univ. Pr., 1975.

Dragon, Dragon and Other Tales. New York: Knopf, 1975.

Gudgekin the Thistle Girl and Other Tales. New York: Knopf, 1976.

October Light. New York: Knopf, 1976.

The King of the Hummingbirds and Other Tales. New York: Knopf, 1977.

The Poetry of Chaucer. Carbondale: Southern Illinois Univ. Pr., 1977.

The Life and Times of Chaucer. New York: Knopf, 1977.

A Child's Bestiary. New York: Knopf, 1977.

In the Suicide Mountains. New York: Knopf, 1977.
On Moral Fiction. New York: Basic Books, 1978.
Poems. Northridge, Calif.: Lord John Pr., 1978.
Rumpelstiltskin. Dallas: New London Pr., 1978.
Frankenstein. Dallas: New London Pr., 1978.
William Wilson. Dallas: New London Pr., 1979.
Vlemk the Box-Painter. Northridge, Calif.: Lord John Pr., 1979.
Freddy's Book. New York: Knopf, 1980.
The Temptation Game. Dallas: New London Pr., 1980.
MSS: A Retrospective. Ed. John Gardner and L. M. Rosenberg. Dallas: New London Pr., 1980.
The Art of Living and Other Stories. New York: Knopf, 1981.
Death and the Maiden. Dallas: New London Pr., 1981.
Mickelsson's Ghosts. New York: Knopf, 1982.
Tengu Child: Stories by Kikuo Itaya. Translated by John Gardner and Nobuko Tsukui. Carbondale: Southern Illinois Univ. Pr., 1983.
On Becoming a Novelist. New York: Harper, 1983.

Criticism and Bibliography

Allen, Bruce. "Settling for Ithaca: The Fictions of John Gardner." *Sewanee Review,* 85 (Summer 1977), 520–531.
Butts, Leonard C. "Locking and Unlocking: Nature as Moral Center in John Gardner's *October Light.*" *Critique,* 22, No. 2 (1980), 47–60.
Cowart, David. "John Champlin Gardner, Jr." In *American Novelists Since World War II.* Vol. II of *Dictionary of Literary Biography.* Ed. Jeffrey Helterman and Richard Layman. Detroit: Gale Research, 1978.
Fitzpatrick, W. P. "John Gardner and the Defense of Fiction." *Midwest Quarterly,* 20 (1979), 405–415.
Harris, Richard C. "Ecclesiastical Wisdom and *Nickel Mountain.*" *Twentieth Century Literature,* 26 (1980), 424–431.
Howell, John M. *John Gardner: A Bibliographical Profile.* Carbondale: Southern Illinois Univ. Pr., 1980.
Hutman, Norma L. "Even Monsters Have Mothers: A Study of *Beowulf* and John Gardner's *Grendel.*" *Mosaic,* 9 (Fall 1975), 19–31.
Maier, John R. "Mesopotamian Names in *The Sunlight Dialogues*: Or MAMA Makes It to Batavia, New York." *Literary Onomastics Studies,* 4 (1977), 33–48.

McConnell, Frank. "Gardner, John (Champlin, Jr.)." In *Contemporary Novelists*. Ed. James Vinson. 2d ed. New York: St. Martin's, 1976, pp. 491–494.

Milosh, Joseph. "John Gardner's *Grendel*: Sources and Analogues." *Contemporary Literature*, 19 (Winter 1978), 48–57.

Minugh, David. "John Gardner Constructs *Grendel*'s Universe." *Studies in English Philology, Linguistics, and Literature: Presented to Alarik Rynell 7 March 1978*. Ed. Mats Rydén and Lennart A. Björk. Stockholm Studies in English, 46. Stockholm: Almqvist & Wiksell, 1978, 125–141.

Morace, Robert A., and Kathryn VanSpanckeren, eds. *John Gardner: Critical Perspectives*. Carbondale: Southern Illinois Univ. Pr., 1982.

Murr, Judy Smith. "John Gardner's Order and Disorder: *Grendel* and *The Sunlight Dialogues*." *Critique*, 18, No. 2 (1976), 97–108.

Rudd, Jay. "Gardner's *Grendel* and *Beowulf*: Humanizing the Monster." *Thoth*, 14 (Spring-Fall 1974), 3–17.

Strehle, Susan. "John Gardner's Novels: Affirmation and the Alien." *Critique*, 18, No. 2 (1976), 86–96.

Stromme, Craig J. "The Twelve Chapters of *Grendel*." *Critique*, 20, No. 1 (1978), 83–92.

Important Interviews

Bellamy, Joe David, and Pat Ensworth. "John Gardner." In *The New Fiction: Interviews with Innovative American Writers*. Ed. Bellamy. Urbana: Univ. of Illinois Pr., 1974, pp. 169–193.

Christian, Ed. "An Interview with John Gardner." *Prairie Schooner*, 54 (1980), 70–73.

Clark, C. E. Frazer, Jr. "John Gardner." In *Conversations with Writers*, Vol. I. Detroit: Gale Research, 1978, pp. 82–103.

Edwards, Don, and Carol Polsgrove. "A Conversation with John Gardner." *Atlantic Monthly*, 239 (May 1977), 43–47.

Ferguson, Paul F., John R. Maier, Frank McConnell, and Sara Matthiessen. "John Gardner: The Art of Fiction LXXIII." *Paris Review*, 21 (Spring 1979), 36–74.

Harvey, Marshall L. "Where Philosophy and Fiction Meet: An Interview with John Gardner." *Chicago Review*, 29 (Spring 1978), 73–87.

Laskin, Daniel. "Challenging the Literary Naysayers." *Horizon*, 21 (July 1978), 32–36.

Natov, Roni, and Geraldine DeLuca. "An Interview with John Gardner." *The Lion and the Unicorn: A Critical Journal of Children's Literature*, 2, No. 1 (1978), 114–136.

Singular, Stephen. "The Sound and Fury Over Fiction." *New York Times Magazine*, 8 July 1979, pp. 13–15, 34, 36–39.

Suplee, Curt. "John Gardner, Flat Out." *Washington Post*, 25 July 1982, Sec. H., pp. 1, 8–9.

Index

Abbot, Sally Page, 112–114, 122–123, 210n.3

abortion: Mickelsson on, 192, 197

absurdity: in "Dragon, Dragon," 130; in "The Pear Tree," 138; in "Queen Louisa," 95

"Abt Vogler" (Browning): compared with "Nimram," 167–168

Achilles: Taggert Hodge as, 62–63; in "The Library Horror," 175, 176

Adam: Old Congressman as, 61, 69; James Page as, 114–116, 118; Gustav Vasa as political, 155; mentioned, 79, 169

Aeneid (Virgil): similarities to *Grendel*, 50

Afanas'ev, Aleksandr, 142

Agaard, Freddy: as artist-historian, 149–151; and "Jack and the Beanstalk," 151; as moral artist, 148, 152, 164

Agaard, Sven, 149, 150, 151, 155, 158, 160, 164

Agathon, 10, 27–32 passim, 84

Alice's Adventures in Wonderland (Carroll), 134, 175

Alliterative Morte Arthure, The, 4

All Saints' Day, 127, 128. *See also* Halloween

America: Bicentennial, 11, 62, 111, 124; in "The King's Indian,'" 99, 101–102, 107–110; in *October Light*, 111–115, 118, 121–122, 128; in *The Sunlight Dialogues*, 66–70; in *The Wreckage of Agathon*, 30–31

anarchism, 10–11, 63–69 passim, 86–87, 102, 109

Anaxagoras, 30

Angst, 1, 8, 94, 120, 123, 153. *See also* existentialism

anomie, 10, 35, 159

Antonucci, Emil, 43

apocalypse: allusions to in *October Light*, 127–128; George Steiner on, 9; in *The Sunlight Dialogues*, 69, 72

Apology for Poetry, An (Sidney), 15

Appearance and Reality (Bradley), 75

Apple, Max: on *On Moral Fiction*, 16

Arcadian Shepherds (Poussin), 22, 23

Armida the Blacksmith's Daughter, 140, 141, 144, 145

ars longa, vita brevis: as theme of "John Napper Sailing Through the Universe," 89

art, moral suasion of, 1–2, 9–10, 14–15, 18–20, 38, 40–41, 53–56, 110, 132, 144, 145, 174. *See also* artist entries; moral fiction; *On Moral Fiction*

artist: benign lunacy of moral, 58–59, 90, 91, 92–96, 97–98, 184, 186; education of, 12; as historian, 149, 150–151; responsibility of, 2, 9–10, 14, 18–19, 40–41, 53–54, 55, 76–77, 83, 89–91, 98–99, 106, 179–182, 204. *See also* Gardner, John Champlin, Jr., philosophy of

artist, bad: Bishop Brask as, 154; composer in "The Music Lover" as, 172–174; Luther Flint as, 12, 19–20, 72, 104–106, 108; Grendel as, 38–41, 73, 84, 173 (*see also* Grendel); in "Vlemk the Box-Painter," 181–182

217

Tarot: Grendel as hanged man, 51
"Tell-Tale Heart, The" (Poe), 175
Tempest, The (Shakespeare): allu-
    sions in "The King's Indian," 105,
    109
"Temptation of St. Ivo, The," 77,
    82–85, 90
Thomas, Dylan, 182
"Thorpe, Dr. William," 12, 80–82,
    84, 135
trickster: Grendel as, 52; Sunlight
    Man as, 67
"Trumpeter": as culmination of
    "Queen Louisa" sequence, 97–98;
    point of view in, 92–93; men-
    tioned, 165, 174, 176, 178
Tuchman, Barbara, 149
Turner, J. M. W., 89
Turn of the Screw, The (James), 93, 149
twentieth century: ills of, 1, 190, 203
Twilight of the Idols (Nietzsche), 190

Übermensch, 198
Ulysses: Chief Clumly as, 61
Unferth: as brother-killer, 42; as
    hero, 55; mentioned, 208n.18
Upchurch, Jonathan: as good artist,
    105; mentioned, 12, 73, 91, 99–110
    passim
Updike, John: on moral fiction, 16,
    53, 124, 206n.22
Utopia, 108–110, 209n.10

Vasa, Gustav: as Adamic politician,
    155–157; guilt of, 161; and propa-
    ganda, 154–155; mentioned, 150
Vergette, Nicholas: Gardner's elegy
    for, 1–2, 3; mentioned, 19, 203

Vietnam, 31, 184, 186
Vlemk the Box-Painter, 12, 173, 179–
    182
"Vlemk the Box-Painter," 165, 179–
    182
Vonnegut, Kurt, 15, 42, 120
Vortrab, 85–88

Waiting for Godot (Beckett), 28
"Warden, The," 77, 85–88, 110
Washington University, 3, 170
Waste Land, The (Eliot), 13, 46, 75,
    104, 171
Watergate, 30
Weber, Max, 113, 155
Wells, Callie, 32–36 passim
West, Nathanael, 42, 118
Whitman, Walt: Whitmanesque
    touches in Gardner, 1, 40, 101, 103
Wilde, Oscar, 179
Winesap, Professor Jack: and histor-
    ical methodology, 150, 151; and
    "Jack and the Beanstalk," 151;
    mentioned, 149, 155, 160, 164, 166
Winfred, 175–176, 183
"Witch's Wish, The," 138–139
Wolfe, Tom, 12–13
Wolff, Geoffrey: on *The Wreckage of
    Agathon*, 5
Woolf, Virginia, 97
Wreckage of Agathon, The: as pastoral,
    21, 27–29, 31; point of view in,
    29–30, 92; political antinomies in,
    30–31; publication and reviews,
    4–5; mentioned, 10, 155

Yeats, William Butler, 25, 95
Yegudkin, Arcady, 169–170